*Faith, Health, and Healing
in African American Life*

Faith, Health, and Healing
in African American Life

Edited by
Stephanie Y. Mitchem and Emilie M. Townes

RELIGION, HEALTH, AND HEALING
Susan Starr Sered and Linda L. Barnes, Series Editors

Westport, Connecticut
London

Library of Congress Cataloging-in-Publication Data

Faith, health, and healing in African American life /
edited by Stephanie Y. Mitchem and Emilie M. Townes.
  p. cm. — (Religion, health, and healing, ISSN 1556–262X)
  Includes bibliographical references and index.
  ISBN-13: 978–0–275–99375–7 (alk. paper)
 1. Spiritual healing—United States. 2. Healing—Religious aspects.
3. African Americans—Religion. I. Mitchem, Stephanie Y., 1950–
II. Townes, Emilie Maureen, 1955–
  BL65.M4F36   2008
  201'.66108996073—dc22   2008016908

British Library Cataloguing in Publication Data is available.

Library of Congress Catalog Card Number: 2008016908
ISBN: 978–0–275–99375–7
ISSN: 1556–262X

First published in 2008

Praeger Publishers, 88 Post Road West, Westport, CT 06881
An imprint of Greenwood Publishing Group, Inc.
www.praeger.com

Printed in the United States of America

The paper used in this book complies with the
Permanent Paper Standard issued by the National
Information Standards Organization (Z39.48–1984).

10 9 8 7 6 5 4 3 2 1

for sula

Contents

Series Foreword

The Religion, Health, and Healing series brings together authors from a variety of academic disciplines and cultural backgrounds, to foster understanding of the meetings between religiously-grounded approaches to health and healing, and different cultural worldviews and experiences. The books in this series offer examples of the meanings associated with religion and spirituality, and curing and healing, in diverse historical and social contexts.

The word "healing," in and of itself, is multi-dimensional, especially in religious settings. It can mean the scientifically measurable cure of physical illnesses. It can mean the alleviation of pain or other symptoms. It can also mean coping, coming to terms with, or learning to live with that which one cannot change (including physical illness and emotional trauma). Healing can mean integration and connection among all the elements of one's being, reestablishment of self-worth, connection with one's tradition, or personal empowerment. Healing can be about relationships with friends, relations, ancestors, the community, the world, the Earth, and/or God. It can refer to developing a sense of well-being or wholeness, whether emotional, social, spiritual, physical, or in relation to other aspects of being that are valued by a particular group. Healing can be about purification, repenting from sin, the cleaning up of one's negative karma, entry into a path of "purer," abstinent, or more moral daily living, eternal salvation, or submission to God's will.

Healing can concern the individual, the family, the community, the nation, the world, or the cosmos as a whole. We think here of healing acts that range from personal spiritual awakenings, to communal and national healing. Perhaps the most common theme in religious accounts of healing is the enactment of change, whether understood as restoration to an earlier state or as transformation to a new one, in relation to the experience of affliction or suffering.[1] The transformation that comes about in the healing process implies movement from one, less desirable state, to another, more desirable state. Even when what is sought is some previous state thought to have been better, it is still pursuit of the more desirable. Thus, the study of religion and healing includes looking at how individuals, communities, and religious traditions diagnose and interpret causes of illness and the sources of affliction, as well as notions of what constitutes health, both ideally and pragmatically. At their core, these different traditions and practices attempt to understand and address suffering in its different forms.

Exploring ways in which biomedicine—the biologically-based system that many people identify simply as "medicine"—converges with different religions in the United States today is another central concern of this series. Some of these interactions are synergistic, while others are antagonistic. Examples of the first include hospital chaplains, interdisciplinary teams on hospital ethics committees, faith-based clinics, and the many health care providers who draw upon their personal spiritual resources in order to provide compassionate care to their patients. Examples of the second include public disputes regarding abortion and end of life, and of the disdain expressed by some members of the medical community for the traditional healing practices of some immigrant groups or some spiritually related healing practices included under the broad heading of "complementary and alternative medicine."

While the series focuses primarily upon the United States, the historical underpinnings and global contexts in which these practices and ideas unfold are an important part of the landscape the series explores as well. Moreover, as globalization continues to unfold, the United States encompasses many of the world's cultures within its own boundaries. Some of these cultural frames of reference have been part of the country's history and heritage from the earliest days, as is the case with what we now commonly refer to as "African American."

Stephanie Y. Mitchem and Emilie M. Townes's new collection, *Faith, Health, and Healing in African American Life*, draws on this heritage. It discusses some of the many ways in which African-descended Americans think about, and address, suffering, sickness, grief, and social-imposed affliction on the one hand and, on the other, bring to bear the depth and range of rich resources rooted in faith and religious life. Some of these approaches are traced back to the ancestors and their legacies; some to the outcomes of dislocation, resettlement, and efforts to preserve and rework traditions. Some focus on the individual, others more on groups. The religious dimensions expressed in each one are different, reminding us that no cultural group is monolithic; rather, each group is made up of its many members, resulting in a tapestry of worldviews which, together, weave a larger, complex umbrella under which the many stand. Mitchem and Townes—both noted womanist theologians—have brought to bear their own years of reflection on such issues, and a circle of colleagues, friends, and companions engaged in thinking about what matters of sickness and healing mean in the lives of black folks—and, by extension, to all other Americans.

We hope that through the publication of this series about diverse healers, healing communities, and healing practices we will offer readers tools to uncover both the common and the uncommon ways in which Americans engage with, find meaning in, and seek to embrace, transcend, or overcome individual and communal suffering.

Susan Starr Sered and Linda L. Barnes

NOTE

1. For more on this, see Linda Barnes and Susan Sered, eds., *Religion and Healing in America* (New York: Oxford University Press, 2005).

Introduction

The traditional medical model that defines health as the absence of disease or illness has a mercurial home in black lives in the United States. This model does not always allow for a more holistic approach that sees the self as an integrated whole and one that is situated in a set of social relationships that includes the family and the community. This is compounded by the fact that black Americans are more likely than whites to die of cancer and heart disease, more likely to get diabetes and asthma, and less likely to get preventive care and screening. Some of this greater morbidity results from education, income level, and environment, as well as from disparities in access to health care. Although the federal government has set a goal of eliminating racial disparities in health care by 2010, researchers are still trying to determine what lies behind the differences. Other studies have shown that access to health insurance is a factor, and some have found that doctors consciously or subconsciously discriminate against black patients. The challenge is to deliver the same quality health care to everyone, despite these factors.

Community-based initiatives have emerged as one key way to address the challenges found in black health care. In cities such as Atlanta, Baltimore, Dallas, and Oakland, residents organize exercise groups, teach one another how to cook with healthy ingredients, and encourage neighbors to get regular checkups. Recently, these models have begun to incorporate churches as a key site for health education, screening, and testing. Another set of responses to the challenge of black health and health care in the United States comes from those who eschew the traditional medical model of disease and cure and its emphasis on the self as a self-contained subject with many different parts—body, mind, soul, and spirit. The emphasis becomes one on health as something that is dependent on social networks, biology, and environment. Often drawing on religious traditions such as beyond traditional Christian thought, these thinkers and practitioners seek to address the whole person in her or his various contexts.

The contributors draw from the fields of anthropology, cultural studies, ethics, history of religions, HIV/AIDS advocacy and research, religion and literature, religion and the arts, religious history, and theology. Given the expertise of the contributors, topics such as affliction, lament, and midwifery join the more traditional topics of healing, HIV/AIDS, and prayer. The authors are representatives from different models of healing and health. They also represent a variety of religious practices found in contemporary black life in the United States.

This collection of chapters gives the reader a better understanding of the varieties of religiously based approaches to healing found in black communities in the United States and alternative models of healing and health. It does not seek to create a hierarchy of perspectives or models. Instead, it assumes one overarching perspective and explores it: that health is not simply the absence of disease, but rather involves a wide range of activities that foster healing and wholeness. Health depends on social networks, biology, and the environment. It is embedded in our social realties and is the integration of the spiritual, the mental, and the biological aspects of our lives.

There are five major parts of this book. The first, "Ancestral Songs," explores hoodoo narratives and folk healing. Yvonne Chireau's chapter, "Natural and Supernatural: African American Hoodoo Narratives of Sickness and Healing," reveals complex visions of the ways by which African Americans have historically identified and addressed affliction and healing. Hoodoo, which is often called folklore, spiritual work, and conjure, emerged from black slave populations in the U.S. South in the early 1800s. It was a way for black slaves and their descendents to manipulate invisible forces to influence their daily lives for empowerment, protection, aggression, and self-defense. As an alternative healing system that features both healing and harm, Hoodoo provides evidence of cultural and spiritual resources that are universally available, which offer the potential means by which one may interpret and address affliction, so as to ultimately manage the forces—be they natural or supernatural—that are believed to eventuate in bodily infirmity.

Dwight N. Hopkins's chapter, "Holistic Health and Healing: Environmental Racism and Ecological Justice," begins with the observation that the U.S. environmental movement falls within two broad trajectories. One public face consists of progressive groups such as Greenpeace and their fight to preserve and conserve Mother Nature. The other takes this crucial focus into consideration while broadening the ecology to include poor people's, Native Americans', and people of color's adverse victimization by racialized processes played out on the level of the environment. Thus holistic health and healing entails simultaneous attention to environmental racism and ecological justice. People of color and Native Americans have been waging a struggle for Mother Earth and the health and healing of human beings long before the popular public forays of Greenpeace and other such organizations. For instance, African Americans have been engaged in the movement around environmental racism and ecological justice since, at least, World War I. Consequently, this essay calls for a combined God-talk, race-talk, and ecological-talk. If the earth and the human species are to achieve a measure of holistic health and healing, we need a black environmental liberation theology.

The second part, "Health and Healing across the Diaspora," the authors focus on the diasporic nature of healing as the intersection between African, European, Native American, and African American communities. Charles H. Long's chapter, "Bodies in Time and the Healing of Spaces: Religion, Temporalities, and Health," looks at the nature of health in the African American communities in the United States during the period of enslavement, after the Civil War, and in two distinct periods—from the reception of scientific medicine by the African American community to the integration of medicine, doctors, and practice on the American scene to extend beyond the ideologies of biomedicine and its techniques as related to the individual body. As a totalizing category, health, like religion in this community, includes the religious institutions, as well as the political, the economic, and the imaginary. He concludes by redirecting the critique of this community away from the understanding that joining the majority population is the only game in town, to an orientation that encourages African American communities to begin to understand the nature of modernity on their own terms. These terms include, but are not restricted to, the Western Enlightenment sciences, but equally encompass their communities' memories and the expressive powers of these memories in their tradition. From this perspective, Long anticipates, one might be able to contemplate that all health is in fact, public, cultural, and social well-being.

In "Spiritual Illness and Healing: 'If the Lord Wills,'" Arvilla Payne-Jackson looks at the ways in which the health culture of African Americans is a complex mixture of African, European colonial, American Indian, and modern medical systems. It includes a tripartite etiology of disease and illness: natural, spiritual, and occult. Payne-Jackson notes the ways in which religious beliefs play an integral part in the perception and interpretation of an illness episode and the cure. In this matrix, practitioners often perceive their abilities to heal as gifts bestowed by God. But, Payne-Jackson argues, it is the will of the Lord that ultimately decides the outcome of an illness episode.

The third part, "The Arts of Ritual and Practice," focuses on depression as a stigma, the power of lament, and power of breathing to promote the health and healing of body, mind, and soul. Carolyn M. Jones's chapter, "The Marking of the Body, Memory, and the Meaning of Suffering in Phyllis Alesia Perry's *Stigmata*," begins this section. Jones investigates African American women's experience with depression. Drawing on the work of Meri Nana-Ama Danquah and others, the chapter investigates the particular problems that African American women experience in diagnosis, in treatment, and with their social lives in dealing with the illness. Jones connects depression to postcolonial melancholia, Paul Gilroy's and Anne Cheng's description of the results of slavery and postcolonial experience and then uses Phyllis Alesia Perry's *Stigmata,* a novel, to think about the links between depression, religion, and culture. While depression is often understood as a stigma, particularly in the African American community, Jones urges African American women to seek treatment and to move toward healing and wholeness.

Emilie M. Townes's chapter, "Just Aweeping and Awailing: Grief, Lament, and Hope as We Face the End of Life," draws on the biblical models of Jeremiah, Ezekiel, and Micah to interrogate the ways in which the issues we face at the end of life are a part of living until we die. Using the framework of grief, lament, and hope, Townes argues that the most healing thing we can do as we face the end of life is to use the power of lament to fall into the hands of God and open ourselves up completely in the hope that we will find a place that breaks our free fall of grief.

In "Honoring the Body: Rituals of Breath and Breathing," C. S'thembile West notes the critical connections between the body, breath, healing, and holistic health maintenance among black women. Her chapter acknowledges the ontological importance of the body in light of an African perspective that prioritizes integration of mind, body, and spirit. West explores the historical patterns sustained by attitudes and behaviors such as race-based social and political constructs that devalue black women and illuminates how black bodies have been devalued in the U.S. context, particularly in light of African enslavement. West's chapter showcases how African aesthetic principles in the New World context comprise marriages between the sacred and secular, and reminds contemporary scholars that, from an African perspective, the body and the culture created through movement functions in the service of daily life.

"Analyzing Social Realities," the fourth part of the book, analyzes the ways in which groups enact healing practices. In "The Destruction of Aunt Ester's House: Faith, Health, and Healing in the African American Community," Terri Baltimore and Mindy Thompson Fullilove consider the break up of several black communities through events like redlining and urban renewal, thereby creating deep bitterness for the members. Baltimore and Fullilove focus on an area known as "The Hill" in Pittsburgh to demonstrate faith-filled possibilities and human agency to heal such social disintegration.

Linda Barnes's chapter, "The Unspoken, the Spoken, and the Affirmed: Meanings of Healing, Same-Gender-Loving African Americans, and Black Churches," examines the interconnection between race and sexual orientation by focusing on the experiences of black gay men and lesbians, and their various understandings of healing and the black church. By exploring the ways in which the Bible and theology can be used to oppress and deny black gay men's and lesbians' humanity and wholeness, the Bible and theology can be the basis for radical inclusivity that leads to healing.

Finally, in "Finding and Making Wellness," the authors consider forms of spiritual and social healing practices. In "Seeking Help for the Body in the Well-Being of the Soul," Rosemary Gooden explores black women's beliefs about and experiences of religious, or spiritual, healing beginning with the nineteenth-century divine-healing movement. She concludes with a discussion of forms of spiritual healing that complement, yet are distinctive from the Christian practice of healing through the prayer of faith that includes the laying on of hands and anointing with oil for healing. Gooden argues that healing includes attending a patient and advocating on behalf of that patient to change the medical establishment. Healing can occur in unexpected and nontraditional places such as prisons and through informal networks such as hair salons that provide education and information about breast cancer. Gooden also looks at the ways in which healing is facilitated by self-help literature, as well as by such complementary therapies as Qigong, meditation, and aromatherapy.

Where does one find a healthy spirituality when one is black, older, and gay? In his chapter, "Too Old for the Club, but Always at Home in the Club: Health, Spirituality, and Social Support among Adult Black Gay Men in Oakland's Cable Reef," D. Mark Wilson notes that African American churches historically have served as centers of healing and spiritual wholeness within African American communities. Yet, this role of black churches is ambiguous, when it comes to creating systems of healing and support for gay, lesbian, bisexual, transgender, intersex, and queer (LGBTIQ) parishioners. Wilson investigates how African American adult gay men experience this dynamic within black congregations. Rather than focusing on how homophobia and heteronormative culture victimizes and causes their health and spirituality to suffer, the cultural and ecological approach Wilson uses highlights how black adult gay men's faith continues to be resilient and thrive as these black gay men move between the organizational structure of churches to cultural spaces of friendship and social support in gay clubs. Wilson argues for a more complex analysis for understanding faith and spirituality experienced on a variety of levels within African American and LGBTIQ communities.

Stephanie Y. Mitchem's chapter, "Healing Hearts and Broken Bodies: An African American Women's Spirituality of Healing," brings this collection to an end. Mitchem explores aspects of often unrecognized and usually undervalued black women's healing work. Black women's healing work has created safe spaces and found ways to hold onto humanity in the face of a world that attempts to destroy the spirit of black people. Black women begin their healing work from a holistic, embodied spirituality that deals honestly with these realities. Healing, in a black women's context, is not just about curing physical ills but also draws from a distinct embodied spirituality. Yet healing of the self from constantly caring for everybody else remains a challenge that black women face.

Rather than look at the individual, the contributors to *Faith, Health, and Healing in African American Life* appeal more to the communal aspects of faith and health. They explore the contexts in which individuals make choices about their health, the roles that institutions play in helping shape these decisions, and the practices in which individuals engage in seeking better health or coping with the health they have. By paying attention to the role of institutions and social factors, we seek to give a fuller sense of varieties of ways black health and health care are perceived and addressed from an inter-religious perspective that spans African-based religions such as the Vodun and Yoruba religions, Christianity, and Islam. We invite you into this exploration of faith, health, and healing.

PART I

Ancestral Songs

CHAPTER 1

⸻ ⧉ ⸻

Natural and Supernatural: African American Hoodoo Narratives of Sickness and Healing

Yvonne P. Chireau

In de days jes' befo' de war I kin' 'member hearin' my dad an' gran-dad tell 'bout ole Dr. Jones, who conjured folks too. He walk 'bout the streets like he in a deep study, an' he wears a black coat like de preachers wear...an he uses roots an' such fer his medicine.

—*Patsy Moses, former slave, early twentieth century*

Accounts of Hoodoo-related illnesses, healing traditions, and practitioners abound in African American narratives like the one above. These stories communicate black American perspectives on sickness and wellness in poignant and powerful ways. As vernacular literature, these oral histories yield insights into the unwritten chronicles of ordinary persons. By their telling and retelling of stories of their own lived experiences, African Americans reconstituted their lived experiences and communicated the elusive realities of embodied sickness and healing in specific contexts, times, and places. In this chapter I examine narrative accounts that describe Hoodoo as a healing tradition that was well known and accessed by black Americans. I will also explore the nature of Hoodoo affliction as both a spiritual and physical phenomenon. My goal is to demonstrate how Hoodoo, in African American culture, has been utilized so as to give meaning to bodily sickness. The strange rituals, the unusual material formulations, and the dramatic repertoire of anomalous Hoodoo practitioners revolved around the goal of addressing human suffering in one form or another. In this sense, "healing" and "health" in the context of Hoodoo practices can be understood as encompassing physical and social dimensions of well-being and constituted by the minimizing of affliction in multiple areas of existence.

What is Hoodoo? Hoodoo has been defined as folklore, as spiritual work, and as cultural performance. It includes a broad complex of ideas and activities. Also referred to as *conjure*, Hoodoo emerged within black slave populations in the southern United States in the early 1800s. Hoodoo was a means by which African American slaves and their descendents sought to manipulate invisible forces so as to influence the human condition for purposes of empowerment and protection, as well as to commit acts of aggression and self-defense. Healing and harming were the most prominent expressions of Hoodoo belief and practice.

Why did healing and harming among black American slaves take this particular form? The conflation of "harming" with "healing" as a cultural practice suggests that a distinctive orientation to affliction characterized black American approaches. A salient element in Hoodoo traditions, for example, is the persistent emphasis on the identification, visualization, and alleviation of sickness. Given the distinctive social conditions and historical circumstances of African Americans both before and after Emancipation in the United States, it is not unusual that such an emphasis would have emerged. In a world of largely unfulfilled aspirations, healing was at the crossroads of faith and active intervention, accessible through specific realms of power.

Although sometimes characterized as superstition by outsiders, Hoodoo cosmology, like many spiritual and religious traditions, recognizes the proximity of the unseen realm and the great many energies that exist therein. The world of the Hoodoo practitioner is densely populated with divine forces, human beings, animals, plants, and elemental powers. As such, Hoodoo places great emphasis upon the efficacious nature of cause and effect through an individual's interactions with invisible agents. As with other traditional religious interventions, Hoodoo also acknowledges the ability of human beings to impact the spiritual realm through words, rituals, and the use of special objects. Understanding this emphasis may require us to adopt a functionalist theory; I have argued elsewhere that Hoodoo was integral to African American religious beliefs in the slavery period, as it addressed the issues of security, protection, and autonomy that arose within the unpredictable domain of bondage. In slavery, one of the primary attractions of Hoodoo had to do with its potential as a force that mediated the inequity of power relations, such as relations between slaves and slave owners and among the slaves themselves. Hoodoo practices also provided an internal impetus that gave many slaves the courage and determination to engage in acts they otherwise would have difficulty committing, including escape, rebellion, and sabotage—acts that undermined the integrity of the so-called peculiar institution. For many African Americans, Hoodoo traditions were utilized, not only because they provided viable alternatives for coping with and resisting domination in situations of limited options, but also because they were validated by enslaved black folk as legitimate sources of power and authority.[1]

Hoodoo was also a pragmatic system. Under slavery, African Americans turned to their own doctors and healers for many health-related concerns.

Even after Emancipation, when African Americans lacked access to professionalized medicine and specialized health care, the relatively low cost and easily acquired formulations of local healers were a sound alternative. Blacks, however, had many reasons for seeking out their own healing practitioners. In the Hoodoo narratives, African Americans speak of the central role of alternative medical and healing practices within black communities: "People couldn't afford doctor," recollected Janie Hunter, a descendent of slaves in South Carolina. "Dey only had homemade medicines," asserted another ex-slave, "and dat is unless dey got sho nuff powerful sick an den dey would to see a doctor." Many slaves and former slaves tended to mistrust white physicians, for many of them, some believed, were disinclined to sufficiently or fairly serve the needs of African Americans. When white doctors were consulted, they often treated black patients with contempt. Their disregard revealed the deeply ingrained prejudices that had been fostered by racist ideologies in science and society in the nineteenth century. Other African Americans were dissuaded by the frightening stories that circulated about physical mutilation, bodily theft, and medical experimentation by health authorities whose intent, many believed, was to deliberately harm unsuspecting patients. Finally, many blacks lacked confidence in the invasive techniques and so-called heroic procedures that were standard in nineteenth- and early-twentieth-century medical practice, preferring more traditional styles of healing. "[D]uh root doctuh was all we needed," explained William Newkirk, an ex-slave in Georgia, speaking in the Gullah dialect of his ancestors. "Dey wuz bettuh dan duh doctuhs now-a-days. Deah wuzn all uh disyuh cuttin an wen yuh sick, duh root doctuh would make some tea an gib yuh sumpm tuh rub wid, an das all." Many African Americans under slavery, and thereafter, would utilize Hoodoo healers, root doctors, and conjurers for their medical needs, not only because they needed these alternatives, but because they shared vital perspectives with these persons on the diagnosis and treatment of their afflictions.[2]

To read the African American narratives of Hoodoo affliction and healing it becomes clear that Hoodoo encompassed a very different kind of therapeutic process than that that existed in the dominant culture. In many reports, actual Hoodoo practices were preceded by a diagnosis in which healers first determined the sources of illness, whether it was natural or supernatural. This was apparently an important distinction for practitioners and patients. Natural afflictions necessitated particular responses, such as herbalism, domestic medicines, and other folk techniques, while supernatural sicknesses required a broader diagnostic framework in order to initiate treatment. African American Hoodoo narratives articulate both emic and etic theories of meaning.

In the first half of the twentieth century, the writer and anthropologist Zora Neale Hurston conducted numerous studies that explored conjure and Hoodoo healing and harming traditions. In her second collection of folklore materials, *Mules and Men*, Hurston provides a brief account of a conversation she had with one of her informants, an African American woman from the local community in which Hurston was embedded. "I was once talking to Mrs. Rachel Silas of Sanford, Florida," she began, "so I asked her where I could find a good Hoodoo doctor." Hurston's intentional request for a Hoodoo *doctor* identifies the authorities in this tradition as healers with something of a professional status. But as the narrative continues, it becomes apparent that Hoodoo is also linked to a particular orientation to affliction as well. As Hurston persists in her quest to find a "good Hoodoo doctor," Mrs. Silas does not disappoint her. The conversation turns after some hedging by the informant, perhaps due to wariness, suspicion, or personal discretion on her part. Mrs. Silas asks, "Do you believe in dat old fogeyism, chile?" Still, Hurston is firm. "Don't fool yourself," Hurston insists. "People can do things. I done seen things happen." It is at this point in the narrative that Hurston tells what she "done seen," and Mrs. Silas, not to be bested, recounts in more detail her own experiences with Hoodoo sickness and affliction: "Oh it kin be done, honey, no effs and 'bout de thing," she agrees. "There's things that kin be done." Here she describes a particular example: "Ah seen uh woman wid uh gopher in her belly," she says, "You could see 'm moving round in her!" She continues with greater specificity:

> And once every day h'ed turn hisself clear over and then you could hear her hollerin for more'n a mile. Dat hard shell would be cuttin' her insides. Way after 'while she took down ill sick from it and died. Ah know de man dat done dat trick. Dat was done in uh dish of hoppin-john.

As narrator of the illness account, Mrs. Silas enhances the plausibility of her story by appealing to the truth of "what she done seen" as she conveys the suffering of the victim in graphic detail. To the outside reader, the narrative might seem fantastic—but what is most unambiguous about this account is its attempt to impose meaning upon the enormous pain and suffering of another human being and upon the afflicted person's own experience of bodily disease. That is what is underscored in the narration of this account: Hoodoo sickness is embodied, and real, even as its meaning is constructed.[3]

In Hurston's *Mules and Men*, we can see an element that is shared in many African American narratives, the idea that affliction of the body can be brought about by mystical or supernatural means, specifically, through a virulent kind of *maleficia*, or magical poisoning. These sorts of sicknesses are traditionally addressed in Hoodoo practice by the use of natural (organic) substances and elements, such as roots and herbs, as well as supernatural (spiritually empowered) individuals, objects, and created articles, such as mojos, tobies, and charms, which are believed to ward off misfortune, physical and otherwise. In theoretical terms, Hoodoo traditions assigned cultural significance to sickness by mapping the human body, both metaphorically and literally. The body enclosed and was enclosed by the supernatural world, while paradoxically, the body was inclusive of the natural (social) worlds in which persons lived and acted. With respect to healing, Hoodoo medicine encompassed both the physiological and spiritual dimensions of sickness, shunning Western scientific definitions that divided organic causes from those that were metaphysical. As we will see, in Hoodoo and Conjuring traditions, illness was often believed to hold social implications. I offer a few cases below to shed further light on this idea.

Consider the following narrative, from an African American woman from Augusta, Georgia, in 1934. The account starts out with a happy story: a couple is newly married. In a few short months after the wedding the woman's spouse starts to desert in her the evenings. He stays away, his bride claims, "'till two and three o'clock...while the next morning, he would get up fussin' and leave." She is pregnant, and before the birth of the child, her husband moves out of the house. It is well known in their neighborhood that he is having an affair, "livin' right 'hind" another woman, as she puts it. She is tormented. She falls ill, dizzy with headaches, and finally she goes deaf. Everyone knows that she has been conjured.

What distinguishes this account as an illness narrative is the focus that it places upon personal suffering and the correlation that it makes between social conflict and physical affliction. Sickness, in this case, was understood as supernaturally induced, precipitated by the acts of betrayal, marital infidelity, and sexual competition that effected the narrator's life. It is a classic example of Hoodoo illness that is described in African American narratives: born of damaged relationships, emotional injury, and most significantly, an unseen, malign force that causes physical suffering. In this narrative Hoodoo is interpreted to be as the direct consequence of human conflict, a kind of supernatural victimization. As understood in Hoodoo narratives, "disease" in the social "body" has both visible and invisible implications in the physical body. What is significant, however, is that with Hoodoo, affliction of the body always manifests in distinctive ways.[4]

Consider, for example, this outlook as it is articulated in the following Hoodoo narrative. Govan Littlejohn of South Carolina, who was emancipated as a youth during the Civil War, recalled how he once believed that he had been conjured when he began to have pain in his foot. First he called a physician to help him. "He lanced my foot three times," Littlejohn explained, "but nothing but blood would come." He then began to suspect that the source of his ailment was the work of a jealous rival. Viewing his affliction from this new perspective, he then sought out the services of a Hoodoo practitioner, who administered natural substances to his injury. "[He]came to see me and said he could cure my foot. He took corn meal poultices, rhubarb roots and some other things, and it wasn't long before my foot got well." Although he was healed, Littlejohn believed that his suspicions of Hoodoo were confirmed, when he later found a bag of "pins, feathers and something else" buried at his front door.[5]

Govan Littlejohn's experience with Hoodoo medicine was similar to that of many other African American patients. For Littlejohn, the painful symptoms of an inflamed foot were linked to a larger world of spiritual beliefs, moral assumptions, and social relations. African American perceptions of health and definitions of illness were related to unique perceptions of the causes of illness, disease, and misfortune as forms of affliction. Each of the elements of Hoodoo—its conceptualization of illness, its beliefs about cause and effect, and the cures offered by Hoodoo doctors to patients—were part of a coherent scheme that provided a theoretical basis for understanding sickness by not only offering an explanation but by providing a practical means of resolution. Littlejohn's illness was not solely a matter of bodily affliction. Littlejohn believed that he was the particular object of resentment and enmity that had produced damaging effects upon his physical person.

There were a number of means by which Hoodoo practitioners distinguished between those illnesses that were considered natural and those involving spiritual forces. In many cases conjure and malign occultism were suspected when affliction was chronic or unresponsive to treatment; when sickness was manifested by unusual signs and symptoms; or when sudden afflictions struck that could not be explained by conventional interpretations. Chronic illness, for example, that was not responsive to treatment by traditional medical techniques was often believed by blacks to have been caused by maleficent forces. "They's lots of those kind of cases the ord'nary person never hear about," said former slave William Adams when questioned about such ailments. "You hear of the cases the doctors can't understand, nor will they 'spond to treatment." A former bondswoman in Yamacraw, Georgia, confirmed the effectiveness of supernatural remedies over seemingly incurable afflictions. She herself had been conjured, and conventional medicine had failed her. "I dohn know who done it, but all ub a sudden muh leg begin tuh swell and swell. I call a regluh doctuh, but he didn seem tuh do no good." She was encouraged by the therapeutic alternatives offered by the folk practitioner. "Tree weeks ago I went tuh a root man," she declared, "...I guess I soon be well."[6]

In some instances a sick patient's condition would deteriorate under the ministrations of regular doctors. "I knew an old lady that had not been able...to even sit up in bed," wrote an observer from Virginia in the late Reconstruction period. "She was pronounced incurable by all the other doctors." Called in at the last minute, a conjurer restored her health. "How he managed to do it," the writer pondered, "I do not know." Hampton Institute teacher Alice Bacon observed that among the freed blacks she knew in southern Virginia that "the surest sign that [a] disease is the result of a spell or trick, is that the patient grows worse rather than better under the treatment of regular physicians." An African American educator working in the south during the late nineteenth century told a story, perhaps derived from her own observations, of an old man who was "ill with palsy," who "after spending much money employing medical doctors and getting no relief," sought a conjurer, who "found the cause of his illness." "Not many days elapsed," she concluded, "before he was walking as well as ever." The frequency of these and similar narratives of illness indicates that simple ailments, as well as more serious diseases, were generally referable to spiritual treatment. Organic, material, and physical explanations in themselves were sometimes limited, according to the cultural perspectives of African American patients, because they did not consider the possibility that there were other, supernatural causes of affliction.[7]

For African Americans, illness that was believed to be caused by Hoodoo often manifested distinctive characteristics. Pellagra, a respiratory disease related to tuberculosis that afflicted many slaves during the nineteenth century, was accompanied in its late stages by symptoms of dementia and insanity. Within African American traditions, this type of madness was often viewed as a definitive by-product of conjure. Other unique diseases associated with Hoodoo included neuralgia, a nerve disorder, which was frequently attributed in illness narratives to the work of sorcerers. Unusual mishaps and accidents were also sometimes conceived as consequences of supernatural maleficia. In one account, an African American teacher stationed in the South in the 1870s told of a young, "well-to-do" woman who had turned her ankle at a local dance. She believed, she said, that the harm had been done by a man who used Hoodoo to try "to win her heart."

Patients with unusual signs and symptoms were prime candidates for treatment by Hoodoo doctors. When freedman Alex Johnson spoke of being conjured he announced that he felt the sensation of "hot feet," like there was "a fire in them":

> I felt the first pain, hoeing in the field; it struck me in the right foot, and then in the left, but most in the right foot, then run over my whole body, and rested in my head; I went home, and knew I was cunjered.

Most frequently, conjure afflictions were described by witnesses in highly graphic images. The most common side effect of supernaturally induced affliction was physical infestation. An article appearing in the school newspaper at Virginia's Hampton Institute in 1878 outlined the process by which it was believed that the intrusion of animal entities came about. In the initial stages, the article noted, there was nearly always a sudden attack, with ensuing physical distress. "The victim is seized with a sharp pain in some part of her body," it stated, "...later, swelling and other symptoms follow...as the disease develops itself the symptoms become more severe and terrible in their nature." African American narratives describe the onset of Hoodoo as an embodied state. A Mississippi police chief told a folklorist in the 1940s of an African American woman he witnessed who had experienced "great agony" because she believed that she had been "hoodooed." "She was screaming and hollering," he said, "[as she] imagined that she had lizards and various other things creeping under her skin and flesh." In disparate accounts, observers would characterize the presence of entities inside of another's body as a sign of a victim's physical, mental, and emotional torment.[8]

The congruence of these narratives suggests that they tapped into a common reservoir of thought concerning the constitution of sickness, spirituality, and the nature of embodiment. For African Americans, it appears that some physical sicknesses were revealed in the body and manifested according to one's understanding of supernatural effects. But how exactly did persons believe that these displayed spiritual invasions of the body came about? Many blacks thought that Hoodoo brought harm to victims by causing misfortune, sickness, or death. Practitioners, most assumed, utilized a variety of measures to afflict their victims. Some used spiritually empowered artifacts, while for others, elaborate oaths and curses were effective vehicles of harm. Usually, however, bodily infestations were believed to be triggered by one of two specific methods: they were either caused by magical substances that were activated by ingestion or by unseen forces, requiring little or no direct contact with the intended victim. Whether the aftermath of poisoning, or just as often the result of a charmed object hidden somewhere in the proximity of the victim, bodily infestation was always accompanied by great physical and mental suffering.

For most observers, the severity of the symptoms confirmed the worst fears that supernatural forces were to blame for the distress of their neighbors, family, and friends. "In 1873 I was going down the street and came across a conjure doctor," related one witness, "and he asked me where did a certain lady live, and I told him and he went there." The woman, he claimed, told him that she had a pain in her head and side and that "something" kept coming up in her throat. The Hoodoo doctor thus determined that she had been poisoned with a cup of tea from another person. According to the account, he gave her his own medicinal formula, told her to drink, and "in five minutes," asserted the observer, "a scorpion came out of her mouth." Former slave Nathaniel John Lewis of Tin City, Georgia, also insisted that he had seen such a bodily intrusion. "My wife Hattie had a spell put on her for three long years with a nest of rattlesnakes inside her," he insisted. "She just lay there and swelled and suffered."

Accounts of Hoodoo sickness routinely testified to plagues of toads, salamanders, spiders, insects, and other creatures in the body. George Little, a root doctor in Brownsville, Georgia, observed the deadly consequences of such infestations. "Frawgs an lizuds and sech tings is injected intuh people's bodies an duh people den fall ill an sometime die," he maintained. Usually, these stories were relayed with the firm conviction of their veracity. "Since I came to talk with such good old Christians who I know would not tell a lie," declared one unidentified writer in a letter to the *Southern Workman* magazine, "they told me they have seen ground puppies jump out of folks' feet, and lizards and snakes." Another reader stated with great confidence that he had viewed a conjurer who treated a patient by pulling "out of her right arm a spool of thread, and out of her leg a lizard…this is the truth," he professed, "what I saw with my own eyes." Ex-slave Estella Jones also insisted on the truth of her account. "Some folk don't believe me, but I ain't telling no tale about it," she maintained. Jones said she had been an eyewitness to several cases of Hoodoo poisoning, and admitted that it was easy for other persons "to put snakes, frogs, turtles, spiders, or most anythin' that you couldn't live with, crawlin' and eatin' on the inside of you." In a Federal Writers Project interview, an Augusta, Georgia, resident described a relative that had been poisoned while drinking alcohol with a jealous neighbor. After he got sick, she said, "He told everybody that asked him…about the frogs in his stomach":

> After he had been sick about four months and the frogs had got to be pretty good size, you could hear them holler every time he opened his mouth. He got to the place where he wouldn't talk much on account of this. His stomach stuck out so far, he looked like he weighed 250 pounds. After these frogs started hollering in him, he lived about three weeks, and before he died you could see the frogs jumping about in him and you could even feel 'em.

With a kind of visual empathy, these descriptions communicate the immediacy of a victim's suffering. The acute distress of the afflicted—persons who are nearly always kin, neighbors, or others known in their community—is made real as their pain is rendered in spectacular form. "In many cases," notes a Hampton Institute report, "snakes and lizards are even known to show their heads from the sufferer's mouth." Another witness described an African American man that had been made ill, he believed, due to the malevolent magic of his rival. "Every time they tried to give him soup or anything to eat, something would come crawling up in his throat," he stated. After he died, others explained to those who asked that a "turtle come up in his throat and choked him to death." In the early 1900s, Newbell Puckett spoke to an ex-slave in Mississippi who suspected that he had been "tricked" by an enemy who put a conjure poison into a glass of whiskey. "He held the glass in his right hand and in a short time that had began to swell," stated Puckett. "Great was his astonishment, on slitting open the palm of his hand with a small knife, to find that the inside…was alive with small black-headed worms." Similar depictions from different times and places, related with near-clinical detail, create a striking picture of the horror experienced by victims of bodily infestation.[9]

What can we conclude about these understandings of illness and the body, experiences that have persisted among black Americans over time and across place? There are several inferences to be drawn concerning the character of affliction as it is represented in the Hoodoo narratives. First, these accounts reveal that African Americans paid particular attention to what they understood to be the social sources of certain kinds of ailments, even as they privileged spiritual interpretations. This is not to say that blacks dismissed scientific etiologies or material explanations when identifying sicknesses that they found unusual; rather, their views of the causes of a sickness were more inclusive of what one might call metaphysical agents. Blacks who believed in the power of Hoodoo to heal and to harm conceived of illness as both physical fact and spiritual reality. From this perspective, conventional medical diagnosis was inadequate because it did not consider the spectrum of possible sources by which a person might become ill. Much like contemporary scientific interpretations that posit the invasion of millions of microscopic substances in the body as the source of an infection, African Americans theorized that the intersection of physical, spiritual, and social forces brought about an invasion and subsequent sickness. Observers and patients alike gave the infecting agents explicit form, often envisioning the body as a living menagerie.

In the Hoodoo understanding of illness, many diseases and ailments were linked to nonphysical sources, whether the acts of an ill-willed enemy or the destructive powers of witchcraft or sorcery. The afflictions themselves varied, but many illuminate social etiologies. The idea that spiritual powers were at the heart of physical afflictions reflects a cosmological vision. The worldview out of which such beliefs emerged was one in which good and evil forces fought for the sovereignty of human territory; their battleground was the body, which exhibited the carnage of supernatural warfare. The powers that afflicted were diverse, but they could be manipulated and controlled by individuals with the spiritual proper skills and techniques. Thus, occurrences of illness, misfortune, and adversity were never random but instead explicable within a broader scheme of Hoodoo beliefs.

Affliction denoted other meanings as well. Explanations for Hoodoo-related illnesses were frequently situated in the social realm. Although conjure was the main vehicle, the source of the bodily ailment or disease was most often believed to lie at the site of human intentions. The envy, fear, greed, and anger that pitted individual against individual ensnared victims of illness in a cycle of pain, suspicion, and violence. Hoodoo was a two-sided system of healing and harming—and as such it gave voice to a variety of impulses.

The pervasiveness of Hoodoo in African American illness narratives raises questions regarding the interpretation of affliction, what is sometimes called theodicy, in the lives of black people. Religion historian Albert Raboteau has argued that Hoodoo and conjure functioned as theories of misfortune for the slaves. He explains that in black folk traditions "the concept of suffering for the guilt of the father is biblical...the concept of being victimized by a 'fix' is Conjure." He adds that "both attempt to locate the cause of irrational suffering." For slaves, and later, for their descendents, Hoodoo located the sources of evil and provided explanations for the occurrence of misfortune in people's lives. Hoodoo thus helped blacks to interpret to define all manner of afflictions and sicknesses, both social and physical, from unanticipated bodily maladies to tragic accidents, to consistent bad luck.[10]

The consequences of Hoodoo in sickness derived from human actions and had both visible and invisible implications. Black slaves and ex-slaves, as did their African forbearers, related the conditions of bodily suffering to the forces—both material and immaterial—around which their lives revolved. In her study of health and sickness on Southern slave plantations, Sharla Fett writes that African American bondspersons shared a "relational vision" by which they interpreted affliction. This vision was shaped and contextualized according to the cultural milieu in which the slaves lived. Black Americans also drew from a broad selection of meanings in their understanding of affliction, with attitudes ranging from strongly predestinarian to stubbornly fatalistic. Some illnesses, for example, were certainly viewed as a form of divine judgment, while others were seen in more personal terms. Sudden, unanticipated sickness, for example, could be a consequence of the evil thoughts of a mean-spirited person, directed through the noxious medium of a conjurer's charm. For many African Americans, sickness was rarely random or abstract, and unusual physical suffering was not attributed to chance. Rather, illness and disease were viewed as encompassing social and spiritual processes. In Hoodoo traditions, physical affliction was the outcome of deadly intent and malicious human actions and motivations, such as jealousy, anger, and revenge.

As we have seen, the direct products of Hoodoo affliction were embodied forms, and the means of affliction were spiritual. Still, even as some ailments were believed to be the product of malevolent forces, others were believed to be sent from God. But most afflictions found their origins within the realm of relationships: relationships between humans and the divine, between humans and their immediate social environment, and between other human beings.

There is much more to be said about African American Hoodoo narratives, which provide unique expressions of experiences of pain, illness, and social disorder, even as they also project relief and healing. Hoodoo narratives provide composite visions of the ways by which African Americans have historically identified and addressed affliction and healing. Further study will shed light on whether there are similar ideas concerning sickness and wellness that intersect with other traditions in the United States. Still, questions remain. How, for example, have indigenous African American understandings and interpretations of Hoodoo medicine persisted into the present day, when education, alternative religious beliefs, and new medical technologies have significantly influenced the ways that persons view themselves, their bodies, their health, and illness? What kind of ideas concerning community does Hoodoo currently offer, when its traditions are now informed and embraced by Americans of all backgrounds and persuasions? It is significant that in slavery and in freedom, the perpetuation of Hoodoo has ensued largely from the myriad physical, spiritual, and social concerns it addressed for African Americans and their descendents. In the present, it might be that as an alternative healing system, Hoodoo provides evidence of cultural and spiritual resources that are universally available, which offer the potential means by which one may interpret and address affliction, so as to ultimately manage the forces—be they natural or supernatural—that are believed to eventuate in bodily infirmity.

NOTES

1. Yvonne Chireau, *Black Magic: Religion and the African American Conjuring Tradition* (Berkeley: University of California Press, 2003).

2. Janie Hunter, quoted in Bruce Jackson, "The Other Kind of Doctor: Conjure and Magic in Black American Folk Medicine," in *American Folk Medicine: A Symposium*, ed. Wayland Hand (Berkeley: University of California Press, 1976), p. 268; William Newkirk, quoted in Georgia Writers Project, *Drums and Shadows: Survival Studies among the Georgia Coastal Negroes* (Athens: University of Georgia Press, 1940), p. 65.

3. Zora Neale Hurston, *Mules and Men* (New York: HarperPerennial, 1990), p. 186. Hoodoo narratives of sickness are found in various sources. See folklore materials by former slaves in the compilation by George Rawick, *The American Slave: A Composite Autobiography, 1972–1977* (Westport, CT: Greenwood, 1972) For later twentieth-century oral accounts, see Harry Middleton Hyatt, *Hoodoo-Conjuration-Witchcraft-Rootwork*, five vols., 1970–1978 (Hannibal, MO: Western Publishing Co, 1970–78).

4. These and other sources can be found by state in the Library of Congress folklore collection. Folklore folder no. 100156, Georgia Narratives, Richmond County, Georgia, Manuscript Division, Library of Congress. Many are reprinted in Rawick, *The American Slave*.

5. See Rawick, *The American Slave*, vol. 2, *South Carolina Narratives*, p. 106.

6. Rawick, *The American Slave*, vol. 7, *Texas Narratives*; Hurston, *Mules and Men*, p. 196; Georgia Writers Project, *Drums and Shadows*, p. 23.

7. *Southern Workman* 24, December 1895, p. 210; *Southern Workman* 7, May 1878, p. 30; *Southern Workman* 28, August 1899, p. 315; *Southern Workman* 24, December, 1895, p. 210; *Southern Workman* 7, May 1878, p. 30. All article references can be found in Donald Waters, *Strange Ways and Sweet Dreams: Afro-American Folklore from the Hampton Institute*, Boston: G. K. Hall, 1983.

8. Rawick, *The American Slave*, vol. 13, *Georgia Narratives*, p. 277. On African American narratives of animal intrusion and sickness, see Yvonne Chireau, "The Body as Menagerie: Sickness and African American Hoodoo Narratives," *Council of Societies for the Study of Religion Bulletin*, February 2007.

9. Newbell N. Puckett, *Folk Beliefs of the Southern Negro* (Chapel Hill: University of North Carolina Press, 1926), p. 435.

10. See Albert Raboteau, "The Afro-American Traditions," in *Caring and Curing: Health and Medicine in the Western Religious Traditions*, ed. Ronald Numbers and Darrel Amundsden (New York: Macmillan Press, 1986), p. 551.

CHAPTER 2

Holistic Health and Healing: Environmental Racism and Ecological Justice

Dwight N. Hopkins

The environmental movement in the United States comprises at least two major sectors. One is known to the public because of its emphasis on the preservation and conservation of Mother Earth; Greenpeace is usually the face of this grouping. The second important dimension of environmental concerns is the struggle against environmental racism and for ecological justice. Here poor and working-class communities of African Americans, Latino–Hispanic Americans, and Native Americans have taken the lead against sickness in human bodies, social relations, and nature.

The Greenpeace wing of the movement has consistently fought for the healing of the planet. It teaches us that "environmental degradation caused by massive pollution of air, water and land threatens the very life of the earth. Rapid depletion of non-renewal resources, indeed of species themselves, the thinning of the ozone layer, exposing all living creatures to the danger of radiation, the buildup of gases exacerbating the greenhouse effect, increasing erosion by the sea—all these are documented by scientific research."[1]

The primary foci of the earth-emphasis environmental wing have been historically "wilderness and wildlife preservation, wise resource management, pollution abatement, and population control." Preservation examples include the spotted owl and the snail darter. The leaders and followers of this movement have mainly been middle and upper income whites with above-average education and easy access to political, cultural, and economic resources.[2]

For instance in April 2007, roughly one thousand scientists from about 74 countries constituted the Intergovernmental Panel on Climate Change. The final report discovered the dire impact of global warming on the earth's ecosystems. Increased populations and growing urbanization coupled with adverse climate changes will eventually result in hazardous flooding, drought, and slow extinction for up to 20 to 30 percent of plant and animal species.[3] More than ever, Mother Earth is sick with acid-rain pollution. The greenhouse effect is increasing; carbon dioxide traps the sun's heat in the atmosphere and consequently warms the earth. Industrial pollution is part of the problem. What many people don't know is that carbon dioxide remains in the atmosphere for about two hundred years. The increase in temperatures and sea levels will give rise to mass famine and damaging flooding. It is possible that in the year 2040, sea ice in the Arctic might disappear totally, preventing polar bears from hunting sea animals on which to live. A radical climate change will drastically lower rainfall in the western United States, and global storms will intensify.[4]

ENVIRONMENTAL RACISM AND ECOLOGICAL JUSTICE

Clearly, the conservation and preservation wing of the environment effort is most widely known in America, which is why many people are surprised to hear that African American communities have been struggling against environmental racism and for ecological justice long before the formal launching of the struggle in the 1980s. Among black people, environmental racism symbolizes profound illness both of the earth and of humans in neighborhoods of people of color. Holistic disease requires ecological justice, that is, holistic health and healing.

For example, Thomas Calhoun Walker was a black man and the Advisor and Consultant of Negro Affairs for the Virginia Emergency Relief Administration in Richmond, Virginia. During World War I, Walker was the architect of environmental initiatives for blacks, including providing black children with access to swimming pools and parks, eliminating rats on wharves, promoting gardening among blacks, and stressing hygienic homes.[5]

Likewise few realize that many of the urban rebellions in the 1960s derived from the anger of black people about lack of garbage collection and sanitation services. And the famous riot at predominantly Texas Southern University in Houston in 1967 erupted partially because community people protested an eight-year-old black girl's drowning at a city garbage dump. Martin Luther King Jr. was assassinated because he was helping black working-class garbage workers in Memphis, Tennessee, who went on strike for a holistic healthy environment. They sought increased wages, the same pay scale as white city workers, and a quality work environment.[6]

However, not all agree that the black community initiated the ecological justice dimension of the environmental movement. Some point to the United Farm Workers struggle against pesticide poisoning in the 1960s. And others mark the fifteenth-century European occupation of Native American lands as the start of environmental justice struggles.

Yet general consensus cites the formal launching of the environmental racism and ecological justice movement in the year 1987. That year the United Church of Christ Commission for Racial Justice (UCC-CRJ) published the landmark study *Toxic Wastes and Race in the United States: A National Report on the Racial and Social-Economic Characteristics of Communities with Hazard Waste Sites.* Rev. Benjamin Chavis (a UCC black clergyman) headed the Commission, whose report substantiated the reality of environmental racism. Having created this new phrase "environmental racism," the report suggested:

> The existence of clear patterns which show that communities with greater minority percentages of the population are more likely to be the sites of commercial hazardous waste facilities. The possibility that these patterns resulted by chance is virtually impossible, strongly suggesting that some underlying factors, which are related to race, played a role in the location of commercial hazardous waste facilities. Therefore the Commission for Racial Justice concludes that, indeed, race has been a factor in the location of hazardous waste facilities in the United States.[7]

The UCC-CRJ (1994) updated study found that the situation had worsened. More people of color were disproportionately living near hazardous waste areas. In seven years, there had been a six percent increase of people of color located near toxic disposal sites.[8]

After releasing their landmark 1987 report, the UCC assembled the historic First National People of Color Environmental Leadership Summit in Washington, D.C., in October 1991. The Summit assembled indigenous peoples, civil rights activists, labor organizers, antitoxic veterans, and academics. A final conference report directly accented the role of race in environmental analysis:

> Environmental inequities cannot be reduced solely to class—the economic ability of people to "vote with their feet" and escape polluted environments. Race interpenetrates class in the United States and is often a more potent predictor of which communities get dumped on and which ones are spared. There is clear evidence that institutional barriers severely limit access to clean environments. Despite the many attempts made by government to level the playing field, all communities are still not equal.

As the head of the UCC-CRJ, Ben Chavis understood the Summit as a key process for people of color to organize self-empowerment and self-determination focused squarely on environmental justice. U.S. minority populations were claiming their own voice and their own agency within the larger environmental effort.[9]

This Summit produced a major document called the "Principles of Environmental Justice." The 17 principles are the plumb line for the environmental racism and ecological justice thrust.[10] With this statement, it becomes crystal clear that ecological justice combines nature with social justice. Both require healing. The ecological justice movement:

does not treat the problem of oppression and social exploitation as separable from the rape and exploitation of the natural world. Instead, it argues that human societies and the natural environment are intricately linked and that the health of one depends on the health of the other. It understands that if the human environment is poisoned, if there are no opportunities for economic survival or nutritional sustenance, or if there are no possibilities to be sheltered, then we have an inadequate environmental program.[11]

Environmental justice activists target the prevention of siting waste facilities in communities of the working class and of people of color. They also broaden their organizing efforts to clean up the toxic impact on Mother Earth. For instance, local communities fight for their participation in decision making on environmental health issues, oversee implementation of governmental and industry policy and guidelines, clean up poisonous industrial areas, and organize to end dangerous practices harming workers on the job. Moreover, the "movement for environmental justice is also about creating clean jobs, building a sustainable economy, guaranteeing safe and affordable housing, and achieving racial and social justice."[12]

FIVE STRANDS WITHIN ECOLOGICAL JUSTICE

The current state of the ecological or environmental justice organizing results from five strands that have coalesced around environmental racism and for a healthy ecology.

The first strand is the 1950s, 1960s, and 1970s civil rights struggle, upon which probably the major foundation the ecological justice movement is built. In fact, the black church and black community's opposition to a PCP dump in Warren County, North Carolina, in 1982 shows a direct tie between civil rights movements and environmental justice movements. It is this history of organizing, sacrificing, and strategizing that grass roots civil rights and church leaders (led by the UCC) bring directly into the ecological justice process. The Warren County protest was initiated by black church women.[13] Likewise, some of the Chicano student leaders of the 1960s Latino civil rights organizations are part of the historical foundation of environmental antiracism efforts.

Second, after the civil rights struggles of blacks and Latinos, grassroots antitoxic activists have brought their wisdom and experience to the ecological justice process. These veterans gathered momentum in the late 1970s in opposition to the construction of incinerators, landfills, and waste facilities. A large representation of women exists here because women were often the ones who rallied to protect the health and lives of their children.

Both the civil rights and antitoxic waste organizers came to understand that their local and specific efforts were linked to a larger systemic and structural problem, complicated by race and the wealthy class.

Third, academics have joined the environmental justice struggle by contributing vital research and providing systemic and structural analyses, publications, lobbying, and networking. The UCC helped to organize academics into conferences to focus on environmental racism.

Fourth, Native American activists have perhaps the longest history of combating environmental racism and building ecological justice. This began 500 years ago with the arrival of European Christian colonialists. In fact the formation of the American Indian Movement (AIM) was influenced by environmental and land demands. A key contribution in the environmental racism–ecological justice philosophy is Native Americans' stress on self-determination; that is to say, oppressed communities must speak for themselves.

And, after American Indians, a fifth strand of the ecological justice organizing has been the labor movement. The United Farm Workers (headed by Cesar Chavez and comprised mainly of Latino farm laborers) built a national network emphasizing both the banning of pesticides and worker input in the decision-making process on their jobs.[14]

CONCRETE EXAMPLES OF ENVIRONMENTAL RACISM

What these five different strands of ecological justice activists recognize is that environmental racism is a profound illness affecting the holistic body of creation. Such life-threatening sickness disproportionately targets people of color and working-class communities. To bring about the needed health and healing work, one has to have a deep appreciation for the depth of the attack on Mother Earth and social dying caused by unchecked individualistic human greed. Examples of environmental racism expose the broad-scale nature of the suffering and sickness. Benjamin F. Chavis Jr. argues the following:

> Millions of African Americans, Latinos, Pacific Islanders, and Native Americans are trapped in polluted environments because of their race and color. Inhabitants of these communities are exposed to greater health and environmental risks than is the general population. Clearly, all Americans do not have the same opportunities to breathe clean air, drink clean water, enjoy clean parks and playgrounds, or work in a clean, safe environment.
>
> Environmental racism is racial discrimination in environmental policymaking. It is racial discrimination in the enforcement of regulations and laws. It is racial discrimination in the deliberate targeting of communities of color for toxic waste disposal and the siting of polluting industries. It is racial discrimination in the official sanctioning of the life-threatening presence of poisons and pollutants in communities of color. And, it is racial discrimination in the history of excluding people of color from the mainstream environmental groups, decisionmaking boards, commissions, and regulatory bodies.[15]

In some cases, environmental racism and the resulting sicknesses it causes are intentional and deliberate policy practices on the part of global financial institutions. For example, Lawrence Summers, chief economist at the World Bank in 1991, released an internal memo that targeted Third World countries, or, in his words "Less Developed Countries." The memo indicates that the primary intent of the World Bank is to make profits for monopoly capitalist corporations at the expense of the health of working-class people and poor countries in the world. Summers begins his memo with the phrase "dirty industries," indicating his awareness of how pollution causes sickness for the earth and for human beings. Because the memo gives an insider's view on the dire implications for health and death, we quote an extended excerpt:

> Dirty Industries: Just between you and me, shouldn't the World Bank be encouraging MORE migration of the dirty industries to the LDCs [Less Developed Countries]? I can think of three reasons:
>
> 1) The measurement of the costs of health impairing pollution depends on the foregone earnings from increased morbidity and mortality. From this point of view a given amount of health impairing pollution should be done in the country with the lowest cost, which will be the country with the lowest wages. I think the economic logic behind dumping a load of toxic waste in the lowest wage country is impeccable and we should face up to that.
> 2) The costs of pollution are likely to be non-linear as the initial increments of pollution probably have very low cost. I've always thought that under-polluted areas in Africa are vastly UNDER-polluted; their air quality is probably vastly inefficiently low compared to Los Angels or Mexico City.
> 3) The demand for a clean environment for aesthetic and health reasons is likely to have very high income elasticity [i.e., meaning in the developed countries of the northern hemisphere]....
>
> The problem with the arguments against all of these proposals for more pollution in LDCs (intrinsic rights to certain goods, moral reasons, social concerns, lack of adequate markets, etc.) could be turned around and used more or less effectively against every [World] Bank proposal.[16]

Larry Summers and the World Bank are plainly considering causing illness and death in the poorer countries of the world in order to make more profits. He calmly offers proposals to dump toxics and pollution in the Third World because the developed countries have high incomes that would cause opposition. And he concludes by rationally calculating how arguments against his proposals for more pollution in Third World countries can be used against the World Bank.

Likewise, in 1975 the Trilateral Commission released its report titled *The Crisis of Democracy*. While the World Bank memo deals with poor people and countries of color internationally, the Trilateral Commission focuses on people of color and other former silent communities within the United States. Yet, the same intentional calculations are at play. The report shares a definition of capitalist elite democracy.

> The vulnerability of democratic government in the United States [thus] comes not primarily from external threats, though such threats are real, nor from internal subversion from the left or the right, although both possibilities could exist, but rather from the internal dynamics of democracy itself in a highly educated, mobilized, and participant society...Previously passive or unorganized groups in the population—Blacks, Indians, Chicanos, white ethnic groups, students, and women—[have] now embarked on concerted efforts to establish their claims to opportunities, positions, rewards, and privileges, to which they had not considered themselves entitled before.[17]

External factors do not threaten American democracy. Rather, the people, the citizens of the United States, are the threat. Clearly the monopoly capitalists' representatives on the Trilateral Commission see democracy from their class perspective. That is why the report states that the "vulnerability of democratic government in the United States [thus] comes not primarily from external threats..., but rather from the internal dynamics of democracy itself." These global capitalist lords are talking about how everyday Americans can threaten bourgeois democracy, the democracy of the monopoly capitalists themselves. Clearly in the eyes of the Trilateral Commission, democracy is not an objective, universal principle, but one deeply ensconced in class interests; that is to say, democracy in America is one of class struggle.

The World Bank represents monopoly capitalists' financial institutions. The Trilateral Commission represents major capitalist governments. But a similar approach is found among experts of environmental systems. For instance, Cerrell Associates, a consulting firm for toxic waste companies, wrote a report suggesting toxic waste companies intentionally "target small, rural communities whose residents are low income, older people, or people with a high school education or less; communities with a high proportion of Catholic residents; and communities whose residents are engaged in resource extractive industries such as agriculture, mining, and forestry. Ideally, the report states, 'Officials and companies should look for lower socioeconomic neighborhoods that are also in a heavy industrial area with little, if any, commercial activity.'"[18] Moreover, other criteria for dumping toxic waste included being near highways and far from schools, nursing homes, and hospitals, all criteria that communities of color lack, and included areas with cheap land values, commercial zoning, and unemployment. The overarching purpose of the report was to advise toxic companies how to bring about toxic sickness in communities that would not cause public opposition. These recommended guidelines for dumping poisonous wastes fit existing California hazardous sites, largely populated by Latinos, and East Coast urban sites, largely populated by blacks.

Given similar worldviews of the capital industry, governments, and private consultants, it should not surprise anyone that the "most polluted urban communities are those with crumbling infrastructure, ongoing economic disinvestment, deteriorating housing, inadequate schools, chronic unemployment, a high poverty rate, and an overloaded health-care system."[19]

The expendability of people of color ends not only with capital, policy, and consultants, but also extends to the practice of the U.S. government's own regulatory agencies. The *National Law Journal*, a leading legal publication, conducted a comprehensive analysis of every U.S. environmental lawsuit from the last seven years. Evidence shows that the U.S. government penalizes at a much higher rate pollution-law violators in white communities than in communities of people of color. In fact, there is a 506-percent disparity between white and black communities. Similarly the *Journal* examined the 12-year history of the federal government's Superfund, an account that provides funds to clean up toxic sites throughout the United States. The review of all residential toxic waste sites showed that "the government takes longer to address hazards in minority communities, and it accepts solutions less stringent than those recommended by the scientific community. This racial imbalance, the investigation found, often occurs whether the community is wealthy or poor."[20] Indeed, sicknesses resulting from environmental racism is about race, as it cuts across class divides within the African American community.

Even studies by official regulatory offices document how African American and Latino communities in California experience closer proximity to toxic industries, comprise the most workers in poisonous work environments, and endure an overall life of unhealthy factors yielding illness of the body and decreased quality of life.[21]

Robert D. Bullard, author of the groundbreaking text, *Dumping in Dixie: Race, Class, and Environmental Quality* (1990), likewise discovered how race trumps class in environmental racism.

> People of color are exposed to greater environmental hazards in their neighborhoods and on the job than are their white counterparts. Studies find elevated exposure levels by race, even when social class is held constant. For example, research indicates race to be independent of class in the distribution of air pollution, contaminated fish consumption, location of municipal landfill and incinerators, abandoned toxic-waste dumps, and lead poisoning in children.[22]

Lead poisoning, for instance, affects children of color at all class levels regardless of their parents' salary and educational status.

The Agency for Toxic Substances Disease Registry concluded "that, for families earning less than $6,000, 68 percent of African American children had lead poisoning, compared with 36 percent for white children. In families with income exceeding $15,000, more than 38 percent of African American children suffer from lead poisoning, compared with 12 percent of whites."[23] Regardless of household income, black children are two to three times more likely than white children to have sicknesses derived from lead poisoning.

What accounts for this across-class illness? Disproportionately, white citizens can leave toxic areas that cause death and not healing. Working-class and poor African Americans and even many black professionals and upper-income households remain stuck in lethal situations due to residential segregation, bank redlining, and housing discrimination. When white families left, blacks moved into harmful areas of stockyards, warehouses, factory pollution, noise, dirt, and railroad tracks. Children grow up exposed to the stench of unhealthy land, water, and air, as well as harmful noise levels.[24] Factually, "an African American who has an income of $50,000 is as residentially segregated as an African American on welfare."[25]

Physical illnesses and death are closely linked to psychological and mental stress-related diseases in areas of concentrated toxicity. Blacks are disproportionately situated in these conditions than whites and, therefore, experience higher levels of stress-related sickness and deaths. "For example, studies of both iron and steel foundry workers and laundry and dry-cleaning industry workers show an increase in the incidence of stress-related mortality and morbidity among blacks as compared to white workers."[26] Consequently, talk of healing from environmental racism has to be a holistic approach encompassing the physical, emotional, and spiritual levels of illnesses among blacks.

Native American and Latino–Hispanic communities are similar. Janet Phoenix (M.D., M.P.H., Ph.D. in children's health) has studied Navajo teenagers and discovered that they have organ cancer 17 times the national average. She concluded also that 50 percent of the nation's youth who suffer from lead paint poison are black.[27] Dr. Phoenix sites the following symptoms of lead poisoning among children of color: behavior challenges, restricted vocabulary, low attention span, "fatigue..., loss of appetite, irritability, sleep disturbance, sudden behavioral change..., development regression...clumsiness, muscular irregularities, weakness, abdominal pain, persistent vomiting, constipation, and changes in consciousness. Lead exposure is particularly harmful to children. It damages their developing brains and nervous systems," which can give rise to emotional disturbances, learning disabilities, and attention disorders.[28] Environmental racism is a severe disease affecting minority children.

Native American nations (called reservations) are receiving increased attention by industrial toxic corporations. The latter view the former as spaces to avoid some of the tougher environmental regulations promulgated by state governments. The weaker federal policies have less bite when applied to Native Americans because of the particular status and nominal sovereignty of Indian nations.[29] Federal governmental offices also are forging ahead to cause sickness and death for Native Americans. Winona LaDuke, co-chair of the Indigenous Women's Network, claims that the "U.S. government recently solicited every Indian tribe within U.S. borders to host a possible nuclear waste storage facility. Officials entice tribes with 'no strings attached' grants of hundreds of thousands of dollars. The federal office of Nuclear Waste Negotiation states its mission as finding 'a state or Indian Tribe willing to host a repository or monitored retrievable storage facility for nuclear waste.'"[30] Given the low wealth and financial base in Indian territories, federal bribery can be enticing. The federal government is persistent because, at least for one reason, two-thirds of all U.S. uranium is under Indian territory. Yet the immediate financial rewards are overshadowed by the health risks. One of the elements that results from the uranium production process remains radioactive for a minimum of 16,000 years.[31]

Latino and Hispanic farm workers are intimately familiar with pesticide production and application. They mix, load, and apply health- and life-threatening pesticides. Latinos and Hispanics are also the flaggers in the fields, the laborers who guide and direct airplanes that spray pesticides over fruit and vegetable fields.

> The highest exposure is from grapes, citrus fruit, peaches, apples, and other tree fruits that grow with a lot of leaves, or from crops that are sprayed often and close to harvest such as strawberries and tomatoes.... Farmworker children are also at high risk of pesticide exposure whether or not they work in the fields alongside their parents. Frequently, young children, including infants and toddlers, are taken to the fields by their parents because childcare is not available. The fetus is exposed as well when pregnant women work in the fields.[32]

Even children not brought to the fields are exposed to the clothing and footprints of their parents' shoes and work outfits. Pesticides cause skin diseases, cancer, male infertility, miscarriage, birth defects, and neurological disorders. In fact, some pesticides sprayed on fruit and vegetables contain a chemical similar to nerve gas. Though there are obvious immediate negative health outcomes, some of the long-term deadly impacts of these pesticides become evident 10 to 20 years after exposure.

Over 95 percent of migrant farm workers are people of color, and 92 percent are Latino and Hispanic laborers. Every day thousands of Spanish-speaking workers and their children are sprayed, infected, and poisoned by the pesticides that go on the fruit and vegetables we eat throughout America.[33]

Like the health of other people of color, Latino health is subject to hazardous dump areas. "California has three Class I toxic waste dumps—the dumps

that can take just about every toxic substance known to science." One is
in Kettleman, which is 95 percent Latino and the largest toxic waste dump
west of Alabama. The second one is in Buttonwillow, whose majority population is Latino. And the third is in Westmorland, with a 72 percent Latino
population.[34] Chemical Waste Management, the company that owns these
California toxic waste dumps, also owns the largest one in the country, found
in Emelle, Alabama. Some suggest that this dump is the largest in the world.
The population here is 95 percent black. Chemical Waste Management also
owned a toxic incinerator on Chicago's south side, which is 55 percent black
and 24 percent Latino; one in Sauget, Illinois, which has a 95 percent black
population; and one in Port Arthur, Texas, comprised of 80 percent Latino
and black residents.

Charles Lee, a Chinese American and the lead author of the landmark
UCC-CRJ report that coined the phrase "environmental racism," sums up
the critical state of toxic health among communities of color:

> Three out of every five African Americans and Hispanic Americans lived in
> communities with uncontrolled toxic waste sites....African Americans were
> heavily overrepresented in the populations of metropolitan areas with the larg-
> est number of uncontrolled toxic waste sites. These areas include: Memphis,
> TN (173 sties); Cleveland, OH (106 sites); St. Louis, MO (160); Chicago, IL
> (103 sites); Houston, TX (152 sites); and Atlanta, GA (94 sites). Los Angeles,
> CA, has more Hispanics living in communities with uncontrolled toxic waste
> sites than any other metropolitan area in the United States. Approximately
> half of all Asians, Pacific Islanders, and Native Americans lived in communi-
> ties with uncontrolled toxic waste sites.[35]

Devastation is an understatement when applied to the holistic health of
people of color, or, that is, their environmental and social wellness. Environmental racism is an underlying cause affecting decisions on contaminated
fish consumption, air pollution, hazardous toxic sites, urban incinerators and
landfills, lead poisoning in children, Native American land rights, the use
of technologies in sustainable development, and farm workers' proximity to
pesticides.[36]

BLACK ENVIRONMENTAL LIBERATION THEOLOGY

Framing environmental racism within the context of holistic environmental and social sickness suggests the important need of holistic healing,
especially for communities of color. Perhaps one move in this direction is the
creation of a black environmental liberation theology (BELT). James H. Cone
hints at this direction when he laments the divide within the United States
between the conservation–preservation and environmental racism–ecological
justice wings of the environmental movement. Cone writes: "Justice fighters
for blacks and the defenders of the earth have tended to ignore each other in

their public discourse and practice. Their separation from each other is unfortunate because they are fighting the same enemy—human beings' domination of one another and nature....Connecting racism with the degradation of the earth is a much-needed work in the African-American community, especially in black liberation theology and the black churches."[37]

This challenge from James H. Cone, the father of black theology of liberation, to link racism and degradation of the earth with black liberation theology can be informed by the teachings of the Bible. Rom. 8:19–23 reveals that the work of Christ includes the redemption of the entire universe, that creation might be freed from decay and share in sacred freedom. Eph. 1:1–10 and Col. 1:15–20 point to Christ kneading together and unifying all that is in heaven and on earth and bringing the entire creation back to God's bosom. And we know Luke 4:18 ff. speaks to Jesus's mission with the oppressed and Matt. 25:31ff. gives the only test to enter heaven. How we spend our earthly lives serving the lowly and healing earth is actually serving Christ. Therefore there "is a unity between the hope for the inward liberation of the children of God and the hope for the liberation of the entire physical creation from its bondage and oppression."[38]

Ps. 24:1–2 reads: "The earth and everything on it belong to the Lord. The world and its people belong to the Lord. The Lord placed it all on the oceans and rivers." To have holistic healing of the environment and social ills, we must unveil the fallacy in an ideology and theology that say monopoly capitalists' corporations, world financial institutions, and governments can own nature and the labor of working people. How is it possible for these megatoxic and deforestation entities to own privately that which was created and still remains in God's hands? It is a sin to monopolize the environmental wealth and resources from earth given to all of creation. So healing can begin on one domain at least—the theological level. Liberation theology can undergird ecological justice.

Indeed, Dianne D. Glave, an African American scholar and a leader in the environmental racism and ecological justice movement, is the first person to advance a BELT. In this manner, hers is a direct response to the aforementioned challenge of James H. Cone. Glave directly references Cone's quote that condemns the racism in the traditional environmental movement and the failure of black theology of liberation to take up environmental justice. Glave unites the environmental efforts with the ecological justice sectors. Hence she attempts to provide a working model for what she calls a "black environmental liberation theology (BELT), a strand of black liberation theology."[39]

Moreover, she claims the following in her constructive BELT:

Black liberation theology, which decries the oppression of African Americans based on biblical principles—is the foundation of BELT, a nascent theology based on environmental justice history and activism by African American Christians. Like black liberation theology, BELT is both a theology and an ideology that is actualized by shielding contemporary African Americans exposed to toxins and pollution from landfills, garbage dumps, and auto mechanics' shops, and sewage plants.[40]

For Glave, BELT is built on three sources: the Bible, history, and grassroots organizing. Glave quotes Gal. 3:28 as a biblical basis for her BELT. "There is neither Jew nor Greek, there is neither slave nor free, there is neither male nor female; for you are all one in Christ Jesus." She complements this text with Ps. 82:3–4, which sides with the oppressed. "Defend the poor and fatherless; Do justice to the afflicted and needy. Deliver the poor and needy; Free them from the hand of the wicked." Yet her foundational biblical text is the Genesis story, where she finds that the earth belongs to God, and Adam and Eve were only given stewardship and not dominion over God's earth.

Regarding the historical basis of BELT, Glave cites "the history of environmental justice by the African American church and Christian organizations. Church environmental justice activists, part of the long history of civil rights in the African American community and an underpinning of BELT, struggled to reverse twentieth-century environmental racism." A prime example was the Memphis black garbage workers' strike. Glave argues that Martin Luther King Jr.'s April 3, 1968, "I've Been To the Mountain Top" speech serves as a "template for the justice of black liberation theology and BELT."[41] This address given the night before King's murder situated the garbage workers' struggles within an ecological lens and as an environmental demand. King's words also expose various forms of white racial discrimination as attacks against nature.

Glave uncovers a history of black church involvement in environmental justice in Rev. Ben Chavis's talk at a national environment conference. Chavis offered a theological interpretation of race and the environment: "'The fact that we [African Americans] are disproportionately dumped on,'" says Chavis, "is just consistent with being in America.... And the demand that God puts on us is that we will face up to the contemporary responsibility that God has given us to not let God's creation be destroyed by sin.... Environmental injustice is sin before God.'"[42]

And regarding her third source for BELT, Glave pinpoints local grassroots activists as they fight against environmental racism. It is this material sector, writes Glave, that defines BELT. Here, too, she notes especially the role of everyday churchgoers struggling alongside clergy and community leaders.

Glave acknowledges that BELT has its origin in black theology of liberation. To transform BELT into what she calls a theology incorporating twenty-first century action, she advances a 12-point environmental justice agenda for action.[43] With her creation of BELT, Glave has advanced not only black theology of liberation. More specifically she provides one way to heal the holistic illnesses caused by environmental racism. Her BELT offers the balm to heal the body, mind, emotions, and feelings of those forging ecological justice on the ground. She acknowledges the component parts of progressive black church leadership, justice biblical warrants, public policy, coalitions of people of color, tactical alliances with mainstream environmental groups, and the plumb line of grassroots efforts. "In response to African Americans being inequitably exposed to toxic chemicals and waste, the church is called to further expand grassroots and national reform looking at BELT—justice, grassroots activism, spirituality, and organization—all based on the Bible. Combined, the history and theology can be a 'spearhead for reform' for African Americans embattled by environmental racism in the future."[44] BELT is part of faith, health, and healing in African American life.

NOTES

1. K. C. Abraham, "A Theological Response to the Ecological Crisis," in *Ecotheology: Voices from South and North*, ed. David G. Hallman (Maryknoll, N.Y.: Orbis Books, 1994), p. 66.

2. Robert D. Bullard, "Anatomy of Environmental Racism and the Environmental Justice Movement," in *Confronting Environmental Racism: Voices from the Grassroots*, ed. Robert D. Bullard (Boston, Mass.: South End Press, 1993), p. 22.

3. *Newsweek* (April 16, 2007): p. 46.

4. *Newsweek* (April 16, 2007): pp. 65–66.

5. Dianne Glave and Mark Stoll, "African American Environmental History: An Introduction," in *"To Love the Wind and the Rain": African Americans and Environmental History*, ed. Dianne Glave and Mark Stoll (Pittsburgh, Penn.: University of Pittsburgh Press, 2006), pp. 1–2.

6. The U.S. National Advisory Commission on Civil Disorders (1968) documented these causes of civil disobedience in black areas; Bullard, *Confronting Environmental Racism*, pp. 9–10.

7. Vernice D. Miller, "Building on Our Past, Planning for Our Future," in *Toxic Struggles: The Theory and Practice of Environmental Justice*, ed. Richard Hofrichter (Philadelphia, Penn.: New Society Publishers, 1993), p. 128.

8. Luke W. Cole and Sheila R. Foster, *From the Ground Up: Environmental Racism and the Rise of the Environmental Justice Movement* (New York: New York University Press, 2001), p. 55.

9. Miller, p. 129.

10. For the "Principles" document, see Hofrichter, *Toxic Struggles*, pp. 237–39.

11. Dorceta E. Taylor, "Environmentalism and the Politics of Inclusion," in Bullard, *Confronting Environmental Racism*, p. 57.

12. Cole and Foster, "Introduction," in *From the Ground Up*, p. 17.

13. Dianne D. Glave, "Black Environmental Liberation Theology," in Glave and Stoll, *"To Love the Wind and the Rain,"* pp. 194–95.

14. Cole and Foster, *From the Ground Up*, pp. 20–28.

15. Rev. Benjamin F. Chavis Jr., "Foreword," in Bullard, *Confronting Environmental Racism*, p. 3.

16. Robert D. Bullard, "Anatomy of Environmental Racism and the Environmental Justice Movement," in Bullard, *Confronting Environmental Racism*, pp. 19–20.

17. Cynthia Hamilton, "Coping with Industrial Exploitation," in Bullard, *Confronting Environmental Racism*, pp. 73–74.

18. Cole and Foster, *From the Ground Up*, pp. 71–72.

19. Robert D. Bullard, "Anatomy of Environmental Racism and the Environmental Justice Movement," in Bullard, *Confronting Environmental Racism*, p. 17.

20. Marianne Lavelle and Marcia A. Coyle, "Unequal Protection: The Racial Divide in Environmental Law," in Hofrichter, *Toxic Struggles*, pp. 136–37.

21. Hamilton, in Bullard, *Confronting Environmental Racism*, p. 70.

22. Robert D. Bullard, "Anatomy of Environmental Racism," in Hofrichter, *Toxic Struggles*, pp. 26–27.

23. Ibid.

24. Hamilton, in Bullard, *Confronting Environmental Racism*, p. 71.

25. Robert D. Bullard, "Anatomy of Environmental Racism," in Hofrichter, *Toxic Struggles*, pp. 26–27.

26. Beverly Hendrix Wright and Robert D. Bullard, "The Effects of Occupational Injury, Illness, and Disease on the Health Statu of Black Americans," in Hofrichter, *Toxic Struggles*, pp. 156, 159.

27. Hamilton, in Bullard, *Confronting Environmental Racism*, p. 68.

28. Janet Phoenix, "Getting the Lead out of the Community," in Bullard, *Confronting Environmental Racism*, p. 77.

29. Robert D. Bullard, "Anatomy of Environmental Racism," in Hofrichter, *Toxic Struggles*, p. 32.

30. Winona LaDuke, "A Society Based on Conquest Cannot Be Sustained," in Hofrichter, *Toxic Struggles*, p. 105.

31. Ibid., 103. LaDuke also writes: "Over fifty million indigenous populations inhabit the world's remaining rain forests; over one million indigenous people will be relecated to allow for the development of hydroelectric dam projects in the next decade; The United States has detonated all its nuclear weapons in the lands of indigenous people...; Two-thirds of all uranium resources within the borders of the United States lie under Native reservations...; One third of all low-sulphur coal in the western United States is on Indian land, with four of the ten largest coal strip mines in these same areas; Fifteen of the current eighteen recipients of nuclear-waste research grants...are Indian communities; and the largest hydroelectric project on the continent, the James Bay project, is on Cree and Inuit lands in northern Canada" (p. 99).

32. Marion Moses, "Farmworkers and Pesticides," in Bullard, *Confronting Environmental Racism*, pp. 165–167.

33. Ibid., p. 162.

34. Cole and Foster, *From the Ground Up*, pp. 2–3.

35. Charles Lee, "Beyond Toxic Wastes and Race," in Bullard, *Confronting Environmental Racism*, p. 49.

36. Robert D. Bullard, "Anatomy of Environmental Racism and the Environmental Justice Movement," in *Confronting Environmental Racism*, p. 21, and Robert D. Bullard, "Introduction," in *Confronting Environmental Racism*, p. 9.

37. James H. Cone, *Risks of Faith: The Emergence of a Black Theology of Liberation, 1968–1998* (Boston: Beacon Press, 1999), pp. 138–39.

38. Abraham, p. 72.

39. Dianne D. Glave, "Black Environmental Liberation Theology," in Glave and Stoll, *"To Love the Wind and the Rain,"* p. 189.

40. Ibid., p. 190.

41. Ibid., p. 193.

42. Ibid., p. 194.

43. Ibid., pp. 197–98.

44. Ibid., pp. 198–99.

PART II

———— ❈ ————

Health and Healing across the Diaspora

CHAPTER 3

———— ❖ ————

Bodies in Time and the Healing of Spaces: Religion, Temporalities, and Health

Charles H. Long

[L]et us make up our faces before the world, and our names shall sound throughout the land with honor! For we ourselves are our true names, not their epithets! So let us say, Make Up Our Faces and Our Minds!
—*Ralph Ellison*

The purpose of this chapter is to address the problematical issue of health within the black community. It is clear that though health and health-related issues are primarily focused upon the individual body, it is possible to see the self as an integrated whole and one that is situated in a set of social relationships that include family and community. These families and communities are situated and defined in specific times and places, which should be seen within a wider order of temporality. The institution of slavery and the subsequent history of oppression within American culture force us to raise issues regarding not simply the meaning of health within the community but the manner in which the issue of health has formed one of the basic meanings of community. According to Townes and Mitchem, "Health depends on social networks, biology, and environment. It is embedded in our social realities and is the integration of the spiritual, the mental, and biological aspects of our lives." Here, I attempt to show how the issue of health arises within the black community and hope from this portrayal to find resources not only for alternative modes of health care but to indicate how the issue of health can define the nature of a moral community itself. Health for the black community has always been defined as an issue of public health and the viability and meaning of the public nature of the black community in this land. A discernment of the history of health within this community affects all the other problems and issues within the black community.

I am, to be sure, concerned about the quality of health care in black communities—the access that black persons have to the various health institutions, as well as the black community's general and chronic malaise as noted by the statistics of HIV-AIDS, hypertension, sickle cell anemia, and so forth. I am equally concerned about the meaning and nature of the moral community in which black persons live and have lived. The nature of biological well-being, the very existence of black bodies in this country always take on the ramifications of political, economic, and social import. And here I have reference to the incidence of homicide among young black males, the rate of their incarceration, and the growing number of children who are not growing up within nurturing and caring communities. These are obviously issues of public health and are related directly and historically to the viability of black persons constituting a moral community.

In a comprehensive and programmatic article, David L. Schoenbrun demonstrates how a "history of public healing reveals compelling notions of public health and forms of power that cut across the colonial period but were transformed by colonialism." This transformation was neither linear nor progressive in the historical sense. Rather, "public healing was wrestled with shifting boundaries between a porous social body's moral communities and the starker outline of an embodied, autonomous individual."[1]

In his discussion, Schoenbrun shows how various scholars of African history have attempted to come to terms with the issue of cultural societal meaning and expression in the colonial encounter. Many have emphasized the African appropriation of Western forms of knowledge, others emphasize precolonial forms of African knowledge, while others see Africans and Europeans engaged in a struggle for power that allows for the emergence of several types of colonial middle figures such as nurses, paramedics, and so forth. In light of the several possible positions of the colonial encounter, Schoenbrun devotes special attention to a summarizing comment by his colleague, Steven Feierman. "[Feierman] worries that the specificities of colonial-cultural mixtures tend to make historical sense in terms of layered narratives that 'originate in Europe,' particularly the narratives of capitalism and of Protestantism, and the implicit, general sense of their historical relations to each other."[2] Feierman does not wish at all to rule out the kind of narratives that originate in Europe, but he fears that the coherence endemic to such narratives fails to see how these kinds of narratives "exist in creative tension with larger historical narratives... the central question is which larger narratives?"[3]

In the case of Africa, some aspects of the efficacious nature of the African traditions were extinguished. While not attempting at all to mitigate the violence done to African traditions, Feierman's point is well taken. Rather than speak of extinctions, the language of "fragmentation of traditions" might be more apt. This fragmentation also represents new forms of adaptation as well as the creation of new and fundamentally new modes of cultural orientation to meet particular challenges. My concern in this chapter is to describe as best I can the kind of entangled and fragmented cultural modes that arose during the time of slavery and the domination of white persons over persons of color in the United States. I agree with Dipesh Chakrabarty when he calls upon us, "to contemplate the necessarily fragmented histories of human belonging that never constitutes a one or a whole."[4]

I have chosen to begin this chapter with an allusion to East Africa not because I wished to establish continuity between East African cultures and those of Africans in North America. My turn to East Africa was out of a concern for certain methodological insights and hints. For some time a group of scholars have attempted to make sense of East African cultures in terms of certain totalities in time and space.[5] What is important in their work is the manner in which they include and regard the long past of the cultures as well as the changes wrought by other Africans and Europeans. This accounts for the fact that a great deal of their data is in the form of oral traditions, sometimes of intra-African derivation, but since the coming of the Europeans, often fragmentary and expressed in nondiscursive modes of song, dance, or rituals.

TIME ON THE CROSS: THE BODY IN BONDAGE

The authors of *Time on the Cross* insist that their cool, analytical, and dispassionate study of American slavery counters arguments that their study tends to make American slavery more acceptable by describing their aims in quite a different manner.[6]

> We have attacked the traditional interpretation of the economics of slavery not in order to resurrect a defunct system, but in order to *correct the perversion of the history of blacks—in order to strike down the view that black Americans were without culture, without achievement, and without development for their first two hundred and fifty years on American soil* (emphasis mine).[7]

I am certain that this was the authors' intent, and from the point of view of economic history their case might be plausible. One problem with this interpretation is that there is no tradition among those who were enslaved that gave expression to such a palatable view of slavery, and, if their interpretations are true, no tradition whether in academic, business, or popular culture ever espoused such a view of the years of slavery. The authors might have added a third volume inquiring into the reasons why the culture, achievement, and creativity of African Americans was not accepted and immediately made a part of the general American culture after the Civil War.

Fogel and Engerman attribute the misunderstanding of the economics of slavery and what they see as the degradation of the enslaved Africans to the influence of the abolitionists. The abolitionists' influence began as a moral indictment and moved into a critique of the economic viability of the slavery system. As we shall see below, this argument did not begin with the abolitionists; it was first made by Southern slave-owning plantation owners during the Constitutional Convention. Fogel and Engerman hope in their study to document the craftsmanship and creativity of African labor and in the process to resurrect the image of the enslaved African. Volume two, *Evidence and Methods*, of their study is devoted to a discussion of their methods and sources. In it they take on other historians' methods and conclusions and devise econometric equations for the positions they take regarding the nature and meaning of slave labor and its ramifications for the subsequent meaning of African American culture in the United States. We are left with the conclusion that enslaved Africans lived more or less like other Americans laborers during various periods of American history, with the exception that the Africans lived under a system of slavery.

Given this conclusion and the methods set forth for it, it is strange that they would entitle their work *Time on the Cross*. We are not told how the authors selected the title or how seriously they took its implications. There is a certain vogue in placing titles that carry a quasi-religious overtone to books related to the study of African Americans, for example, Eugene Genovese's *Roll, Jordan Roll*, Sylvia Frye's *Water from the Rock*, or Taylor Branch's *Parting the Waters*, for example. In some cases, the text and the suggestive intent of the title are congruent. There might be a slight congruency in the Fogel and Engerman volumes in so far as part of their discussion has to do with the exploitation of enslaved Africans. The more fundamental sense of any meaning of the notion of "time on the cross" is not carried through, however. The theological and iconographic meaning of the phrase is the passion and suffering of Jesus, the Christ, for the salvation of the world. The major image for this meaning is a crucifix—the suffering body of Jesus pierced by thorns and spear, abandoned and left to die on the cross. Little of the implications of these meanings are present in this work.

Allow me to suggest another, albeit deeper, implication. Here, I reference the way the authors have made the identification between time and history. They have assumed that there is only one order and structure of time and it is expressed in their notion of history; though it includes the enslaved, they are not the actors or protagonists of this time as history. Their actions and voices have been made passive and silenced by the makers of history.

Ira Berlin reminds us of the totalizing effect of American slavery. Berlin tells us that two markers should be to the fore in understanding the first centuries of American slavery: the first was a distinction between a society with slaves and a "slave society."

> What distinguished societies with slaves was the fact that slaves were marginal to the central productive processes; slavery was just one form of labor among many...In societies with slaves, no one presumed the master-slave to be the social exemplar...In slave societies, by contrast, slavery stood at the center of

economic production, and the master-slave relationship provided the model for all social relationships, husband and wife, parent and child, employer and employee, teacher and student. From the most intimate connections between men and women to the most public ones of ruler and ruled, all relationships mimicked slavery. As Frank Tannebaum said, "Nothing escaped, nothing, and no one."[8]

Berlin's second distinctive mark regarding American slavery was the coincidence of slavery with the revolutions of the eighteenth century; these included the American, French, and Haitian revolutions. In the case of the Haitian revolution, the slave system was toppled. In the American Revolution, slavery was legitimated and preserved. For the American Republic this meant that the major societal and cultural institutions that developed from its founding obscured the fact of slavery the same moment that it legitimated the system of slavery. Though there is no explicit mention or language of "slave" or "slavery" in the founding documents, the issue of slavery was debated in the Constitutional Convention on an almost daily basis since "this peculiar property" was part and parcel of the debates that had to do with taxation, representation, states rights, and so forth.[9]

Obviously, the period of slavery was not a caring time for Africans in the American Republic. By and large the rhetoric surrounding the enslaved during the founding conventions depicted them as lazy, shiftless, and a burden upon the owners. One might have thought that this would be one of the primary reasons for the abolition of the institution. The slave owners attempted to demonize the enslaved precisely to save the institution of slavery and through its preservation, to enhance their political power, wealth, and cultural prestige. Robin Einhorn reports the refrain of many southern delegates to the Constitutional Convention. "The main point...was that southern slaveholders were victims of slavery—and therefore should gain a tax break at the expense of northerners who did not suffer from owning unproductive workers. This was an outrageous argument, and the southern delegates made it one after the other."[10]

Some variation or derivative of this kind of outrageous statement of the Southern slave owners became a staple of a great deal of the rhetoric of American historiography. W.E.B. Du Bois's *Black Reconstruction*, published in 1935, was an attempt to counter this style in American historiography. Since that time a number of American historians have attempted to rectify this style of American historical writing; there is, however, a deeper issue. I pose it in this manner—regardless of how one might structure the American historical narrative, is it possible for the *passion* of the *time on the cross* to stylize, inform, and engage in a therapeutic of history? The American Republic in its founding and in the ordering of its institutions was consciously set up to place the enslaved Africans in a situation of dis-ease and imbalance, a most unhealthy situation.

Enslaved Africans existed as the private property of the owners. The concern for their care and well-being was identical with what was good for those who owned them. Slaves were under the constant surveillance of their owners. As such, the masters or mistresses diagnosed their illnesses in light of the capacity they had to carry out the duties of the owners. Diagnoses were based upon various ideologies of the black body—its capabilities, strengths, weaknesses, and so forth. These ideologies of the black body were at the same time part and parcel of the apologia that affirmed the necessity for the system of slavery. Owners, as part of their diagnoses, were especially alert to discern the difference between what they thought was feigned illness as opposed to an authentic issue of health. Determination of illness, feigned or otherwise, was made in accord with the owner's prerogatives. In all cases of diagnosis and treatment, the owners were concerned that their actions reinforced the hierarchy necessary for the maintenance of the slave system.

Care for and healing of the body is normally exercised within an intimate and responsible community, usually the family unit. While several relatively stable unions of slaves existed, it is difficult to refer to them as families. And this is because all members of this so-called family unit, including offspring, were owned by another human being or family. The owner of the enslaved enjoyed the consciousness of determining the total consciousness of all the human beings in his possession. It was the slave masters and mistresses that made decisions in *history*; though the enslaved might carry out the actions, the origin and goal of these actions were determined by the owners. Obviously, husbands were sold away from their wives; children were sold away from parents, and so forth. This was the terror that lay at the heart of any and every intimate relationship among and between the enslaved.

The very notion of family was highly ambiguous during slavery. Though the family was a normal and publicly recognized institution, many owners had two families: one African and enslaved, the other free and white; one legitimate, the other illegal and illegitimate. In addition, Nell Painter has pointed out the highly ambiguous psychological atmosphere created by the tensions and emotions evoked by the male and female owners, their enslaved paramours, and the offspring of these unions.[11] In spite of this, many stable relationships analogous to the family unit existed among the enslaved during the period of slavery. Such unions were not inherent to the slave system and one can not credit the slave owners for the viability of the slave family. This is a point overlooked by Fogel and Engerman. Herbert G. Gutman speaks directly to this point. The slave system, whether seen as demonic or benign, was the context for the unions, but Gutman explains: "The study of slave 'treatment' is in itself invaluable, it is not the same as the study of a viable slave culture with its own standards of correct behaviour, what the anthropologist Sidney Mintz describes as 'the repertory of socially-learned and inculcated resources of the enslaved.'"[12] To the extent that there was care and healing during the period of slavery, it was due to the creation of a moral community by the enslaved within the structures of slavery. This moral community cannot easily be elided to the kind of "time on the cross" history that is represented by Fogel and Engerman.

Schoenbrun raises this issue as it relates to Africa in this way:

> Health in Africa implicates histories of the environment, of the state, of gender, it is a social history. Healing in African history implicates other histories too—of morality, of the body, of the person, of relations between life and death, of notions of efficacy and capacity. They are histories of practical reason—as much as they are histories of the forces that cause illness and sustain wellness. African histories of healing intersect with all these larger narratives, but they must grapple with concepts of causality not easily translated across cultures and forms of action greatly concerned with' *social embeddedness of suffering and misfortune* (emphasis mine).[13]

One of the issues in the discussion of health and wellness in an enslaved community arises around the proper locus of the healing process. It cannot be that of private health because the slave possessed no privacy and while the institution of slavery was a public and legal institution, the enslaved person had no public persona. Thus, the health of the enslaved always redounded to the situation of the owner. Only within the orders of a moral community created by the enslaved themselves does a self or soul as the human locus requiring compassion, care, and concern appear.

CONJURING, CARE, AND COMMUNITY

Salo Baron, who held the first chair in Jewish Studies in an American university, set the stage for his intellectual orientation in an programmatic article, "Ghetto and Emancipation," published in the journal *Menorah* in 1928. In this article Baron undertook a critique of Jewish intellectuals who tended to interpret the history of the Jews as a tale of suffering and woe— what he referred to as a "lachrymose history." In a concluding part of this article, he writes, "Surely it is time to break with the lachrymose history of pre-Revolutionary woe; and to adopt a view more in accord with historic truth."[14]

I open with this allusion to the problem of Jewish history since it poses the issue of how a dispossessed and oppressed moral community deals with the meaning of its past even as it seeks to promote the goals of freedom. There are several profound differences between the Jewish and black experiences. First and foremost, the Jewish community has been able to maintain their traditions and languages well over a millennium even though for most of this time they lived in hostile territory. The similarity lies in the temptation or possibility of losing their identity through becoming a part of the majority culture that is the source of their oppression. I shall return to this topic as a methodological horizon in the last part of this chapter. I wish now to dwell upon the meaning of a "lachrymose African American history" in relationship to care, health, and healing.

The origin of the African American communities in the United States must be seen against a backdrop of a sustained history of terrorism and violence. In another place I have suggested that African Americans' beginnings as a moral community took place in the bowels of slave ships that brought them across the ocean.[15] Sterling Stuckey makes this meaning more explicit: "The final gift of African 'tribalism' in the nineteenth century was its life as a lingering memory in the minds of American slaves. That memory enabled them to go back to the sense of community in the traditional African setting and to include all Africans in their common experience of oppression in North America."[16] Stuckey goes on in his analysis of African American folklore to decipher the meaning of Africa in the traditions of the enslaved communities. He places particular emphasis on the inclusive and incorporating ritual of the ring shout.

> In these areas, [West Africa] an integral part of religion and culture was movement in a ring during ceremonies honoring the ancestors. There is, in fact, substantial evidence for the importance of the ancestral function of the circle in West Africa but the circle ritual imported by Africans from the Congo region was so powerful in its elaboration of an African vision that it contributed disproportionately to the centrality of the circle in slavery... Wherever in Africa the counterclockwise dance ceremony was performed—it is called the ring shout in North America—the dancing and singing were directed to the ancestors and the gods, the tempo and revolution of the circle quickening during the course of the movement.[17]

Stuckey maintains that it was through the ring shout that newly arrived Africans were introduced and welcomed into the moral community of the enslaved on the plantation by other enslaved Africans. He shows how the ring shout expressed itself in many and varied forms of African American culture, within and without the Christian congregations, and in music, folklore and folk drama.

In a recent doctoral dissertation, *Doctoring Freedom: The Politics of African American Medical Care, 1840–1910*, Margaret Geneva Long surveys the history of medical care in the African American community from 1840 to 1910. She gives several examples of the health care, thought, and rhetoric that the owners used to justify the treatment of the slaves. Much of the rationale for care was stated within a rhetoric of contestation. Margaret Long notes that plantation owners gained a great deal of information from agricultural journals of the day such as *DeBow's Review* and *Southern Planter*. These journals gave advice on topics such as the feeding of slaves, the number of hours of sleep they should receive, and how much leisure should be allotted to the enslaved.

Throughout the journals the writers hasten to assure their readers that African Americans have few resources for internal control—food must be rationed out frequently, lest slaves gobble it up at once and become ill. All fruit in the slaves' garden patches must be inspected lest the greedy slave eat unripe watermelon. The exertions of the master in discipline, surveillance, and the encouragement of religion, are the only safeguards that slaves have against their own natures.[18]

The legitimacy of the institution of chattel slavery in a country founded on revolutionary principles of democratic freedom was the great contradiction and fundamental evil flaw of the American Republic. This contradiction was expressed on the mundane level on every slave-owning plantation. The wellness of the enslaved was designed to enhance the owner's property, but the enslaved must never have been *too well*, lest such wellness lead them to contemplate notions of independence and freedom.[19] Slavery and its practice defined an agonistic site—a battlefield, or better a minefield, that camouflaged and obscured within its pacific domesticity a strange and depressing dialectic of evil. This constituted a very complex situation for the enslaved person, who had to come to a knowledge of his or her situation as an enslaved person and had to invent modes of communication with his or her owners. The enslaved equally had to establish a way of being with and understanding those who shared their common fate and in the midst of this find some region of consciousness and public space for the exercise of their inherent value as human beings. It is from this context that the modality of African American conjure emerges.

Yvonne Chireau, in her excellent study of African American conjure, offers us several definitions and explanations of conjure and conjuring.[20] I shall put together several statements that exemplify her position.

> Conjure is a magical tradition in which spiritual power is invoked for various purposes, such as healing, protection, and self defense.... It is clear that in many cases, supernatural beliefs served to mediate relations between blacks and whites. Conjure also might have allowed black people to attain a measure of control over their lives, as bondspersons. The world that the slaves inhabited was unpredictable and uncertain. Anxiety over inevitable violence, separation from loved ones, or the unforeseeable risks of escape must have engendered persistent insecurity for African American slaves...Conjuring constituted a pragmatic and realistic method, given a situation of extremely limited alternatives, that slaves could use to cope with their masters. Nevertheless, slaveholders often found that the dilemma posed by Conjure lay not in the question of direct efficacy—that is to say, whether such practices "worked" against them—but in the ways that the slaves utilized these beliefs to challenge their authority.[21]

Conjuring was a practice; it also constituted a divinatory epistemology and a deciphering process. Conjuring techniques, while heavily African in style, borrowed from European, Native American, and Christian notions and rituals. Chireau quotes with approval Albert Raboteau's statement that conjure served as an alternative religious theory of misfortune for the slaves. Raboteau stated that "The concept of suffering for the guilt of the father is biblical; the concept of being victimized by a 'fix' is Conjure." Raboteau adds, "Both attempt to locate the cause of irrational suffering."[22]

The black body, individually and collectively, centered all the important dimensions of social life—politics, economics, and sexuality, as well as the range of exchanges of materials and affections that make up a human community. These dimensions were present for the enslaved and their owners but in quite different ways and for different purposes. Thus the health, disease, and wellness of the black body was not simply another dimension of societal life; the black body brought everything together into a single focus. Conjure expressed another source of power available to the enslaved, and this power was directly related to the body of the slave and to the total situation of enslavement. Conjure was theoretical and practical. In many cases it involved a precise knowledge of the effect of plants, herbs, and other potions on the body. The conjurer was also an adept social psychologist, able to read the moods of owners as well as the enslaved. The conjurer acted to provide so-called medicine for the body physical and the body social.

Conjuring was based upon a body of knowledge, but like all knowledge of this kind, it changed over the course of time and from one place to another. What was sustaining in conjure was the orientation that it expressed. This orientation, this deciphering and divining another power of being, lay at the heart of the enslaved persons as the basis for a moral community. One should see conjure in the same way as Sterling Stuckey's account of the ring shout referred to above. The ring shout dance, a movement remembered by the body from Africa, became the initiatory rhythm that brought new Africans into the moral community created by enslaved Africans in America. Thus, in this one rhythmic movement of the body, the newly enslaved Africans recreated Africa in the same moment that they became American. This is a powerful legerdemain, paralleling or even surpassing the Cartesian cogito for it takes place within a public and contested arena and not in the private abstractness of the individual consciousness; both the ring shout and the *cogito* have had profound ramifications for the modern world.

The subversive and legerdemain character of conjure explains why it evokes the notion and concept of magic. This has been followed through in Yvonne Chireau's book on conjuring, *Black Magic.* Only in the subtitle, *Religion and the African American Conjuring Tradition,* does the notion of conjuring appear. Whether from an authentic intellectual concern or from a marketing strategy, it is assumed that American popular culture is familiar with the notion of so-called black magic. While this may be true, the notion and practice of magic is complex—present in almost all cultures, thus creating a very long history.[23]

Magic appears to be an aspect of all cultures past and present. In the modern period, magic tends to be discussed either in the context of Western cultures of the past or its occurrence within non-Western cultures. This modern interest in magic reflects the dominance of science and scientific thinking as the norm of modernity. Theories and practices of magic are thus relegated to a nonscientific and nonrational mode of being in the world. This is not the occasion to review the various theories and practices of magic. Suffice it to say that magic is most often discussed in relation to and in distinction from science and religion. From the point of view of prominent contemporary anthropologists, both religion and magic rest upon the basis of the existence of a mystical and transcendent reality. Religion, from their point of view, expresses the manner in which a community participates and acknowledges this reality. Magic, while acknowledging this reality, relates to it privately and secretively for utilitarian purposes. Bronislav Malinowski tells us that this penchant for the practical and concrete shows that magic, from this perspective, is somewhat akin to science.[24] Modern theories of magic have, for the most part, come from anthropologists who describe and discuss the practice of magic in societies outside of the West. Implicit in their theories is that modern science and the rationalism of scientific thinking has replaced the necessity for magic and magical modes of thought and action. Hardly any notion or theory of magic pays attention to the inordinate and pervasive prevalence of magic in the astrology, games of chance, and the like in modern Western societies, nor has any theory of magic related it to colonialism or slavery in the modern period.

Conjuring as a form of magic reveals a great deal about contemporary Western culture and its influence and impact upon the world during the period of Western colonialism and slavery. The magical modality is not simply a so-called child of deprivation; it expresses a critical and creative role in the cultures of the colonized and oppressed by deciphering and divining new and alternate understandings of the human mode of being that refuses to prioritize social engineering and futuristic promises of happiness predicated on the continual conquest of nature and other human societies. In the case of African Americans, magic retained its secretive and individual modes but in addition opened up and created possibilities of freedom that belied the spurious rhetoric and practices of the American Republic.

Margaret Geneva Long in her research on the history of African American medical practices describes how African Americans took on the mantle of "official medical care" based upon the scientific model. Obviously African Americans did not immediately, nor gradually, for that matter, become members of medical societies and groups. While these medical societies and groups were scientific associations, most still maintained an ideological and stereotypical view of black bodies. African American medical associations grew out of the older communities of African societies. In the antebellum North, there were several societies of freedpersons. These societies spawned mutual aid, benevolent, and burial societies, and in the case of the African society in Philadelphia, the African Methodist Episcopal (AME) church.

These societies were not religious in the same way as were the Christian churches. They were not at all in opposition to the Christian church; indeed the orientation of the African societies expressed the profound orientation of African people in the United States. In speaking about the medical societies of African Americans, Margaret Long, speaking about the difference between black associations and the Christian church, puts it this way:

> Black associations had no such ideological burden to bear. Although [Christian] congregations and societies often overlapped, their purposes and organization did not hold an outright spiritual charge. They were called into being to provide for the members in this world, and to provide a fitting sendoff to the next. The provision of medical and funerary benefits as well as fellowship had a decided secular focus. Their extension of charity to the wider community may well have sprung from a sense of Christian obligation, but it also reflected a consciousness of racial identity and an emergent sense of formalized obligation to a "community." Their aid in times of distress was on their own terms and was more concrete and exclusive than that of the black congregations from which they often sprung.[25]

While I am in basic agreement with Margaret Long's statement regarding the distinction between Christian churches and African societies, it does not define a distinction between the secular and the religious. The African societies express a form of religion—religion as ultimate orientation. The African American community in the United States, through the period of slavery and afterward, expressed a profound and specific ordering in the world, which is the source and resource of its identity. This orientation may be expressed in various religious organizations, as well as in music, dance, literature, and so forth. While conjuring did entail healing and a practice of medicine, this knowledge or practice was not posed by the African American community as an impediment to the knowledge and practice of official scientific medicine. Conjuring as an African American cultural hermeneutic enabled Africans in America to realize their true situation with all its limitations and resources and to create a viable human community from them.

This modality of the meaning of conjuring enabled Africans in America to create not only another American culture but another meaning of American history.

DIVINING TIME, REMEMBERING BODIES

In her novel *Beloved*, Toni Morrison describes a scene where Baby Suggs, an old black matriarch, brings the community together:

> After situating herself on a huge flat-sided rock, Baby Suggs bowed her head and prayed silently. The company watched her from the trees. They knew she was ready when she put her stick down. Then she shouted, "Let the children

come!" and they ran from the trees toward her. "Let the mothers hear you laugh," she told them, and the woods rang. The adults looked on and could not help smiling. Then "Let the grown men come," she shouted. They stepped out one by one among the ringing trees. "Let your wives and your children see you dance," she told them, and the groundlife shuddered under their feet. Finally she called the women to her. "Cry," she told them. "For the living and the dead. Just cry." And without covering their eyes the women let loose.

Morrison goes on to describe the sermon Baby Suggs preached.

She did not tell them to clean up their lives or to go and sin no more. She did not tell them they were blessed of the earth, its inheriting meek or its glory-bound pure. She told them that the only grace they could have was the grace they could imagine. That if they could not see it, they would not have it.

Baby Suggs then reminds them of the nature of this gathering.

"Here," she said, "in this here place, we flesh: flesh that weeps, laughs; flesh that dances on bare feet in grass. Love it. Love it hard. Yonder they do not love your flesh. They despise it. They don't love your eyes; they'd just soon pick them out. No more do they love the skin on your back. Yonder they flay it. And O my people they do not love your hands. Those they only use, tie, bind, chop off and leave empty. Love your hands! Love them. Raise them up and kiss them. Touch others with them, pat them together, stroke them on your face 'cause they don't love that either. *You* got to love it, *you!*"

The remainder of Baby Suggs's sermon consists of an anatomical poesis of the black body and the need of love and care for it by black persons.

This is flesh I'm talking about here. Flesh that needs to be loved…So love your neck…And all your inside parts…The dark, dark liver—love it, love it, and the beat and beating heart, love that too. More than eyes or feet. More than lungs that yet have to draw free air. More than your life-holding womb and your life-giving private parts, hear me now, love your heart. For this is the prize.[26]

This passage in Morrison's novel expresses that form of religiousness that comes into being from conjuring the mystery of the presence and experiences of the African people in America. The English word "religion" is a derivative of the Latin term *religare*. One of the central meanings of *religare* is binding, and one of the purposes of religion is to bind together a group of persons around some fundamental and primordial orientation to the world. In the previously cited sermon, Baby Suggs calls upon those gathered to bind themselves together through dance, laughter, tears, and loving their black bodies, individually and collectively. In this sermon and ceremony the black body becomes the site of memory for an alternative meaning of the time and space of America. It is clear in Baby Suggs's refrains that in the "yonder out there" they don't love your body, your mouth, eyes, flesh, your neck, and so forth; she is speaking about a yonder out there of history—of time on the cross. It is clear that the black body cannot become a body of health, individually or collectively, within the modality of the yonder, out there of time as history. Another meaning of temporality is called for if there are to be healthy social bodies in time.

In Morrison's novel, Baby Suggs conjures time, bringing into existence another meaning and mode of temporality—a temporality that is able to remember and recognize the individual and social bodies of black persons. Baby Suggs does not shrink from the meaning and necessity of the yonder out there—this time on the cross, this lachrymose history of blacks. She reminds the congregation that having endured this time, it can become the site of healing, critique, and creativity.

I was recently reminded of this issue when I read the essay of the African American cultural critic, Nelson George. In one of his comments, he says:

> Remember black Republicans? Some of the those early '80s curiosities hold high positions in government in this tumultuous young century. But Condi Rice and Clarence Thomas prove that success of one or two individuals, the old role model ideology, sometimes has precious little positive effect on the masses. In the end it seems, for blacks to participate in this tenuous experiment called American democracy no longer takes exceptional skill or protest marches or the marshaling of moral suasion. It seems all you need now is a desire to fit in and embrace the values of a flawed nation that loves technology, materialism, vast military budgets, false piety, and interventionist foreign policy and hates visionary social programs, independent third world countries, and paying attention to the views of those who don't accept American values. Mediocrity is a national obsession and, from top to bottom, African Americans joined the chase. And what of post-soul? I think that African Americans have passed through that phase and, in the twenty-first century are grappling with a new set of identity issues.[27]

If we juxtapose Baby Suggs's sermon with Nelson George's comment we seem to be facing the dilemma of a choice between the degrading time on the cross of history or becoming a part of its vanguard of oppression. This was alluded to as the temptation of method in Schoenbrun's quote from Steve Feierman—that of falling into narratives of capitalism or Protestantism or both.[28] The temptation is certainly there; indeed it was specified and discussed quite thoroughly by W.E.B. Du Bois in *Souls of Black Folk*. In a recent article dealing with Du Bois's notion of the "Talented Tenth," Carole L. Stewart shows how Du Bois faced the temptation of having to choose between the authority of a capitalistic Protestant ethic represented by Booker T. Washington on the one hand and a civilizing and triumphant Christianity as expressed by his friend, Alexander Crummel, on the other. Stewart makes clear that it was through Du Bois's deciphering of the spirituals, the sorrow songs, those deeply poignant expressions of the lachrymose history of African American slavery, that he is able to specify another mode of temporality.[29]

Du Bois's recourse to the spirituals are reflected in the attention Schoenbrun gives to what he refers to as "poetic stories."

> Existentially poetic stories of the fragmentary are also stories of struggle. Flawed and freighted, history of public healing emphasizes the discourses and practices that people used in the "boundary-crossing struggle over the conceptual and moral bases of political and social organization"...Constituting the sources to meet these challenges—and asking how the sources have been constituted—is a necessary first step in exploring the multiple temporalities recognizable today in the moral community and collective action at the core of public healing.[30]

Precisely how are these sources constituted? I contend that we must imagine a modality of the temporal process that is capable of knowing and understanding the black body in the rhetoric of Baby Suggs's sermon.

These new and other sources will be recognized only within a new kind of time and space where black bodies appear in their authenticity within the modern world. I am defining this new time–space as a temporality that is congruent to the conjure mode of being and knowing. I am not for one minute recommending a contest between an old conjuring method of healing and contemporary biological medical practices, though I think that all modes of healing should be taken seriously. The basic point I wish to make here is that a healing and caring situation is a fundamental ingredient in the nature and meaning of community. Margaret Long's research shows us that historically black bodies were bodies of the enslaved chattel; then during the Civil War they were war contraband; and after Reconstruction they were second-class or quasi-citizens. The black body has always appeared as a fetishized body within the American Republic. As a form of fetish matter, it carried all the characteristics of any fetishized body—portable, with no inherent value, fluctuating between the notions of desire, exorcism, denial, and invisibility, yet possessing an overwhelming materiality.

Lawrence Jones, former Dean of the Howard University Divinity School, described the conversion of enslaved Africans with this phrase: "they overheard the Gospel." Jones describes something both simple and complex. It was simple in the sense that the enslaved African heard the Gospel from within their situation and not from the point of view of the intent presupposed by the bearers of the message. And this was not only the specific words but also the notion of the book and writing and notions such as the holy, the sacred, or freedom. All of these meanings had to be conjured by a people in slavery. The complexity involved the world of meaning that was intended by American meanings of salvation and freedom. And finally, how did any or all of this relate to the nature and meaning of their black bodies that were dominated by other human beings? They overheard the Gospel, which means that they did not hear the Gospel with the same ears as the history makers who preached it to them. The phrase "overhearing the Gospel" evokes eavesdropping, the sense of something subversive, of learning the true secret that is not known by all.

In another place I described the situation of the dominated and oppressed in the modern period through the metaphor or speaking and specified the time–space of their being as the pause, the silence, between each word—a pause that is necessary for coherent speech. "The fact that silence presupposes words is what gives it this ironic twist. Without words there can be no silence, yet the sheer absence of words is not silence. Silence forces us to realize that our words, the units of our naming and recognition in the world, presuppose a reality which is prior to our naming and doing."[31]

Kathleen Biddick raises a similar point when she notes the difference between the Jewish and Christian modes of coming to terms with modernity. In this discussion she has recourse to the Enlightenment Jewish philosopher, Moses Mendelssohn, and she contrasts his way of thinking with that of Immanuel Kant, who comes from a Protestant Christian tradition. She tells us that Mendelssohn, in his treatise, *Jerusalem,* posited something between speech and writing. In working out this meaning through the theological and psychoanalytic literature, she calls this in-betweeness the "Echo."

> It is Echo, too, who now needs to intervene among the contemporary historicists who eschew lachrymose history without acknowledging the historiographical problem of thinking Enlightenment and Haskalah together. Mendelssohn's understanding of Jewish speech and writing ask us to think of Echo as an unhistorical acoustic between speech and writing, between the circumcision of the foreskin and of the heart.[32]

And, I might add, between the blackness of our bodies and the nature and meaning of freedom and care.

It is interesting to note how the probing for an authentic time–space for the individual and social bodies of the oppressed and dominated have tended toward various metaphors related to language, whether written or oral. Jones spoke of "overhearing"; Charles Long of "pauses between words"; and Kathleen Biddick of an "unhistorical acoustic between speech and writing." I think that all have reference to a new kind of temporality in the world. While cognizant of the "master narratives of the Makers of History," and living within that matrix, there is the desire and necessity to seek a more authentic ordering of time. It is clear that as individual and social bodies they can never become a part of history as authentic human beings. They are nevertheless a part of this history by virtue of not being a part of it. This is the history of Baby Suggs's yonder, out there. The new nonhistorical temporality is nurtured by the oppressed's various indigenous and lachrymose pasts where they were known and dealt with as authentic human beings.

In the United States, the black body as individual person and as part of moral communities in time define a site for remembering the truth of the past of this land and also as a critical and creative renewal of the human venture. I have put forth the notion of conjuring as not only a technique of healing but equally as an epistemology and a hermeneutic of remembering. It was during the time of African Americans' "weary years and silent tears"—their lachrymose history where they learned that the black body was not only the locus and site for health and the curing arts, but it was also simultaneously a site of memory. It was from within this mode of temporality that the black body escaped its fetishistic mode and ceased to be merely a pawn of the American constitutional order. Many of us who were born during the time of segregation and intense discrimination are appalled not only by the empirical situations that are rampant within the black communities throughout the country. Could it be that we as a moral community have forgotten the meaning of freedom, that we think that we can learn more about freedom from those who enslaved us rather than from those who cared for us? David Brion Davis told us some time ago that in the modern world it is only those who have been enslaved who know the meaning of freedom.[33]

In 1900, at the turn of the century, James Weldon and John Rosamond Johnson wrote the great hymn of our lachrymose time, "Lift Every Voice and Sing." Three year later, in 1903, Du Bois published his famous text, *Souls of Black Folk*. Both of these texts set forth a new position within the modern world. The Johnson brothers gave back in song the resource of an ordeal that African Americans had undergone, but not in the sense of a conquering progress in the pursuit of happiness. The song ask us to reflect upon where we are, why we were there, and invited us to ponder the meaning of freedom from this perspective. Du Bois's *Souls* anticipated much of what makes up postcolonial thought today. To make use of the language of Kathleen Biddick, Du Bois's *Souls* invited us into "the risk of thinking about 'unhistorical' temporalities—ones not about divisions between then and now, but about passages, thresholds, gaps, intervals, in-betweeness. These unhistorical temporalities that do not use time as a utilitarian resource to ground identity are temporalities that are not one."[34]

Margaret Geneva Long titled her history of African American medical care and practice "Doctoring Freedom." It is clear that she saw the issue of health care as part and parcel of the meaning, nature, and fortunes of the black body in the time and space of the American Republic. Her work echoes the pervasive description of slavery by Ira Berlin noted above. The last chapter of her dissertation is entitled, "The Fictional Black Doctor: Issues of Science and Medicine in Progressive-Era African American Fiction." In this chapter she analyzes the role and practice of black doctors in the novels of Charles Chestnutt and Pauline Hopkins.

I see her inclusion of fictive material as one way of coming to terms with other narratives and temporal modes of understanding the nature of health and healing within the black communities. Margaret Long ask this rhetorical question:

> And what of black healers in our era?...The problematic relationship between black doctors and a black folk, and the promises, or threats, of science to African American culture remain, but in a changed form...More than a century after Chestnutt's and Harper's novels were published, public health statistics—rates of unintended pregnancy, smoking, obesity, and heart disease—continue, and efforts to ground public policy in the body, now abstracted to genetics, continue to impinge on discussions of race in America.[35]

The nondiscursive, nonscientific expressions fit well into the stylistics of conjuring that I have attempted to set forth. In like manner, Nell Painter, in her survey of African American history, *Creating Black Americans: African-American History and Its Meanings, 1619 to the Present*, includes over one hundred examples of African American artists. Nell Painter makes it clear that the inclusion of the artwork was not an afterthought. As a matter of fact, she tells us that she would have included more if such inclusion had not made the price of the text almost prohibitive. The artwork is as necessary to her text as is the discursive historical narrative.

> Although the selection of artwork is limited, readers will notice that black artists have preferred certain subjects to others. Throughout the twentieth century, for example, black visual artists depicted two kinds of images repeatedly that were seldom features in American fine art: ordinary working people and violence inflicted upon people of African descent. Black artists illustrated—literally—the importance of these two themes. [Her book] *Creating Black Americans* reflects the abundance of these images by emphasizing the lives of ordinary people and the violence so common in their lives.[36]

The black body remains a site of memory—a body of the in-betweenness that tells another story of modern times. The black body is the site for diagnosis, critique, and creativity. As Du Bois put it at the beginning of the twentieth century, "the problem of the twentieth century is the problem of the color line." Upon the wellness of these black bodies, a great deal of the well-being of the world depends.

NOTES

1. David L. Schoenbrun, "Conjuring the Modern in Africa: Durability and Rupture in Histories of Public Healing between the Great Lakes of East Africa," *American Historical Review*, 3, no. 5 (December 2006): pp. 1403–439.

2. See Schoenbrun, "Conjuring the Modern in Africa," p. 1405.

3. Ibid., p. 1405.

4. Dipesh Chakrabarty, *Provincializing Europe, Postcolonial Thought and Historical Difference* (Princeton, N.J.: Princeton University Press, 2000), p. 255.

5. I refer to a tradition of scholarship that can be identified with the late T. O. Ranger. They include I. A. Kimambo, Bethwell Ogot, and Matthew Schoffler. See T. O. Ranger and Isara Kimambo, eds., *The Historical Study of African Religion* (Berkeley: University of California Press, 1974) and T. O. Ranger, *Dance and Society in East Africa* (Berkeley: University of California Press, 1975).

6. The title of this section, "Time on the Cross," is taken from the controversial study of slavery of cliometric historians, Robert William Fogel and Stanley L. Engerman. See *Time on the Cross*, 2 vols. (Boston: Little, Brown, 1974).

7. Fogel and Engerman, *Time on the Cross*, vol. 1, p. 258.

8. Ira Berlin, *Many Thousand Gone* (Cambridge: The Belnap Press of Harvard University Press), p. 8.

9. See Robin L. Einhorn, *American Taxation, American Slavery* (Chicago: University of Chicago Press, 2006) for a thorough discussion of the role slavery played in the discussion on the Articles of Confederation and how slavery was implicated and resolved in the Constitution, especially as it was related to voting, taxation, and the significance of the House of Representatives as the branch of government that is able to propose taxation.

10. Einhorn, *American Taxation*, p. 123.

11. See Nell Irvin Painter, "On Soul Murder and Slavery," Africana America, http://www.Africans in America/Part4/Nell Irvin Painter on soul murder and slavery. htm.

12. Herbert G. Gutman, *The Black Family in Slavery and Freedom, 1750–1925* (New York: Pantheon, 1976), p. 32.

13. Schoenbrun, "Conjuring the Modern in Africa," p. 1417.

14. This quote and the discussion of Salo Baron is taken from her book, *The Typological Imaginary: Circumcision, Technology, History* (Philadelphia: University of Pennsylvania Press, 2003), chap. 4, p. 78.

15. Charles H. Long, "Passage and Prayer: The Origins of Religion in the Atlantic World," in *The Courage to Hope, from Black Suffering to Human Redemption*, ed. Quinton Hosford Dixie and Cornel West (Boston: Beacon Press, 1999), pp. 11–21.

16. Sterling Stuckey, *Slave Culture: Nationalist Theory & The Foundations of Black America* (New York: Oxford University Press, 1987), p. 3.

17. Ibid., p. 12.

18. Margaret Geneva Long, "Doctoring Freedom: The Politics of African American Medical Care," 1840–1910 (Ph.D. diss., The University of Chicago, August 2004), pp. 18–19.

19. After hearing so many Southern delegates at the Constitutional Convention minimizing the ownership of Africans as no more than that of sheep, cattle, or horses,

Benjamin Franklin refused to mince words. "Sheep were totally different from slaves: sheep will never make any Insurrections." Quoted by Einhorn, *American Taxation*, p. 122.

20. Yvonne P. Chireau, *Black Magic, Religion and the African American Conjuring Tradition* (Berkeley: University of California, 2003).

21. Chiraeu, *Black Magic*, pp. 12, 17.

22. Quoted by Chireau, *Black Magic*, pp. 77–78.

23. A reliable reference is the articles devoted to magic in *Encyclopedia of Religion*, 2nd ed., ed. Lindsay Jones (Farmington Hills, Mich.: Thomas Gale Co., 2005), vol. 8, pp. 5562–94. The articles are "Theories of Magic," "Magic in Indigenous Societies," "Magic in Graeco-Roman Antiquity," "Magic in Medieval and Renaissance Europe," "Magic in Eastern Europe," "Magic in Islam," "Magic in South Asia," and "Magic in East Asia."

24. See John Middleton's discussion of Malinowski in "Theories of Magic," in Jones, *Encyclopedia of Religion*, p. 5566.

25. See Margaret Long, "Doctoring Freedom," p. 134.

26. Toni Morrison, *Beloved* (New York: Penguin Putman, 1987), pp. 92–94.

27. Nelson George, *Post Soul Nation: The Explosive, Contradictory, Triumph and Tragic 1980s as Experienced by African Americans (Previously Known as Blacks and before that Negroes)* (New York: Viking Press, 2004), p. 229.

28. Ibid., p. 2.

29. Carole Lynn Stewart, "Challenging Liberal Justice: The Talented Tenth Revisited," in *Re-cognizing W.E.B. Du Bois in the Twenty-First Century: Essays on W.E.B. Du Bois*, ed. Mary Keller and Chester Fontenot Jr. (Macon, Ga.: Mercer University Press, 2007), pp. 112–41, esp. 137–39.

30. Schoenbrun, "Conjuring the Modern in Africa," p. 1411.

31. Charles H. Long, *Significations, Signs, Symbols, and Images in the Study of Religion*, 2nd ed. (Aurora, Colo.: The Davies Group Publishers, 1999), p. 67.

32. Kathleen Biddick, *The Typological Imaginary, Circumcision, Technology, History* (Philadelphia: University of Pennsylvania Press, 2003), p. 90.

33. See David Brion Davis, *The Problem of Slavery in the Age of Revolution, 1770–1823* (Ithaca, N.Y.: Cornell University Press, 1975), p. 564.

34. See Biddick, *The Typological Imaginary*, p. 2.

35. Margaret Geneva Long, "Doctoring Freedom," pp. 292–93.

36. Nell Irvin Painter, *Creating Black Americans, African-American History and Its meanings, 1519 to the Present* (New York: Oxford University Press, 2006), p. xii.

CHAPTER 4

———— ⌖ ————

Spiritual Illness and Healing: "If the Lord Wills"

Arvilla Payne-Jackson

The worldview of a culture encompasses its belief system, the cognitive perception of the natural world, and its relationship to the supernatural world. One function of belief systems is to make sense of experience.[1] This includes the perception and interpretation of religious beliefs and healing practices utilized in medical systems. Barfield defines a medical system as being the following:

> Comprised of both cognitive and behavioral components...The cognitive component of a medical system centers upon theories of etiology or causation of *illness* and usually involves a taxonomy of *disease* categories grouped by a causal agent...The behavioral component of medical systems concerns the social interactions of healers and their patients in a cultural and economic context.[2]

Theologically, healing occurs once an individual is restored to wholeness or well-being, which is characterized by obtaining an equilibrium or balance of mind, body, and spirit.[3]

Early studies of traditional medical practices and beliefs were filtered through the lens of religion because "healing serves as a fruitful entrée to the study of religion, because it is integral to many if not most religious traditions."[4] Sickness and therapeutic rituals are viewed as a way to understand underlying cosmological beliefs and cultural values.[5] In more recent years, the study of medical systems has refocused on "the study of cultural knowledge about illness and its linkage to differential diagnosis and curative actions," what is called ethnomedicine.[6]

AFRICAN AMERICAN ETHNOMEDICINE

The African American ethnomedical system (AAES) has a distinctive core of perceptions and practices, the central core of which developed from a combination of intercultural theoretical and practical techniques from African, European Colonial, and American Indian healing systems.[7] Loudell Snow, a medical anthropologist, describes the AAES as the following:

> A composite of classical medicine of an earlier day, European folklore regarding the natural world, rare African traits, and selected beliefs derived from modern scientific medicine. The whole is inextricably blended with the tenets of fundamentalist Christianity, elements of the Voodoo religion of the West Indies, and the added spice of sympathetic magic. It is a coherent system and not a ragtag collection of isolated superstitions.[8]

Medical anthropologists recognize that there are distinct differences between disease and illness. Horacio Fabegra differentiated disease and illness. "Disease refers to bodily events and processes conceptualized in terms of a scientific framework; while illness designates the socioculturally structured behaviors and interpretations of persons which are a response to these processes."[9] This distinction between disease and illness reflects different illness models that are related to the perceived causes of the problem being treated.[10]

George Foster[11] in his research on non-Western or traditional medical systems put forth an etiological model of disease in which illnesses were either of a naturalistic or personalistic nature. Naturalistic disease results from natural forces or conditions such as sudden changes in exposure to cold or heat, being caught in a draft or wind, or coming into contact with dampness such as night dew, and, most importantly, any imbalance of basic body elements. Personalistic disease, on the other hand, can result from two sources: (1) an occult source in which a human, for example, a witch or a sorcerer (known as a root doctor or a hoodoo voodoo man in AAES), plays an active role in causing the illness using magic, rituals, potions, or poison, among other elements; and (2) a spiritual source or supernatural force in which spiritual agents such as God, Satan, demons, or evil spirits can cause an illness.[12]

In the AAES, natural illness is primarily the result of an imbalance in the blood or a build up of cold in the body (phlegm). An imbalance of natural elements is a remnant of the Hippocratic humoral system of medicine brought over with the Europeans. The state of the blood is described in terms of binary qualities: good/bad (blood purity), hot/cold (temperature), thick/thin (viscosity), high/low (quantity), and fast/slow (circulation).[13]

Spiritual sources of illness include God, who sends illness as a "person's cross to bear," as a way to "bear witness," or as "penalty for sin." One person cited in Snow's work assessed that

> [t]he prevention and treatment of health problems was almost entirely of a religious nature. She was one of 14 children in a household where health care was the herbal remedies of her parents and trusting in "Doctor Jesus." And she

was still depending on Doctor Jesus. She saw sickness as a form of weakness that is very nearly the same as sin and, as such, as something that is not allowed in her house.[14]

Another patient refused surgery as she perceived her illness to be "a tangible sign of divine displeasure" and that her illness was "the deserved outcome of some unstated sinful behavior" and that God would heal her "should it be His will."[15]

Surviving a serious illness or accident is frequently attributed to the Lord. When Mr. Johnson[16] (interviewed by the author in 1994) was working at a saw mill, a young man cut down a tree too close to where he was working and it fell on him, breaking three ribs off of his backbone, bursting his left kidney, and paralyzing his left arm. "Well, I didn't think I would live till I got to the hospital. The Lord was with me and I did survive. And I'm still doing along pretty good today."

The power of Satan to derail the saints into sin and subsequent illness of body and spirit is a common theme in church services. Demon possession is one explanation for mental health problems and physical addictions. Exorcism, prayer, and laying on of hands are treatments for illness, whether of a natural or supernatural etiology. According to Mr. John Lee, an herbal healer in North Carolina, one of the most important elements in how one's health is maintained is whether or not people are treated with love.

> Love makes a difference too. A lot of people say, "How can I love you? You did me wrong." You supposed to forgive. If you don't love man, you don't love God. Take a person who doesn't treat you like you think they ought to. We supposed to love one another. That's the way it works. If we don't live right, you gonna have to pay for it. There's a whole lot of different ways that you look into sin. You say sin is sin, but they's a lot of things you can do that's more grievous than others.

Occult causes of illness are the result of so-called rooting, or sorcery by a root doctor. Jealousy, envy, greed, revenge, and control are among the primary motives of a person who seeks the services of a root doctor. Ms. Jones (interviewed by author in 1994) stated why people go to the root doctor. "When people go to the root doctor, they go to get someone to hurt somebody, or maybe get some help for theirselves. They get some root or some hair. Take a chicken. This has been goin' on for years, before Christ's time. The devil plays his part. That's all devil work."

Root doctors or hoodoo voodoo practitioners practice the occult arts. They use formulas, magic, powders, potions, and other paraphernalia to put so-called roots on a person. They use both imitative magic and contagious magic as a means of effectuating the roots. Sympathetic magic works on the principle of like produces like, and contagious magic works on the principle that once two objects have been in contact they remain in contact. In the case of the latter, a person may be asked to collect something that belongs to an individual and bring it to the root doctor, for example, hair, nail clippings, sweat, semen, blood, or clothing. These are used to prepare the rooting. Consequently, many people are careful to collect and dispose of their own hair and nail clippings so that they cannot be used against them.

Food is another source of rooting, and many young men are warned not to eat food prepared by women, especially those who may have ulterior motives. As reported by one individual, interviewed by the author (1992), her friend mixed her menstrual blood into the spaghetti sauce she served her boyfriend in an effort to keep him from wandering.

Any individual in a community who works with herbs and roots is likely to be considered to be a root doctor by the community-at-large. Ms. Mays, an herbalist, pointed out one way to identify root doctors as different from herbalists.

> If I was a root doctor my yard would be full [of people]. They'd be here from every which way. A root doctor would be more powerful. Somebody [a client, may be] trying to get ahead; or they want to fix somebody else, they tryin' to get a lucky root, or they tryin to do something. Or somebody did something to 'em. You just can't hardly get in there for all the people.

Mr. Lee (interviewed by author in 1988) traced the origins of rooting back to the times of Genesis. "Rachel was the beloved wife and her sister was jealous. She told her maid to go out and get mandrake (ginseng). That has the reputation to make you fall in love. It raises blood pressure."

One incident recorded in North Carolina by the author in 1982 relates an illness experience brought on by a greedy landlady in the 1940s, who took out an insurance policy on one of her boarders without his knowledge.

> A woman tried to mess me up one time. I knew something was wrong. I had a very heavy feeling. It was just as hard for me to breathe as it would be for me to try to go through this ceiling. Oh, it was gettin' on me. I was just too strong to give up on it. She had a little jar, about that long [4"] and about that big around [2"]. And she put it over on the other side of my bed. Well, at that time every once in a while I'd wear a brace on my back. She had taken one of the straps that I had fastened back here to hold it down and cut it up and put it in this jar with some other stuff and a gold colored liquid. It just happened that the Lord fixed it so I would find it. I was makin' my bed one morning and flicked the covers stronger than usual and this jar rolled out. If I hadn't found it, I don't know what would have happened because it was getting' worse every day. I don't know how long she had it back there, maybe two or three weeks probably. But every day I would get worse and worse. And I was wondering about it.
>
> Most of the time when people is bein' fixed, it's like that. They don't know what's getting' wrong with them. It look like I had a fever, and it came to me 'bout me bein' like I was.

I left there that morning. I told her husband I was goin'. And she came up there where I was workin'. Oh, she kept callin' for me, 'cause they had to call me on the intercom. I wouldn't go up there and talk with her. Course, I had the jar with me, that's what she wanted. Well, I could have fixed her if I had been dirty as she was. I could have taken and threw the bottle out there in the water, and what I would have did is put her name to it before it hit the water. She'd a been crazy today [imitative magic]. But, I said, "No, I'm not gonna do that." I taken it and carried it to the toilet and put it in the east corner and I named it up there and left it there. I begin to get better, every day I get better, better and better. It wasn't too long before they tore the toilet down.

When doctors are not able to help a person, the ultimate conclusion some may come to is that he or she has been rooted. This was the case of one young woman in North Carolina.

We went to see her. She'd been in the hospital and she got out. And she was sick. And we were there with her and she said, "Ms. M., do something for me, please do something for me. I ain't never done nothin' to nobody in my life. Please do something for me." She said she felt like something was comin' up choking her and she's sittin' up on the side of the bed and she just went back like that on the bed. They had one of these old night pots, you know what we used to call slop jars. And she sit down on that thing, and she had a bowel movement, and it look like it was as black as that box over there under your hat. They carried her on to the hospital. She died that night. But I just felt like, because of all that black stuff come out of her like it did, that somebody might have did something to her. That was one thing she said that worried me. She said, "Please do something for me. I ain't never did nothin' to nobody in my life." And that made me think she thought it. And she might have been right because they're the ones down there where they have that pot of roots boiling all the time. And my mama said, she heard the boys sayin' they had the medicine that she got from the doctor, and they said, "When you got some of that mess in you, doctor medicine is against you. He kill you faster than anything." And that made me think she thought it.

RECEIVING THE CALL

Practitioners of AAES receive their calls through acceptable cultural and religious experiences. Some healers are recognized at birth as having a special calling by unusual signs such as being born with the veil (caul or placenta over the face). Such an individual is considered to have the gift of clairvoyance and in some instances the ability to see into a person in order to determine the cause of the illness. In earlier times, lay midwives would take a part of the placenta and make a tea and give some to the infant in order to give him or her the ability to deal with the spirit world.[17]

Another healer, interviewed by the author in 1989, was reported to be born with nine teeth, another was the seventh son of the seventh son, which indicated that he had special powers. Near-death experiences may result in healers striking a bargain with God that if He will cure them then they will serve Him as healers. Natural and spiritual healers often perceive their work as a gift from God, or a calling by God.

In some instances healing is passed down family lines. Ms. Dolly, a practicing African American lay midwife in North Carolina in the 1980s, was selected at birth by her grandmother to carry on her work. A few days after she was born Ms. Dolly's grandmother took her out into the yard, anointed her body with oil, and presented her to God. She then told Ms. Dolly's mother that she could now rest as she had found the child who would carry on her work. She died a few days later. Ms. Dolly was not told about this event until after she had decided to become a midwife many years later. Like many other lay midwives, she considered her calling to come from the Lord. She learned her trade through apprenticeship to other midwives and in later years (the 1940s) acquired the state license to practice.

Mr. John Lee came from a family of healers. His father and brother were herbalists who served their community, and his mother and sister were lay midwives. Mr. Lee was born with the veil. He considered his gift to be from God so he could help and serve people. His gift of clairvoyance allowed him to "see into a person" and tell what the problem was.

> I can tell if a person has bad blood by how they talk, how they look. But I can look at 'em and just tell when I see 'em. I just have that gift you know. I used to tell you anything in the world you'd want to know about yourself or anybody else. But I had to stop that. It was too strong for me. It begin to work on my heart. I had to get rid of some of that power 'cause it was comin' on me too much. When I was about ten what I did, I takin' a baby's hand, the baby wasn't too old, maybe two, three months old, and the baby was dead. They told me to take this baby's hand, and carry it over my face like this [from the chin to the forehead] three times. It taken a lot of it away 'cause it was just gettin' too strong on me.
>
> I could stand things better. I didn't see things like I had seen. Before I could see things, hear things, talk to things. I didn't want to talk with them [spirits], but they would talk with me. Scared me so bad. See that's why I had to get rid of some of that stuff, it was getting too strong on me.

Even though his power was reduced people still came to him looking for answers to questions about their personal lives and health.

> A lot of people would come and they would ask me questions. Black and white would come. This man one time, a white fellow, came here and was sitting in this room here. He said, "Can you tell me how long I'm gonna live?" My wife heard him. She came in there and said, "Don't tell him, don't tell him." I was gonna tell him because he asked me. He asked me about his girlfriend. I told him how she looked. He said, "What do you think about her?" I said, "Well,

she's alright, but she's usin' you right now." He said, "I know it. How did you know it?" It didn't bother me to tell 'em, I was just tryin' to help them, let them see their sins.

Mr. Lee also used dreams as an aide in diagnosing causes of illness.

When these things come to me plain, it's just like we're talking now. Looks like I can just see it, feel it. And I can sit down and talk with a person, but it's in my dream. And I can look at them and tell there's something bad about them. Sometimes I see a shadow. I know what they want, and what they come to see me for. It look like sometime something's following me, and I can see it. I had a dream about this man that I was tellin' you about his leg. That man followed me around, I didn't know he was dead at the time I dreamed about him. He didn't hurt me, or anything, but it looked like it was something that he wanted to tell me. The way I felt like, it was witchcraft stuff. And finally I woke up. That stayed with me all that day about this man. But I've had dreams like that several times. Sometimes before they die. Sometimes after they die.

The way I feel about it, God just leads me to the right thing. He guides me in doing this. It looks like it just comes to me. He just gives me that much power to do these things. It just come natural. I would say about 90%, 95% of my ability is spiritual because I don't try to overdo a thing. I do go to church and I do feel the Lord has blessed me by knowin' some of these things. After I get an idea and see that I have helped these people I feel justified in getting these things [herbs] for them. And when I get these things and it does help them, I say, "Well, I've been blessed. If the Lord wills, I can help."

One distinction between spiritual healers and occult healers is that the former do not require payment for their services, although donations may be acceptable, while occult healers require monetary payment for their services and these payments often are very high.

"The belief in the efficacy of power or healing touch of a minister of God adds another dimension to the restoration of balance."[18] Ministers and spiritual healers may be called on to drive out demons that cause illness or remove roots that have been put on a person.[19] One incident of rooting in which a minister was called on to remove the roots was recounted to the author in 1978 on a field trip to the Southeast Lowlands of the United States.

One young African American woman wanted to keep her child's father from leaving her. She collected sweat from his groin on a handkerchief and took it to a root doctor, who then performed a ritual that created an unnatural need for the young man to be close to her at all times. The young man recognized that his feelings were unnatural and oppressive and realized that he had been rooted. If he went to his grandfather, who was a root doctor, he was afraid that he would counter-root and nullify the effect of the original root, cause her great harm, or even kill her. Instead, he chose to go to a Baptist minister, who told him how to undo the rooting, but warned him that the result would "turn back on her" and she would not be able to be in his presence. He followed the minister's instructions and took three items[20] to the river, turned his back to the river, and threw them over his left shoulder while calling on the name of the Father, Son, and Holy Ghost. This resulted in the reversal of the original rooting, and the woman could not stand to be in his presence. She was reported to have backed her car up two blocks when she saw him coming to the house.

A variety of commercial products incorporating elements of religion and magic are also available to individuals who need help in dealing with everyday life. Specialty stores usually found in urban areas are the primary source for these items.[21] Powders, candles, potions, herbs, amulets, talismans, crystals, and herbs are purported to help overcome personal weaknesses, gain prosperity, bring good luck, or increase wealth. These products can also be used to prevent harm or illness compelled on an individual by another person or root doctor with the intention of causing mental anguish or illness, to ward off evil, and to protect against rooting. Books based on the Psalms are also found in these stores. Psalms are believed to be a good and positive supernatural source of protection against evil and negative elements that can cause harm, illness, or death.[22]

The author interviewed three specialist practitioners in the AAES system: blood stoppers, wart removers, and practitioners who talk out fire. Blood stoppers repeat the biblical verse, Ezekiel 16:6, over a bleeding wound to stop the blood flow. Wart removers use a piece of animal bone to mark the sign of the cross three times over the wart while repeating a silent prayer. Specialists who talk out fire repeat a silent prayer while blowing over the burned area. This prevents blistering and scarring. One individual recounted to the author (1989) how a man from Virginia, when he was a young boy, was taken to an old African American healer after he fell into a campfire. His father wrapped him in a sheet and drove him to the healer's home. The healer blew over the young boy's body. As he blew, the pain left and the blisters disappeared and he was left with no scars.

Different types of practitioners in the AAES system are called on to solve different problems. The perceived cause and seriousness of an illness frequently determines the choice of healer(s), who may be consulted either sequentially or concurrently. Family members or community elders, or both, are the first source of counsel. Prayers and laying on of hands of church members and the minister are sought as an aide in healing for both supernatural and natural illness. If home remedies are not effective, a biomedical practitioner is the most likely next step in the health care process. Unbeknown to most biomedical practitioners, when they announce that they cannot find out what is wrong with a patient they may confirm for the patient and family that the person has been either rooted through sorcery or that the illness is of a spiritual nature. Either a minister or another root doctor is sought out for help.[23] Others see biomedical practitioners simply as technicians or instruments of God and that it is God who does the healing, performs the surgeries, and creates the miracles.

Just as God is consulted in the event of illness, the cure is also believed to be at hand. A common belief that was voiced by one herbal practitioner interviewed by the author in 1994 and echoed by many people interviewed over the years is the following:

> The Lord, he put something here for everything. There are plants for everything. The Lord put these things here and that's what we used in the beginning. That's all we had to use. We didn't have the pills and all the things, and even the people who used to sell this patent medicine, they would fix it in the bottles and they would carry it around and sell it.

Persistence of the AAES system is due in part to the distrust of the traditional biomedical system. A recurring theme among people interviewed in the Southeast Lowlands between 1978 and 2000 was that "The doctor's medicine helps with one thing, but kills you in another way." The warnings issued for medicines on television ads were given as evidence of this belief. The system also continues to exist because, unlike biomedicine, it is not restricted to dealing with matters of health and illness.[24]

The underlying worldview in the AAES is that God is the source of healing and He provides the means to fight against illnesses of both natural and supernatural etiology. Illness can result not only from an imbalance brought on by outside elements but also by sin that has entered one's life. The cure for either naturalistic or personalistic illness is best summed up as follows—If the Lord wills, health will be restored.

NOTES

1. Loudell Snow, *Walkin' over Medicine* (Boulder, Colo.: Westview Press, 1993), p. 17.

2. Thomas Barfield, ed., *The Dictionary of Anthropology* (Oxford: Blackwell Publishers, Ltd., 2001), p. 318.

3. See Linda Barnes and Ines Talamantez, eds., *Teaching Religion and Healing* (Oxford: Oxford University Press, 2006); Arvilla Payne-Jackson and John Lee, *Folk Wisdom and Mother Wit: John Lee—An African American Healer* (Westport, Conn.: Greenwood Press, 1993).

4. Barnes and Talamantez, *Teaching Religion*.

5. Horacio Fabrega, "Some Features of Zinacanecan Medical Knowledge," *Ethnology* 10 (1971): pp. 1–24.

6. Barfield, *The Dictionary of Anthropology*, p. 318.

7. Payne-Jackson and Lee, *Folk Wisdom and Mother Wit*; Faith Mitchell, *Hoodoo Medicine: Sea Islands Herbal Remedies* (Berkeley: Reed, Cannon and Johnson, 1978); Wilbur Watson, *Black Folk Medicine: The Therapeutic Significance of Faith and Trust* (New Brunswick, N.J.: Transactions, 1984).

8. Loudell Snow, "Folk Medical Beliefs and Their Implications for Care and Patients," *Annals of Internal Medicine* 81, no. 1 (1974): p. 83.

9. Horacio Fabrega, "On the Specificity of Folk Illness," in *Culture, Disease and Healing: Studies in Medical Anthropology,* ed. David Landy (New York: Macmillian Publishing Co., 1977), p. 274; see also David Mechanic, "The Concept of Illness Behavior," *Journal of Chronic Diseases* 15 (1962): pp. 189–94; Arthur Kleinman, *Patients and Healers in the Context of Culture* (Berkeley: University of California Press, 1980).

10. See Barnes and Talamantez, *Teaching Religion.*

11. George Foster, "Disease Etiologies in Northwestern Medical Systems," *American Anthropologist* 78 (1976): p. 775.

12. See also Payne-Jackson and Lee, *Folk Wisdom and Mother Wit;* Faith Mitchell, *Hoodoo Medicine: Sea Islands Herbal Remedies* (Berkeley: Reed, Cannon and Johnson, 1978); Watson, *Black Folk Medicine;* Snow, "Folk Medical Beliefs," p. 83.

13. Snow, "Folk Medical Beliefs"; Snow, *Walkin';* Payne-Jackson and Lee, *Folk Wisdom and Mother Wit.*

14. Snow, *Walkin',* p. 29.

15. Ibid., p. 43.

16. Quotes about illness incidents attributed to individuals are from interviews conducted in the Southeast Lowlands between 1977 and 2000. All names, except those of Mr. John Lee, are pseudonyms.

17. Payne-Jackson and Lee, *Folk Wisdom and Mother Wit.*

18. Snow, *Walkin',* p. 133.

19. See Linda Camino, *Ethnomedical Illnesses and Non-Orthodox Healing Practices in the American South: How They Work and What They Mean* (Ph.D. diss., University of Michigan, Ann Arbor, 1986).

20. He would not reveal what the three items were.

21. The *Candle Shop* in Washington, D.C., that was in business until the late 1990s is featured in the video *African Roots to American Roots: A Story of Folk Medicine in America* produced in 1994 by the author as part of a commissioned exhibit for the U.S. National Park Service at Ellis Island on immigrants' contributions to the health care system. It includes pictures of the items that could be used to affect one's own health or induce desired results in the behavior of another. Barrels of powders with labels such as love, money, and good luck, as well as potions, candles, minerals, and bottled herbs were part of the shop's magical paraphernalia. In addition, written materials including books on the Psalms were also available.

22. See Arthur Hall and Peter Bourne, "Indigenous Therapists in a Southern Black Urban Community," *Archives of General Psychiatry* 28 (1973): pp. 137–42; Snow, *Walkin';* Payne-Jackson and Lee, *Folk Wisdom and Mother Wit.*

23. Charles Erasmus, "Changing Folk Beliefs and the Relativity of Empirical Knowledge," *Southwestern Journal of Anthropology* 8 (1952): pp. 411–28; David Landy, *Culture, Disease and Healing;* and Camino, *Ethnomedical Illnesses.*

24. Snow, *Walkin',* p. 133.

PART III

The Arts of Ritual and Practice

CHAPTER 5

——— ✝ ———

The Marking of the Body, Memory, and the Meaning of Suffering in Phyllis Alesia Perry's *Stigmata*

Carolyn M. Jones

I have always felt that maybe God hated me and that he chose me to carry a burden of pain for the rest of the world.[1]

—Jade, *Willow Weep for Me*

Who were these Saints? These crazy, loony, pitiful women? Some of them, without a doubt, were our mothers and grandmothers.[2]

—*Alice Walker, In Search of Our Mother's Gardens*

Phyllis Alesia Perry's novel *Stigmata* is about marking, mental illness, and memory. The novel repeats many of the themes of African American women's literature. A quilt, as in Alice Walker's "Everyday Use"[3] and Toni Morrison's *Beloved*,[4] is a major image in the novel. Women's arts—quilting, painting, and writing, particularly—break the silence of suffering present in the novel. The continuing presence of the slave past that separates mother and daughter and the Middle Passage are key to the novel. Nonlinear time and multidimensional space open the possibility for exploration of the suffering of black women: "'You have no idea how complex the universe really is,'" Lizzie tells us.[5] Perry's protagonist, Lizzie DuBose, is the one who makes the movement across time and space, transforming stigma, a sign of disgrace, into stigmata, a sign of grace.

Lizzie has spent most of her adult life in mental hospitals because she exhibits what a Catholic priest will name for her: stigmata, the marking of the body. She exhibits depression's most violent features: delusions and suicidal tendencies. This chapter examines depression and African American women, utilizing the novel, and focuses on the cultural context that generates what postcolonial critics are calling, using Freud, melancholia. We will turn, finally, to the title essay of Alice Walker's *In Search of Our Mother's*

Gardens to think about the silent black women saints that have come before us, their suffering, and its meaning and beauty.

Depression, as the *Diagnostic Statistical Manual of Mental Disorders, Fourth Edition* (DSM-IV) defines it, is a mood disorder, affecting about 17 million people per year. As "Fighting 'the blues' in African Americans" argues, "If you are an average black person in America, you are more likely than an average white person to suffer depression."[6] Yet, as Barbara Jones Warren, a clinical psychiatric nurse who works with African American patients, notes, statistics on depression in African American women are "either non-existent or uncertain," and the research is scarce.[7] Warren writes that the available statistics support what she has found in her practice: "That African American women report more depressive symptoms than African American men or European-American women or men, and that these women have a depression rate twice that of Euro-American women."[8] African Americans, in general, however, do not seek treatment. Dr. Frieda Lewis-Hall, a medical doctor who has worked for the National Institute of Mental Health, says that "Most either believe that depression, or 'the blues,' is a necessary condition of life and must be endured, or they fear being labeled as insane."[9]

Depression does seem to mirror the blues—the melancholy of the poor and oppressed.[10] But it is a particular illness that involves two essential features: depressed mood and loss of pleasure in one's activities.[11] One of these two must be present for the diagnosis of depression to be determined, and "[f]or the symptom to meet the criteria towards a diagnosis of major depression, a person must have had a depressed mood for most of the day, nearly every day for a two-week period of time."[12] In addition, the depressed person may manifest a variety of symptoms. First, one may experience feelings of hopelessness, helplessness, or both, including a negative view of the future, a sense of dissatisfaction or failure, and a negative view of the self.[13] Meri Nana-Ama Danquah wrote the following in *Willow Weep for Me*, an autobiography about her own experiences with depression:

> Depression is a very *"me"* disease. There is an enormous amount of self-criticism, self-loathing, and low self-esteem. Everything revolves around the perception of self. Most depressives find themselves—as much to their own disgust as to everybody else's—annoyingly and negatively self-obsessed.[14]

Warren gives important insight into this focus on self:

> African-American women...are survivors and innovators who historically have been involved in the development of family and group survival strategies. However, women may experience increased stress, guilt, and depressive symptoms when they have role conflicts between their family's survival and their own developmental needs. It is this cumulative stress which takes a toll on the

strengths of African-American women and can produce erosion of emotional and physical health.[15]

Second, one may also experience loss of interest or pleasure in what one once found enjoyable, particularly sexuality.[16] Depression may bring about a change in appetite and weight. Hunger may increase or decrease. A change in weight of more than 5 percent in a month may indicate depression.[17] Third, a depressed person may develop sleeping problems. Disruption of sleep patterns is common: waking in the middle of the night, the inability to return to sleep, or oversleeping. Depression may also make one feel agitated or slowed down. The depressed person may feel tired, even when not having engaged in any physical activity. This may not be "necessarily observable by others" and depends on report.[18]

Depression also causes feelings of worthlessness or guilt. One may become preoccupied with past perceived failures or have an unrealistic sense of personal responsibility.[19] This can lead to problems in thinking, including negative thoughts as well as difficulty in thinking clearly, in concentration, or in decision making. Memory may suffer, creating problems for those in vocations that involve intellectual activity. For teenagers, a drop in grades is often an indicator.[20]

Thoughts of death and suicide and suicide attempts may occur in the clinically depressed. Ironically, those who are severely depressed are at a lower risk for suicide because they lack the energy or motivation to commit the act. The *DSM-IV* stresses that those who are at high risk are individuals "who have made plans to kill themselves and who seem to have a brighter mood after deciding to do so."[21]

About 15 percent of depressed people suffer from delusions, hallucinations, or both.

These are psychotic features of major depressive disorders. Since these symptoms interfere with decision making and judgment, hospitalization is required. Lizzie in *Stigmata* suffers this disorder.

More common are physical aches and pains. Depressed persons often seek help from their primary care physicians for other symptoms like "chronic aches and pains, headaches, stomachaches, and gastrointestinal problems. Women's menstrual periods may be affected, becoming either painful or irregular."[22] For African American women, this tends to be a point of misdiagnosis. Warren writes that African American women are

[f]requently told that they are hypertensive, run down, or tense and nervous. They may be prescribed antihypertensives, vitamins, or mood elevating pills; or they may be informed to lose weight, learn to relax, get a change of scenery, or get more exercise. The root of their symptoms frequently is not explored; and these women continue to complain of being tired, weary, empty, lonely, sad.

Other women friends and family members may say, "We all feel this way some-times, it's just the way it is for us Black women."[23]

Meri Nana-Ama Danquah chronicles her struggle with crippling depres-sion and exhibits many of these symptoms. She records her reluctance to enter therapy.[24] She openly talks about her struggle with taking drugs, such as Zoloft—which made her so anxious that she tempered it with alcohol to function. Finally, Danquah recognizes the pattern of depression in her family, when her sister Paula confesses her own struggles.[25] She argues that depres-sion in African Americans is an issue that has been unexplored:

> Add to all this the social and economic realities of women, blacks, single par-ents, or any combination of the three, and my chances for a life that is free of depression appear to be slim. I, and others like me, seem to be doomed from the get-go.[26]

Danquah writes:

> White people take prescription drugs with gentle, melodic names; they go to therapy once or twice a week in nice, paneled offices. Black people take illicit drugs with names as harsh as the streets on which they are bought. We build churches and sing songs that tell us to "Go Tell It on the Mountain." Either that or we march. Left, right, left, from city to city, for justice and for peace. We are the walking wounded. And we suffer alone because we don't know that there are others like us.[27]

Dealing with white caregivers, as Danquah does, "ethnic, cultural, and/or gender needs" may be unmet.[28] Warren strongly suggests that, for African American women, treatment needs to be consistent with cultural and ethnic values.[29]

Danquah links depression with racism. In her autobiography and in an-other essay, she records two opposing but complementary reactions from white people to her public acknowledgement that she suffers from depres-sion. The first came at a dinner party. The only person of color in the room, Danquah got a very aggressive, sarcastic response from an "older, heavily perfumed" white woman. "*Black* women and depression?...Isn't that kinda redundant?...Don't get me wrong...It's just that when *black* women start going on Prozac, you know the whole world is falling apart."[30] The response rightfully angered Danquah, who responded that when a black woman suffers from any mental illness, "The overwhelming opinion is that she is weak. And weakness in black women is intolerable."[31]

The white woman seems, to me, however, to be saying more: she is sug-gesting that black women's lives *are* ones in which anyone would become depressed. It is to suggest that depression can and should be *acknowledged* as "redundant." I read this to mean, "We all know it's true, but we would rather not face it so things can go on as they are." Acknowledged weakness in black women, therefore, is a cultural threat, a threat to the order of things, and, as Danquah argues in "Writing the Wrongs of Identity," there are, therefore, no images of black women's wellness that have to do with really being well.[32]

Black people also buy into this pathology. Danquah tells us that black men and women reacted negatively to her as well.

> I've frequently been told things like, "Girl, you've been hanging out with too many white folk"; "What do you have to be depressed about? If our people could make it through slavery, we can make it through anything"; "Take your troubles to Jesus, not no damn psychiatrist."[33]

Religion plays both a positive and negative role for African Americans in dealing with depression. Positively, a University of Chicago study reports that a belief in God "can have a powerful impact on reducing depression, particularly among African Americans," in contrast to white subjects of the study for whom such a belief has negligible benefit.[34] The researchers found, unsurprisingly, that African Americans report higher levels of alienation, but, as John Cacioppo, an expert on loneliness and health, concluded:

> When one's group is the target of cultural bias, connection with one's countrymen may not be sufficient to reduce feelings of alienation. Reliance on a power that supercedes that of the country, God, may be beneficial, however...Thus, the consequences of a personal relationship with God may confer benefits in circumstances beyond the reach of relationships with individuals.[35]

For other African Americans, however, as the comments to Danquah suggest, religion can be an impediment to seeking care and moving toward health.

The second reaction to Danquah's admission came from Robert Bly, who said, "Whew. That's going to be one really long book,"[36] acknowledging the reality of black women's lives hidden behind the myths.[37] Danquah argues that it is beneficial to society not to acknowledge African American women's depression, their melancholia, as Paul Gilroy and Anne Cheng call it, as it is connected intimately to racism. Danquah writes:

> You see, the mask of depression is not all that different from the mask of race...Racism is also an illness...To contend with either is bad enough. To grapple with both at the same time...that's enough to drive a person—pardon the expression—"crazy."[38]

Paul Gilroy in *Postcolonial Melancholia* and Anne Anglin Cheng in *The Melancholy of Race* unpack the connection between race and depression and suggest that modern civilization predisposes human beings to depression.

Gilroy is writing about Great Britain and Europe, but postcolonial culture—
that is, the culture that emerged after World War II as colonized places, such
as India, began to find independence—focuses the work. He, recognizing the
violence that has emerged as these new nation-states have developed, urges
us to think in what he calls a "planetary" way, in a mode that is capable of
"comprehending the universality of our elemental vulnerability to the wrongs
we visit upon each other."[39] Such an acknowledgement can open up avenues
of movement. Gilroy fears that we seem incapable of planetary humanism,
and racism is a factor in our limitations. Gilroy reminds us that race is a constructed category; we tend to use race negatively when we are xenophobic,
or afraid of the "other," and race is an "unstable product" of our fear.[40] The
stranger and those who are threatening to "us" are "fixed under the sign of
race."[41] Fear of the other becomes racism when our presuppositions take on
their own institutional lives and support the hierarchical structures, such as
governmental ones, in absolute cultures.[42]

Absolute cultures are ones that Gilroy defines as having closed national
borders. They deny cosmopolitan hopes—that is to say, they believe that their
way is the only and best way. Absolute cultures affirm that national, local,
and ethnic connections and loyalties constitute "the individual." Absolute
cultures that resist dissent and a civilization based on such factors will also
resist self-examination.[43] Rather than address racism, therefore, an absolute
culture either "doses" it[44] or dismisses it as an attempt on the part of the other
to claim victimhood. In Lizzie's case, in *Stigmata*, both are thought true.

The category of race used without facing racism creates what Gilroy
calls "postimperial melancholia."[45] It emerges when those who have been
oppressed start to make demands and as the dominant culture resists a "new
map" of reality that would include those demands.[46] Melancholia, an inability to mourn and an inability to change, demands that culture "Carry on!" as
it had been before.[47]

Gilroy and Cheng scrutinize the implications of colonial power and of living with a double consciousness. Both the Hegelian mastery of others that
creates a simultaneous loss of self and offers a weird unusable power to the
slave and the result that W.E.B. Du Bois predicted—the African American's
living in eternal two-ness—provoke personal and cultural definitional crises.

Melancholia is, therefore, a crisis in self-definition for person and nation.
For Gilroy, melancholia emerges when the postcolonial culture cannot solve
or face the structures its power generated in the colonial situation and therefore sinks into an obsessive "national pathology"[48] that attempts to say who
"we" are. What the culture holding onto the "absolute" cannot face is twofold. First, that its signifier, its way of defining itself, is not useful. For Europe,
Gilroy writes, "the synonymy of the terms 'European' and 'white' cannot continue."[49] Second, the implications of that reality are not just local but global:
they compromise national morality.[50]

On the level of the human person, race is necessarily tied to identity. Postcolonial persons experience what W.E.B. Du Bois called "double consciousness" in *The Souls of Black Folk* and stand both inside and outside the political life and institutional rhythms the inability to mourn creates.[51] This subject position can be unacknowledged and benign or pathological. It is somewhat benign in "convivial" interactions, local "processes of cohabitation and interaction that have made multiculture a part of [our lives]."[52] For example, when I taught at Louisiana State University, an African American student told me that anyone will "party" with anyone at festivals, what Gilroy would call a "convivial interaction," but that the associations do not go beyond that moment. These convivial forms, however, are interpersonal, and, as my student's comment suggests, do not mean that racism or intolerance are absent, just benign. Such interactions are not performed in the absence of racism or in a context of tolerance.

As Gilroy points out, however, the double location of "minority" persons can also be incredibly pathological.[53] A culture in fear can create new, marginal spaces for the stranger. Racism can generate special places outside the rules and define these strangers as "third things," Gilroy argues, using Du Bois's term.[54] Places like Guantanamo Bay, Cuba, where those charged with terrorist activity but who are denied their rights are held, is such a special place housing these third things.

Slavery, in the American context, defined Africans and African Americans as these third things. Anne Cheng turns our focus to the American context and to person as well as structure, arguing that identity is the ground upon which political progress and societal discriminations are made.[55] She points out that assimilation—the idea of the American so-called melting pot—is a fiction in which we can never be secure.[56] This is true because racism is factor used to keep certain institutions and culturalist racism forms in place. She builds on the work of Toni Morrison in *Playing in the Dark: Whiteness and the Literary Imagination* to explore the "racial rejection and desire" in the American psyche.[57]

Morrison's thesis is that the identity of the "American" cannot be imagined without the "shadow" of the African American presence. The contemplation of the black presence is central to any understanding of our national literature, she writes, and "also a way of organizing American coherence."[58] The African presence is a way for white writers—and white Americans, Cheng argues, by extension—to imagine themselves.[59]

What Morrison so astutely points out is that white Americans project onto the Africanist presence what they fear. "Nothing highlighted freedom," Morrison comments, "if it did not in fact create it—like slavery."[60] The exemplary qualities of the American personality, therefore, have their shadow sides. Autonomy and individualism become solitariness, alienation, and malcontent. Newness is translated into an uncritical innocence that cannot self-assess and becomes infantile. Distinctiveness becomes crippling difference, the "strange and threatening...sign of race."[61] Authority becomes absolute power, which Morrison calls a romantic, conquering heroism that is expressed in virility and in wielding power over the lives of others.[62]

Cheng, also thinking through Du Bois's haunting construction of the double consciousness, asks what happens to the psyche of the ethnic and racial minority in this context, using Freud's "Mourning and Melancholia." Mourning, Freud argued, is a healthy response to loss. It is finite and accepts substitution—that the lost object can be replaced. For the person mourning, the *world* is empty and poor.[63] The melancholic, in contrast, is trapped in a pathological state. Grief is interminable, substitution is rejected, and the *ego itself* is poor and empty.[64] Melancholy involves loss; melancholia, ultimately, involves exclusion as the melancholic takes into the self, internalizes what is loved and lost, and attempts to sustain the self through the ghostly emptiness of a "lost other."[65]

Dominant white America, Cheng argues, operates in melancholia. Melancholia is the way American whiteness "goes on" in the face of the transgressions of the past.[66] The "other," defined by her race, is the foreigner within, the devoured object that white America both internalizes and rejects; paralleling Morrison, Cheng writes, "racial exclusion is the condition of American freedom."[67] American freedom maintains the other within the existing order, in an "imbricated but denied relationship."[68] Violence erupts at the points of contact with that willed invisibility.[69]

Let me give an example. Many young white men pattern themselves on hip-hop artists in clothing, in speech, and in style. However, this imitation, this internalized image of the black male, does not mean, necessarily, that the white men change their attitudes in terms of issues such as affirmative action. They take what they like, in terms of personal identity, while potentially rejecting the very persons that they mimic.

For the racialized other, this means that a series of complex psychic negotiations is ongoing, negotiations that express both agency, assertion of the self, and abjection, or self-hatred.[70] Using Toni Morrison's *The Bluest Eye*, Cheng shows us that melancholia is, for the raced subject, twofold. In terms of the body itself, "the assimilating racial and ethnic body is trained to be preoccupied with its non-legitimacy and authenticity."[71] And, second, psychically, there is an internalization of a scripted context of perception, a script for how to see and read the world. This double bind—being both familiar and strange, both desired and rejected—makes the raced subject both the one lost and the one losing.[72] This creates "the imaginative loss of a never-possible perfection whose loss the [raced subject] must come to identify as the rejection of the self."[73] The resulting anger or grief has no place to go and so goes into hiding—creating depression—and keeping the racialized subject in "ambulatory despair."[74]

Cheng is clear that the socialization of different minority groups is "distinct but related."[75] African Americans, however, carry a particular burden because racism in America is constructed as black and white, without "paying attention to the *shades* between where the real battles are fought."[76]

How can this be addressed? Gilroy argues that we should do two things. First, we need to keep telling the story. In a sense, *Stigmata*, repeating motifs from the works of many black women writers, is doing just this. Representation, as Cheng argues, becomes a strategy. It delineates both presence and absence and, thereby, is both the problem (effect) and its critique (affect).[77] The marginalized other must remember that he or she is an agent as well. That is to say, even though one is being looked at, one is always also looking back. This looking back has incredible power: it can reject the definitions imposed on one or it can expose the motives and true power of the one looking. If there is no gaze that is not already mirrored by another, even the gaze of the invisible can reflect back, making "visible the contingency of distinction and pervert the lines of power," exposing power as positionality.[78] This countergaze can create a border position that is another kind of double, one that neither denies nor participates fully in the structures that generate melancholia and that, thereby, can claim a different kind of power to define the self and culture. One might think of Ice-T's early raps, like "Cop Killer," as the oppositional gaze, for example. His work exposed tension and fear in the majority culture. Ice-T said of that work, "I'm singing in the first person as a character who is fed up with police brutality."[79]

Second, Gilroy argues that this retelling and redirection of the gaze requires that we "step back audaciously into the past"[80]—or crawl back through history, as Charles H. Long puts it.[81] Gilroy emphasizes here, as in *The Black Atlantic*,[82] that art is one site at which openness to the other is apparent. He suggests that, rather than letting such openness remain either convivial or be co-opted by corporations, we might put it to political and social uses. The crawling back is not just to rediscover the past, the boundaries of the postcolonial present, but to bring more incidences of past openness forward. We have a hybrid history; what we need to do is to see that history as a resource, hidden in convivial culture, for creating a counterhistory.[83] Crawling back can "provide an opening onto the multicultural promise" of the present world as we acknowledge what the presence of "strangers, aliens, and blacks"[84] and their interaction with colonial or slave cultures has *already* contributed to existing institutional and cultural forms.

STIGMATA

Beginning in the thirteenth century, with St. Francis of Assisi, stigmatists exhibited the wounds of Christ in hands or wrists, feet, and sides. Over three hundred incidences of stigmata have been recorded, and of these, about

90 percent occurred in women.[85] Stigmata are visible suffering and a sign of grace: "the substance of this grace consists of pity for Christ, participation in His sufferings, sorrows, and for the same end—the expiation of sins unceasingly committed in the world."[86] The wounds have legitimacy because of human suffering: "If the sufferings were absent, the wounds would be but an empty symbol, theatrical representation, conducing to pride."[87] The wounds themselves are intensely painful. They do not heal, yet they do not give off a "fetid odor,"[88] and some give off fragrance. The life of a stigmatist, therefore, is usually one of physical and psychic pain. Many have been sainted, though the Catholic Church has made no infallible declaration about this phenomenon.[89] Some stigmatists have incredible powers, like Padre Pio of Pietrelcina, who was able to bilocate and heal.

The scientific explanation for stigmata is that it is generated by autosuggestion, by nervousness, or by cataleptic hysteria.[90] Lizzie manifests stigmata, as Father Tom Jay identifies it, in her wrists and ankles, from shackles put on her ancestor Ayo, and back, from a whipping Ayo suffered. Stigmata, in the novel, are a sign of ongoing suffering and mourning and simultaneously a sign of grace.

Lizzie's marks are a sign of Grace, her grandmother. At age 34, Lizzie leaves, after 14 years of hospitalization, the last of a series of mental hospitals, and comes home. Her melancholia[91] begins when she is 20 and inherits Grace's trunk. It contains a quilt that Grace made to record Ayo's, her grandmother's, story, and a diary, written by Ayo's daughter Joy to record Ayo's story. The quilt and diary are "keys"[92] that open the door to the past. Lizzie begins to manifest the stigmata and to remember—even to step into—the lives of Grace and Ayo.

Lizzie's cousin Ruth, her great-aunt Eva and a mental patient, Mrs. Corday, are the three people who believe her. Ruth is puzzled. "How," she asks, "is it that you can step into the life of a woman who died before you were born?"[93] Mrs. Corday can see all the women Lizzie is and wants to know how to do it: "I wish I knew how you do that...Change like that...One day you're a woman, today you're a girl. And a dark little thing at that."[94]

Aunt Eva knows that Grace has something left undone that Lizzie must accomplish. Grace wants to reconcile with her husband, George, whom she left when she became terrified by her own manifestation of Ayo who is "all pain."[95] Ayo's curiosity established the pattern of traveling in the women. Ayo's leaving her mother in the market of her African village makes her vulnerable to capture, and she enters "the land of ghosts."[96] Grace leaves George, and Lizzie will leave Anthony Paul. Grace and Ayo seem to become ghosts themselves, haunting Lizzie. Lizzie must crawl back into this ghost land, experience the pain—Ayo's attempt to kill herself on the slave ship, the whippings she endures, and her psychic pain, all passed to Grace—and then come out.

Lizzie accomplishes the reconciliation between Grace and George in her love for Anthony Paul. Anthony knows and remembers her from their past lives but finds it difficult to believe what is happening. More important, Grace must let her daughter—Lizzie's mother, Sarah—know why she left. Lizzie becomes Grace, and the reconciliation is accomplished when Lizzie makes her own quilt, or when Grace makes another quilt. The project draws in Lizzie's middle-class parents, particularly Sarah, who begins to help. Sarah's reconciliation with Grace through Lizzie and her acceptance that Lizzie is also Grace heals both women. Sarah asks Grace why she left. When Grace explains, Sarah says, "I used to beg God to send you back to me." Grace answers, "I came as soon as I could."[97]

Lizzie is the nexus of multiple planes of time and space and is multiple people: she is Lizzie, Ayo, and Grace. In the reconciliation with Grace is the eternal return; time closes and reopens. Lizzie thinks, "I am the circle," and she is.[98] The past is materially represented by an insubstantial two-inch scrap of indigo cloth from a garment that Ayo's mother dyed.[99] It is the physical link to the past, and Lizzie tells Sarah, "That's what this quilt is about. The past. And putting the past aside when we're through."[100]

The choice of "aside" rather than "away" is important. Peter Homans writes, "The creation of meaning is a process which breaks radically with the past and yet also reappropriates that very past."[101] To make meaning out of what has been denied and, potentially, forgotten, Lizzie must make another quilt and use it as the vehicle where mourning can take place. Quilting, Sarah and her daughter immerse themselves in the past (the loss itself), move on into the present (the construction of the monument), and from there to release into the future."[102] The quilt opens the mourning process and stimulates the

> uncanny feeling, which can at times intensify to the point of irrefutable conviction, that we are, in some mysterious and disturbingly inexplicable way, "a part of all that," and further, that apart from "all that" we might not be at all...[S]uch experiences also suggest that in some way or other our essence is constituted as much by "all that out there" as it is by "all this in here"; it is only that we did not understand this very well, before we had this experience.[103]

Perry brings together the stigmatist and the quilt to remind us, I think, of Alice Walker's notion of female ancestors as saints, not mad women. Walker writes in "In Search of Our Mothers' Gardens":

> When Jean Toomer walked through the South in the early twenties, he discovered a curious thing: black women whose spirituality was so intense, so deep, so *unconscious*, that they were themselves unaware of the richness they held. They stumbled blindly through their lives: creatures so abused and mutilated in body, so dimmed and confused by pain, that they considered themselves

unworthy even of hope. In the selfless abstractions their bodies became to the men who used them, they became more than "sexual objects," more even than mere women: they became "Saints." Instead of being perceived as whole persons, their bodies became shrines: what were thought to be their minds became temples suitable for worship. These crazy Saints stared out at the world, wildly, like lunatics—or quietly, like suicides; and the "God" that was in their gaze was as mute as a great stone.

Who were these Saints? These crazy, loony, pitiful women? Some of them, without a doubt, were our mothers and grandmothers.[104]

Black women, Walker argues, in their everyday arts, kept alive black women's history and *"the notion of song."*[105] The price of keeping the bloodlines connected was high, as it is for Lizzie, and "cruel enough to stop the blood."[106] Yet, the women persisted in these discredited ordinary rites. In *Stigmata*, when Ayo dies, Joy records, "I could not make myself *rite*" (emphasis mine).[107] Art as rite and the diary and novel written make right: talk back to history and challenge Enlightenment reason as the only way to know and be, using writing and reason, the master's tools.

Perry suggests that the blood *is* stopped, in a sense: history seems to be a burden, and modern science defines Lizzie's experience as pathological. Ayo and Grace, without being understood, cannot fully join the ancestors. Joy (for me, the unsung heroine of the novel), who records Ayo's story and Lizzie, who quilts, journals, and paints, helps the women in their family become ancestors. Their rite-ing/writing facilitates the "march with the saints."[108] Ayo chooses to remember; this sets her apart;[109] Joy and Lizzie "rite" this memory so that it can become a source of healing and joy, the name of the linking child, the promise that is not just pain.

For the promise to be fulfilled, stigma must become stigmata. Once Father Tom Jay gives Lizzie a name for her melancholia, she can accept it and use it to heal. Lizzie tells Father Tom that she is "an old soul in a young body, and I don't know what to do about it and nobody else does either."[110] When Lizzie shows Father Tom her scars, he tells her that there was a monk (I think he means Padre Pio) who had the marks of Christ and that what she has is stigmata. He gives her a name and a meaning.

This person, this ancestor, is with you in some way, just as Christ was with the monk. The merging of spirits and all that. I don't know if that is reincarnation or something else. In any case, no one considered the monk insane. He was practically considered a saint, a healer.[111]

Father Tom likens the mental hospital to a monastery, giving Lizzie separation and permission to engage in quiet contemplation.[112] Armed with this redefinition, Lizzie takes art classes, begins to journal, and sketches past-life experiences.[113] She grows in faith: "'True faith is belief in the midst of unrelenting pressure,' Father Tom wrote to me. 'You are clearing a path to your place among the saints.'"[114]

Lizzie does not quite believe this, but armed with a name other than "crazy," Lizzie understands that she is not just wounded, she is "marked."[115] While Father Tom says he is honored to meet Lizzie, Lizzie's psychiatrist is not impressed. She, nevertheless, helps Lizzie associate prayer with memory. Lizzie says, "I wasn't praying when it happened...I was remembering. Remembering something unbelievably traumatic."[116]

This remembering may explain why Perry places a Catholic presence—often maligned like the Africanist one—in her novel. Lizzie goes to Catholic school and participates in Catholic festivals. Catholic rites and practices, from the Eucharist, to the Stations of the Cross, to the rosary engage the whole self in an act of memory. Remembering is a physical as well as psychical quality of the Catholic imagination that urges adherents toward identification with Christ. It puts the Catholic *there*—as does ultimately, all religious ritual—to generate compassion, the quality Gilroy suggests we need for a planetary humanism. The person does not just cross the boundaries of time and space but becomes a transitional point, as Lizzie does in the novel. Homans writes that, "The response to loss opens up the transitional space...and in this space, persons construct a bridge of symbols...."[117] The artistic construction of symbols is a of the truth of the human relationship with God and is a form of practical wisdom in Catholic thought.[118] There is no stigma, to pun, on such activity.

Catholicism retains, along with indigenous religions, ancestors. We call them saints but they are ancestors: people who have lived on earth, who are part of our extended family, and who intercede for us with God. Perhaps Perry wants to suggest that Lizzie is a catholic, a universally human experience. Lizzie is becoming ancestor, interceding for Ayo and Grace—and ultimately, Joy. Joy cannot "rite" anymore after Ayo dies,[119] though she believes that she should "see [Ayo's] story to the end."[120] Lizzie does this for her. At the end of the novel, Lizzie is in the hospital, painting Ayo's past that Grace is remembering in her: "I take up another brush to paint a gray ship and a brown girl standing at the rail."[121]

That the novel ends in the beginning signals the ritual significance of human creativity and the presence of the ancestor who, as Anthony Ephirim-Donkor suggests, is the sign of a cyclically constructed cosmos but with a thrust toward the future.[122] The ancestor is, Ephirim-Donkor argues, the maturation of the human being, and Lizzie, with a name for her condition, is maturing, getting free.

What Lizzie DuBose brings to her family—and to the reader—is the ability to mourn. We crawl back through history with Lizzie, experience her depression and her finding a way to heal. Depression and melancholia develop when there is nothing to do with the anger or fear that oppression creates but turn it inward, striking at the self, or outward, at the other who is the rejected image of the self. Lizzie's stigmata signals the pain suffered by her ancestors. When she takes it on, she becomes, as Karla F. C. Holloway would put it, a translucent and diffusive presence who "moors" the "nature of spiritual and psychic fracture," revealing its multiple layers.[123] This anchoring opens up a space in which one can mourn, healing anger and pain—but not without scars.

The consciousness of the slave, Gilroy writes in *The Black Atlantic*, is an extended act of mourning. The slave, Ayo, is marked—stigmatized. One definition of stigma is "a brand impressed with a red-hot iron on slaves... a brand of disgrace." It is a sign of shame and separation. Stigmata, in contrast, is a form of marking, but it is, as we have seen in Lizzie, a sign of grace and of hope. This may seem awful—though I remember one student, when a class of mine read "Agnes of God," almost weeping at the beauty of Agnes Dei, the Lamb of God's stigmata. But the wound, the stigmata, is the sign of presence that, acknowledged, is the beginning of the ability to mourn, the foundational capacity necessary for a planetary compassion, to borrow Gilroy's term. That kind of compassion might facilitate the formation of a new, beloved, cosmopolis. Stigmata, working us through depression to expression, suggests, as Deborah McDowell put it so beautifully in her work on *Sula*, that "the process of mourning and remembering... leads to intimacy with the self, which is all that makes intimacy with others possible."[124]

CONCLUSION

Memory, rightly confronted and integrated into one's personal and communal story, can lead to a deep understanding and transformation of both culture and self. For African American women living with depression, intimacy with the self, gained through talk therapy, is one way that they may find an opening to understand personal identity and, perhaps, more important, relief from pain. Father Tom, in *Stigmata*, is that compassionate listener who helps Lizzie see that her pain is part of her power. Indeed, depression is often connected to creativity. Nell Casey's edited work, *Unholy Ghost*, shows us the link between depression and the work of the artist in the lives of many powerful writers.

Casey also shows us how depression cripples. And, for many African American women, those silent saints, the crippling side of depression is what they most experience, even as they go about their daily tasks, seemingly fine. Though one may be predisposed to depression, by family history, for example, it is not a disease that has to be endured. Stigmata, in one sense, means stigma, and many depressed African American women fear be stigmatized, fear the sense that they are not in control. Depression, however, is disease, like high blood pressure. It is not the person's fault, and though the condition may be ongoing, it is also treatable, with therapy, both person-to person and group, and, when necessary, with pharmacological drugs.

The drugs that are now prescribed to treat depression are more effective and generate fewer side effects than the ones that Meri Nana-Ama Danquah took, even a few years ago. No one should have to suffer the crippling effects of even minor depression. There is help. Only in taking care of ourselves and helping each other can we live full lives in the Spirit, whose fruits are love and wholeness and who, as Mary Townes urges us in "Looking to Your Tomorrows Today" in *Embracing the Spirit*, moves us to "stand tall, to smile tall, to live tall, and to think tall."[125]

NOTES

1. Danquah Meri Nana-Ama, *Willow Weep for Me: A Black Woman's Journey through Depression* (New York: Ballentine/One World, 1999), p. 82.

2. Alice Walker, *In Search of Our Mothers' Gardens: Womanist Prose* (New York: Harcourt, Brace and Company, 1984), pp. 231–32.

3. Alice Walker, "Everyday Use," in *In Love and Trouble: Stories of Black Women* (New York: Harcourt Brace and Company, 1967), pp. 47–59.

4. Toni Morrison, *Beloved* (New York: Plume/New American Library, 1987).

5. Phyllis Alesia Perry, *Stigmata* (New York: Hyperion, 1988), p. 203.

6. "Fighting 'the Blues' in African Americans." http://www.healthyplace.com/Communities/depression/minorities_9.asp (accessed January 7, 2007).

7. Barbara Jones Warren, "Examining Depression among African American Woman Using Womanist and Psychiatric Mental Health Nursing Perspectives," Womanist Theory and Research Web site, http://www.uga.edu/~womanist/warren1.2.thm (accessed January 1, 2007).

8. Ibid.

9. "Fighting 'the Blues,'" p. 1.

10. Anne Anglin Cheng, *The Melancholy of Race: Psychoanalysis, Assimilation, and Hidden Grief* (New York: Oxford University Press, 2001), p. 20; Paul Gilroy, *Postcolonial Melancholia* (New York: Columbia University Press, 2005), p. 91.

11. "Depressed Mood," http://www.allaboutdepression.com/dia_12html (accessed January 24, 2007), p. 1.

12. Ibid., p. 1.

13. Ibid., p. 1.

14. Danquah, *Willow Weep for Me*, p. 31.

15. Warren, "Examining Depression," p. 3.

16. "Depressed Mood," p. 2.

17. Ibid., p. 2.

18. Ibid., p. 3.

19. Ibid., p. 4.

20. Ibid., p. 4.

21. Ibid., p. 5.

22. Ibid., p. 6.

23. Warren, "Examining Depression," p. 1.

24. Danquah, *Willow Weep for Me*, p. 147.

25. Ibid., pp. 210–213.

26. Ibid., p. 257.

27. Ibid., p. 184.

28. Warren, "Examining Depression," p. 2.

29. Ibid., 3.

30. Danquah, *Willow Weep for Me*, pp. 19–20.

31. Ibid., p. 20.

32. Mari Nana-Ama Danquah, "Writing the Wrongs of Identity," in *Unholy Ghost: Writers on Depression*, ed. Nell Casey (New York: Harper Perennial, 2002), p. 175.

33. Danquah, *Willow Weep for Me*, p. 21.

34. "Religious Faith Has Big Impact on Reducing Depression among African Americans," University of Chicago Research Shows, http://www.news.chicaog.edu/releases/05/050413.data.shtml (accessed January 1, 2007), p. 1.

35. Ibid., p. 1.

36. Danquah, "Writing the Wrongs," p. 178.

37. Ibid., p. 179.

38. Ibid., p. 175.

39. Gilroy, *Postcolonial Melancholia*, p. 2.

40. Ibid., p. 14.

41. Ibid., p. 144.

42. Ibid., p. 12.

43. Ibid., pp. 23–24.

44. Ibid., p. 13.

45. Ibid., p. 91.

46. Ibid., p. 92.

47. Ibid., p. 133.

48. Ibid., pp. 114, 140.

49. Ibid., p. 141.

50. Ibid., p. 143.

51. Ibid., p. 22.

52. Ibid., p. xv.

53. Ibid., p. 8.

54. Ibid., p. 11.

55. Cheng, *The Melancholy of Race*, p. 24.

56. Ibid., p. 80.

57. Toni Morrison, *Playing in the Dark: Whiteness and the Literary Imagination* (Cambridge: Harvard University Press, 1992), p. xi.

58. Ibid., p. 8.

59. Ibid., p. 48.

60. Ibid., p. 38.

61. Gilroy, *Postcolonial Melancholia*, p. 144.

62. Morrison, *Playing in the Dark*, p. 45.

63. Cheng, *The Melancholy of Race*, p. 7. Sigmund Freud, "Mourning and Melancholia," in *Sigmund Freud: 11. On Metapsychology*, ed. Angela Richards, trans. James Strachey (New York: Penguin Books, 1984), p. 254.

64. Cheng, *The Melancholy of Race*, p. 8. Freud, "Mourning and Melancholia," p. 256.

65. Cheng, *The Melancholy of Race*, p. 9.

66. Ibid., p. 11.

67. Ibid., p. 10.

68. Ibid., p. 12.

69. Ibid., p. 16.

70. Ibid., pp. 21, 17.

71. Ibid., p. 72.

72. Ibid., p. 17.

73. Ibid., p. 17.

74. Ibid., p. 23.

75. Ibid., p. 21.

76. Ibid., p. 22.

77. Gilroy, *Postcolonial Melancholia*, p. 130.

78. Ibid., p. 132.

79. "Gangster Lyrics," http://it.uwp.edu/gangsters/ice-t.cop.killer.html.

80. Gilroy, *Postcolonial Melancholia*, p. 142.

81. Charles H. Long, *Significations: Signs, Symbols, and Images in the Interpretation of Religion* (Philadelphia: Fortress Press, 1986), p. 9.

82. Paul Gilroy, *The Black Atlantic: Modernity and Double Consciousness* (Cambridge: Harvard University Press, 1993).

83. Gilroy, *Postcolonial Melancholia*, p. 145.

84. Ibid., p. 142.

85. "Stigmata/Stigmatist," http://www.catholicforum.com/Saints/define10.htm (accessed January 25, 2007), p. 1.

86. "Mystical Stigmata," http://www.newadvent.org/cathen/14294b.htm (accessed January 25, 2007), p. 1.

87. Ibid., p. 1.

88. Ibid., p. 3.

89. "Stigmata/Stigmatist," p. 1.

90. "Stigmata," http://www.answere.com/topic/stigmata (accessed January 25, 2007), p. 1.

91. Perry, *Stigmata*, p. 142. Like Freud, Perry uses melancholia for depression.

92. Ibid., p. 118.

93. Ibid., p. 84.

94. Ibid., p. 175.

95. Ibid., p. 144.

96. Ibid., p. 98.

97. Ibid., p. 230.

98. Ibid., p. 94.

99. Ibid., p. 229.

100. Ibid., p. 228.

101. Peter Homans, *The Ability to Mourn: Disillusionment and the Social Origins of Psychoanalysis* (Chicago: University of Chicago Press, 1989), p. 269.

102. Ibid., p. 271.

103. Ibid., p. 272.

104. Walker, pp. 231–32.

105. Ibid., p. 237.

106. Ibid., p. 223.

107. Perry, *Stigmata*, p. 230.

108. Ibid., p. 218.

109. Ibid., p. 17.

110. Ibid., p. 211.

111. Ibid., p. 212.

112. Ibid., p. 233.

113. Ibid., p. 232.

114. Ibid., p. 232.

115. Ibid., p. 213.

116. Ibid., p. 214.

117. Homans, *The Ability to Mourn*, p. 333.

118. *Catechism of the Catholic Church*, 2nd ed. (Washington, D.C: United States Catholic Conference, Inc., 1997).

119. Perry, *Stigmata*, pp. 230–31.

120. Ibid., p. 230.

121. Ibid., p. 235.

122. Anthony Ephirim-Donkor, *On Becoming Ancestors* (Trenton, N.J.: African World Press, 1997), pp. 5, 11.

123. Karla F. C. Holloway, *Moorings and Metaphors: Figures of Culture and Gender in Black Women's Literature* (New York: Rutgers University Press, 1992), 116–117.

124. Deborah E. McDowell, "The 'Self and the Other'": Reading Toni Morrison's *Sula* and the Black Female Text," in *Critical Essays on Toni Morrison*, ed. Nellie Y. McKay (Boston: Hall, 1998), p. 85.

125. Mary M. Townes, "Looking To Your Tomorrows Today," in *Embracing the Spirit: Womanist Perspectives on Hope, Salvation and Transformation*, ed. Emilie M. Townes (New York: Maryknoll, 1997), p. 5.

CHAPTER 6

—— ❖ ——

Just Awailing and Aweeping: Grief, Lament, and Hope as We Face the End of Life

Emilie M. Townes

I am often struck, as a sometime-archetypical grumpy and never quite satisfied ethicist, with the drive we have as meaning makers and moral agents to make sense out of chaos and disaster and uncertainty. Our need for order sometimes drives us to acts of justice, or ill-conceived passions, or ethical hubris, or moral strength and resilience, or great care and compassion. Sometimes we commit brave acts even when we do not have a burning bush to guide our way. In short, we humans are a rather creative lot. We never quite know what we will do next at times because just when we think we have ourselves figured out, we commit the unfathomable.

I begin with these observations because to write about the power of grief, lament, and hope as we face the end of life, be it our own or that of others, is not easy for me. It means that I must call to the front of my head and heart my own experiences of grief and lament and confess that I do not have this all figured out. However, I offer my observations about what I have learned and am learning about bone-deep sorrow and the hard decisions I have made in burying both my parents. It means that I consciously reenter the grieving process in ways that are far from intellectual but are as present for me as my breathing in and out and the pounding of my still-broken heart.

I am moving from grief to lament and lament to grief, and then they are all mixed up at times. This is not a linear process, not exactly a loop, not wholly a curlicue, not accurately described as a whirlwind. It is what it is, and perhaps the best description is that it's a part of living and being. Hence, this chapter is not solely an intellectual exercise. It is painful and I am continuing to try to make meaning out of that hurt so that I do not remain wedged at 7:00 A.M. on July 11, 1990, or 10:30 P.M. on January 14, 2003. To do so, I begin with a light tracing of the outlines of three biblical chroniclers of disaster, lament, and hope to guide the way.

THREE GUIDES FROM THE HEBREW BIBLE

Perhaps it is disaster that shapes us—that cosmic crumbling that is relentless in its precision in interrupting, disrupting, and changing our lives. Jeremiah is the book of oracles, the chronicler of lament, the one who names the spiritual struggle with God with meticulous wording—reward, punishment, payment for good and evil and faithfulness and disobedience. The book of Jeremiah is a call to meaning-filled and faith-filled living, a call to a more enduring relationship with God.

In Jeremiah, we read and can picture the disaster. The people are wounded survivors, and Jeremiah is not afraid to use the rhetoric of blame as he tells the people that they are responsible for the disaster crashing down on their heads. This is not God's doing, but yours—deal with it. Jeremiah forces us to deal with disturbing questions: What does it mean that we are to take on the blame for disasters? Is this not a divine form of blaming the victim? Moreover, if we do take this on, does it challenge us to rethink our larger worldviews because after all, the fault resides in us...doesn't it?

However, in Jeremiah we also see the wounded survivor, the one of unswerving loyalty to God, the one who resists monarchical and religious powers, and the one who survives with the help of the community and others. Jeremiah establishes a vision of a future community on new ethical footing, and disaster does not consume it. In this new community, we die for our sins, not for those who have gone before us. This is a community of absolute devotion as we take responsibility for our actions and the consequences of them. In effect, the book of Jeremiah performs the collapse of the world. It forces us to live *with* Judah and Jerusalem and face soul-deep questions. The words of this prophet tell us that we must make sense of our disasters as we survive them.

The prophet Ezekiel forces us to consider what it means that we cannot mourn and explores what forces of nature or the divine are at work that prevent us from forming our grief into groans of anguish, loss, and chaos. Ezekiel invites us to explore if the way to re-forming ourselves is by placing ourselves into a cataclysm of the primal where reason and rationality hold no sway. In this place, we are not allowed to structure or to order our loss. Instead, we must twist and turn into the collapse of our worlds. We are left with the horror of questions formed out of the absolute confusion we have when we are observers at the accident scene, when we realize that the wail of sirens in the background are from the horns of the rescue squad coming from us.

We are the wailers, the questioners in modern and postmodern smugness at times that is now worn thin by the demands of living our survival. Rather than escape into neat discourses or familiar rituals, we must make meaning out of the worlds destroyed, the health that has vanished like a thief in the night or slowly and sometimes painfully leaked away, or the loss raged and fought against with all that we have within us and beyond.

Micah, the advocate of pure worship and social justice, proclaims judgment, divine forgiveness, and hope. With him, we can ponder notions of the good and the ways in which the goodness can be a supreme end. Further, we explore the ways in which the good can be juxtaposed to justice and how it is inseparable from the inner person.

Micah also reminds us that we should never forget the power of stories. They can help establish identity and location, locate us in time (past, present, and future), and clarify the ways in which we are accountable for our thoughts, wishes, desires, and actions. In Micah's hands, the power of stories and the concept of the good join forces such that the good is something that the people should already know. The book's marvelous formula captures this: do justice, love mercy, and be humble. These concrete acts, these practices, are the stuff of moral formation for Micah and not liturgies that are actually self-condemning or worse—displeasing to God.

GRIEF AND LAMENT

Biblical prophets such as Ezekiel, Jeremiah, and Micah remind us that the issues we often face at the end of care are not exceptional; they are a part of living until we die. As harsh as this may sound to some, and as hard as it is for me to accept at times, death is natural—it is a part of our rising and dying in Christ for those of us who are Christians. Perhaps, then, the question is the way in which we die and how humane and compassionate care should be a part of it for however long or short the time is when we do it.

This question involves exploring the ethics of the end of care. In order to do so, I begin with grief, that great sadness, the realm of deep and profound sorrow. In Brazilian Portuguese, they use the word *saudade* to convey this. *Saudade* communicates emotion rather than reason, and when you say it, all those who hear it know that something bone deep is at work with you and you are being invited to share the loss, the sorry, the regret, and the sadness of the speaker.

Grief is the emotion of loss or impending loss, the place where we often cannot name what is happening. In the face of the loss of life, we must find ways to shake ourselves from our nocturnes of mediocrity, our jazz riffs of reason and rationality, our strident chords searching for control and order. What we must turn to is our faith—its depths *and* its shallows. Ezekiel, Jeremiah, and Micah give us powerful nudges in this direction.

Grief takes certainty and turns us on our heads. We cannot always rely on the formulas of living that serve us so well. We tumble, stumble, fall, or place ourselves in the hands of a presence greater than us and somehow enact our faith—perhaps against our will—to see us through and help us find the way again. In doing so, we become fuller, richer people because our grief gives us a chance to grow in our faith. We now know that we can wail and rage and even walk away from God; we know God carries all the pain, the questions, and yes, even the celebration until we can bear our loss with God. Our grief gives us the chance to grow our faith into our living a bit more deeply and perhaps more wisely.

To move into our faith through grief is to find the lament within us. In the Hebrew Bible (Old Testament), laments mark the *beginning* of the healing process, and people need and want to be healed. If we learn anything from prophets like Ezekiel, it is to know that the healing of brokenness and injustice, of social sin and degradation, of fractured relationships, of spiritual doubts and fears, and of the body begins with an unrestrained lament—one that starts from our toenails and is a shout by the time it gets to the ends of the strands of our hair. This is a lament of faith to the God of faith that we need help, that we can't do this alone. We ache, with every fiber of our being, with grief and sorrow. We cannot fight off the hordes of anguish with a big stick, and we need *divine* help.

Biblical scholar Claus Westermann maintains that no worship observance in ancient Israel is better known to us today than the rite of lament.[1] The cry of distress gives lament its power. As Ezekiel, Jeremiah, and Micah present situations of crisis and distress, lament comes forth in potent language that is unequivocal in its anguish. However, this rending of the heart belongs to the events of deliverance.[2]

Walter Brueggemann tells us that lament is formful.[3] By putting our suffering into the form of lament, we first have to acknowledge that we are going through some mess. Lament helps us put words to our suffering, and when we can name it, we begin to see the contours of allowing our faith to help us *into* the loss—whatever its extent—to help us bear it.

Brueggemann notes that laments are genuine pastoral activities.[4] In an essay in which he reflects on our contemporary moves away from genuine lament, Brueggemann suggests that this loss of lament is also a loss of genuine covenant interaction with God.[5] For him, the petitioner either becomes voiceless or has a voice permitted to speak only praise. When lament is absent, covenant is created *only* as celebration of joy and well-being. Without lament, covenant is a practice of denial and pretense that sanctions social control.[6]

Lament enables us and even requires us to acknowledge and to experience our suffering or the suffering of others—to walk or crawl or roll into grieving. Lament helps us move to responsible faith—one of praise and thanksgiving *and* grief and mourning. Further, lament in our contemporary world helps us ask questions of justice and good health care as we remain in the stream of our religious traditions as Christians. When Israel used lament as a rite and in worship on a regular basis, it kept the question of justice visible and legitimate.[7]

I want to extend these ideas to informed compassionate care as we face the end of life—not only as individuals, but in a network of caring that involves family, friends, religious communities, medical staff, the community, and on and on. The formfulness of communal lament has a deep moral character. We are drawn to explore anew what lament can mean for us as a part of care at the end of life. As important is it is for us to walk into our own grief to begin lamentation, I want to stress the importance of communal lament as we do this. We cannot do this alone, and it is vitally important, I believe, that we also arc into a corporate experience of calling for healing in all its various forms. When we grieve and when we lament, we acknowledge and live the experience rather than try to hold it away from us out of some misguided notion of being objective, strong, or rational. We hurt; something is wrong in and with our bodies and spirits, with someone we love, with someone we care for, or with someone we are treating or with whom we are in ministry. We must name suffering as grieving and acknowledge the very human need to lament.

To acknowledge such is to dare the unthinkable in our postmodern culture—to feel life deeply and join others in the depths of their emotions, which is not a narcissistic cavalcade of sentiments that masquerade as the therapeutic but rather arrives out of a deep sense of community and accountability to and with each other. It models the best of what care can be for all of us. The prophetic in this is that we dare to call others and ourselves into the lament.

HOPE

To live with and through grieving to get to lament, we need something to hold onto that is more than the so-called facts of health. This something lets us know that although we may not be able to see the light at the end of the tunnel, it is possible to take the weight from around our hearts and minds.

For me, that something is hope.

when i was a little girl
   i spent a good deal of time trying to conjure up heaven
i thought that if i could just imagine those angels, those harps, those clouds
   then i wouldn't be so scared of this big angry white-haired, white-bearded,
      white furrow-browed God the minister preachified about on those sunday
      mornings in southern pines, north carolina
i thought if i could see those fluffy clouds
   sit on those soft-with-goose-down couches
   move around with grace and style as my walk was a *glide* all over heaven
   always being good, never having to worry about being bad
   smell the tasty (cause i just knew anything that had to do with heaven
      had to be tasty) food
      the fried chicken
      the hot-with-butter rolls
      the spoon bread
    the gravy made from chicken grease
      the fresh greens

> the fresh string beans
> the big-grained rice
> the macaroni and cheese
> the mashed potatoes
> the candied yams, coming right from the ground
> the rib roast
> the salmon croquettes
> the salads—lettuce and tomato
> the cakes—pound, coconut, chocolate
> the pies—apple, sweet potato, chess, pecan
> the kool-aid
> the lemonade
> the sweetened tea ('cause there was no such thing as *un*sweetened tea when
>   i was growing up)
> and butter, butter, butter, butter
>   i realize now that i was associating heaven with the way my grandmama's
>   house smelled on saturday night and sunday
> i thought if i could hear the good music—'cause even my playmates and i knew
>   that all angels knew the beat, could carry a tune and played a mean harp
>   then i wouldn't worry so much
>   when the men in white sheets marched through the black section of town
>   where my grandmother and all the other loving people i knew lived
> i thought if i could just conjure up heaven in my mind
>   and in my heart
>   and in my prayers
>   then maybe
>   just maybe...[8]

That maybe, just maybe, is hope. Allowing hope to shape our grief and lament is a bold thing to do because it can, and perhaps must, conjure up the ghosts, the terrors in our lives that come as dancing specters, haunting goblins, or moaning trolls who remind us again and again that we are far too human to try to do this life all by ourselves. Lament is a good thing because lament is often the sign that we are seeking, yearning, and chasing hope.

This hope is not only in God but also in the fact that God loves us, rocks us, cares for us, heals us—but perhaps not in the ways we expect or want. More importantly, it is a hope that God does not leave us even when we feel abandoned and alone. It is here, particularly here—just as we have reached so deeply into lament because it is the only thing that quenches our thirst—that God comes to us.

But alas, lament does not let things come so easily most times because to lament means we have opened our eyes, hearts, minds, souls, and very spirits and now see and feel and touch and smell the joy and the agony living in the fractures of creation. This is often easier said than done. Moreover, there is irony in lament. In our yearning for hope, we often walk far away from it as we try to come home to it. We often live into the small and narrow spaces of life that stunt our growth and demand far too little of us because far too little is expected of us or far too little is deemed comfortable.

This makes it imperative that we see that lament is not a force outside of ourselves or a sign of our natural depravity or hopeless sinfulness. Engaging lament means that we have the wisdom, intuition, courage, or faith to open ourselves in the full force of the emotions that are aswirl in our loss. Rather than being exceptional, lament becomes one more piece to the fabric of our universe, one more way to signal this restless journey we are on, one more sign that Emmaus is not the end of the journey but its beginning.

In short, lament is not the end product on the assembly line of our lives; it is a part of the journey. It is part of the way in which we come to know God's way in our lives with a richness that ripens and deepens. This richness often disquiets us when we learn that there is nothing more that can be done by intelligence and skill to extend our lives or change our health. This richness often disrupts our ability to control because we are now staring into the cold, hard eye of the uncontrollable; the cold, hard eye of death. This richness lets us know that that we are *not* alone as children of God and an enormous part of our task as members of faith communities is to make sure that no one is alone because we must be there as witnesses and disciples, perfect and deeply imperfect, physically present or there in spirit, but willing to *be* there fully as the passage of this side of the Jordan crosses to the next takes place in our dying.

SAYING GOODBYE

My sister and two aunts (my mother's sisters) were able to hold and touch my mother as she died in that bed in cardiac intensive care at Durham Country Hospital in North Carolina. The respirator gave her breath, so we could only watch the monitors and talk with her, stroke her, tell her how much her going would cause us grief, and finally say goodbye to her and let her go. We watched as each monitor indicating a vital sign went flat and the only sound in the room was the working of the respirator. We could not leave her that night with the image of that machine pumping false life into her. We returned after the nurse—as he said—had "cleaned her up" to say goodbye and to see for ourselves that there was no breathing in and out—that sign of life we knew and trusted.

God held my sister, my two aunts, and me that night—and my mother. As minister of our family, I did what ministers do. I began the tasks: following her wishes to have her body cremated, planned her memorial service, canceled my speaking engagements, and found others to do the work to which I had committed. I consulted with my family about various things—legal and otherwise, and cared for my family and checked in with my sister. It was not until we were recessing to the back of the auditorium at North Carolina Central University, my mother's beloved school where we held the memorial service, that I began a death wail. I had done it when my mother called me in 1990 to tell me of my father's passing, and now I marked hers.

It came with little warning and was completely unplanned. The funeral home directors closed the auditorium doors to keep folks out of the vestibule where I stood in such deep and profound lament—weeping and wailing—that I can only remember colors and that my sister and aunts surrounded me and held me as I mourned the loss of not only my mother but a woman to whom I looked as mentor and friend. It hurt then, and it hurts now.

Yes, it was my lament, but the community of the faithful (in this case my family) held me and did not tell me to stop, that it would be okay, that this was not dignified, or that I would be all right. They let the grieving find its form in lamentation. In large ways and small, the task is to create spaces of grace and grief so that people can find their way into lament and begin to heal. Lament, then, is a natural mark of our humanity. It is not a sign of moral failing. Rather it gives us the chance to learn a master class lesson: when we accept the fullness of our humanity in those moments of grief and then realize that we cannot bear the sorrow alone, we are caught in the web of creation. This is a is a magnificent web woven with the tensile threads of creation unfolding into creation as we breathe in and out as a testament to God's grace alive in our living—the being and the doing and yes, even in our lament.

What brilliant places we can go if see lament as a mark of grace as it welcomes us into a soul-deep relationship with ourselves and a God who never lets us go and never lets us down morning by morning and day by day. The reality is that the complexity of balancing mercy and justice, forgiveness and accountability, freedom and responsibility, can make our collective heads spin. Any religion that suppresses lament and any church that feels the grieving mind and heart is a threat to God is most likely a pitiful wasteland that consecrates blindness as faithfulness, timidity as love, and arrogance as hope.

We do not follow Jesus's model when we try to quash lament. He was untroubled by it and he gives us a most profound model for lament from the cross: "My God, my God, why have you forsaken me? (Matt. 27:46). Lament can be a gateway *into* hope, and hope, in this case, is another way to say faith. This is a faith forged on the hard work of living it rather than having it handed to us in doctrine or dogmatics. Lament, earnest and soul-deep searching, can hold us in our loss and into the days beyond it where we begin again and again to step out of the folds of old wounds and live anew.

STEPPING INTO LAMENT

I end by returning to Ezekiel (Eze. 37) and his dream of the valley of dry bones that recognizes the need for lament before healing. The vision of the valley of dry bones is more than a story about reconnecting some sun-bleached ivory. It is the revelation of the transforming power of God's spirit within our suffering.

True, those bones are castanets of grief, but because the focus of this chapter is on grief and lament, it is important to remember that God looked at the bones and asked Ezekiel: "Can these bones live?" What a marvelous invitation to lament! However, my hunch is that Ezekiel wanted to say no because he *knew* the list of sins that had made those bones dry. So he replied, "O God, you know." Theologically, this is known as buying some time. However, he does prophesy to the bones. In calling out to the bones, Ezekiel enacts lament.

Like Ezekiel, we have to stand in the *midst* of the valley with God and talk with and through our grief that can then become lament.

grief, oh grief, i feel your presence and you won't leave me alone
   i can't make it through the day without you reminding me that you're still
      there sometimes you come when i don't love myself enough to realize that
      God loves me sometimes you come when i close my heart and mind to the
      pain of the loss i am feeling grief, oh grief
   i can't let anyone too close
   because you might destroy them too
grief, i'm tired of living the folds of these old wounds
grief, i'm tired of living in a silence that is not golden
   it's got me wrapped up in indifference
   it's making me cantankerous
   i'm living in the backwaters of fear
   and i'm scared to come out of the house
grief, i'm tired of this silence
   that is like a mimed compassion
      that's killing and maiming my spirit
   and leaving me empty and hollow and mean as a snake
grief, i'm tired of living in this muzzled life you've got me in
   where i have no voice
      except for laissez-faire postmodern platitudes
      that just seem to hide out in the wastelands of my heart
grief, i'm tired of living my life on the altars of spectacular requiems
so i'm naming what i feel and what i know about this valley you've got me in
   i've driven off my friends
   i've made my life partner mad
   i've become the kind of person that folk talk about behind my back
      hell, i talk about myself behind my own back
and i've come to tell you
   i'm lamenting for my life and soul
   i'm reaching into the depths of my sorrow to find the light on the other side
   that is healing
   i'm learning to live with this loss and not be bound by it

     to stop in those moments when i remember and cry
       when i remember and laugh
       when i remember and feel blessed to have loved someone so much that
         their memory still calls forth deep emotions and strong conviction
i'm walking into my own death
  sometimes with fear
  sometimes in pain
  sometimes with courage
  being fully human and not necessarily strong
grief, i'm holding on the watch light of hope
i'm making my stand with God
  i'm gonna live a life that is filled by God's breath until i die
  i'm gonna have a witness that is woven by the sinews that comes from the
    almighty
  i'm gonna have a faith that is covered by the flesh the Holy Spirit gave me
can you hear these bones of mine rattling
  with the promise of salvation
come on winds of deliverance
  God's grace is getting good to me now
God's grace
  there in the laughter and through the tears
  there in the agony
  there in the ecstasy
  there in the morning
  there in the night
  there in the fear
  there in the boldness
  there in the earth, wind, rain *and* fire

Sometimes the unfathomable thing that we do is to fall into the hands of
God and open the utter depths of who we are in the hope that we will find a
place that breaks our free fall of grief. Lament gives us a way to craft a living
hope in this that not only understands but also *believes* that healing will come
in its own way and time.

NOTES

    1. Claus Westermann, *The Psalms: Structure, Content and Message*, trans. Ralph D.
Gehrke (Minneapolis: Augsburg Publishing House, 1980), p. 32.

    2. Westermann, "The Role of Lament," in Gehrke, *The Psalms*, p. 21.

    3. Walter Brueggemann, "The Formfulness of Grief," *Interpretation: A Journal of
Bible and Theology* XXXI, no. 3 (July 1977): p. 265. Although Brueggemann uses the
word grief in this essay, I believe that his remarks also closely parallel the process of
lament.

    4. Walter Brueggemann, "The Costly Loss of Lament," *Journal for the Study of the
Old Testament* no. 36 (1986): p. 59.

5. Ibid., p. 60.

6. Ibid., p. 60.

7. Ibid., p. 63.

8. Emilie M. Townes, *Breaking the Fine Rain of Death: African American Health Issues and a Womanist Ethic of Care* (New York: Continuum, 1998; repr., Eugene, OR: Wipf and Stock, 2006), pp. 168–69.

CHAPTER 7

———— ❖ ————

Honoring the Body: Rituals of Breath and Breathing

C. S'thembile West

The celebration of black bodies, particularly Black women's bodies, has been long overdue. A plethora of scholarship engages conversation from varying perspectives—gender, class, race, sex—about the devaluation of Black women's bodies vis-à-vis enslavement and Jim Crow. Attitudes concretized during enslavement in the United States were institutionalized across society. Debunking historical depictions, imagery, and assumptions about black bodies are important and necessary routes to squelch degrading, myth-based portrayals and ideas about African American women. Equally critical, however, is identifying, honoring, and concretizing how the body as text illuminates and reflects the sacred in African women's bodies, both philosophically and ontologically, especially in relationship to an African-derived worldview.

As such, the focus of this chapter is to identify critical connections between the body, breath, healing, and holistic health maintenance in the context of an African cosmology and epistemology. Engaging spirit, mind, and body is ontologically important in order to maximize life chances. In fact, it is in the merging of the sacred and secular that African-derived cultures have not only distinguished themselves within the human family but have also sustained the wherewithal to resist oppressive forces such as enslavement, discrimination, and dehumanization. In an African ontological and epistemological framework of being and knowing, one defines oneself and thereby asserts autonomy in oral as well as physical expression. It is in the context of ritual song-dance-chant[1] that one fashions sacred sensibilities into practical tools for living. Examples of such formations are found in Negro spirituals, hymns, and prayers that inspire hope, in dances that lift the spirit, and in stories that instill values. These examples stand as demonstrable legacies of an African aesthetic at work in contemporary U.S. culture. They will be used to showcase how marriages between sacred and secular comprise not only an African-derived way of being in the world but also an orientation to everyday life that facilitates and supports a measure of balance and health.

To frame this analysis, first, I will briefly discuss ancient Egyptian-Kemetic philosophy and its emphasis on the integration of body, mind, and spirit. Next, I will provide examples of how an African aesthetic contributes to and guides somatic expressiveness among people of African descent. The intent is to illuminate not only the holistic orientation of the body as text but to also open a window onto ways that much of the stylistic movement among Africans in the Diaspora functions in the service of everyday life.

Lastly, after brief discussion of the health conditions—hypertension, high blood pressure, and obesity—that are disproportionately represented among African American women, I will focus on consistent, conscious development of individual programs of relaxation and breathing exercises that African American women can engage to counteract stress and increase longevity. Honoring the body constitutes an integral component of the sacred act of loving the self, regardless.[2] In recognizing that the body is, indeed, sacred, then honoring it becomes part of a personal mandate and motivation to initiate and maintain a lifestyle that fosters wholeness, health, and healing.

KEMETIC ROOTS: BODY, MIND, AND SPIRIT

According to Maulana Karenga, an activist 1960s scholar who conceptualized Kwanzaa and its seven key principles, Nguza Saba, emphasized that "the heart of ancient Egyptian ethics and spiritual striving is maat."[3] *Maat* identifies truth, justice, beauty, and balance. Maat is the central guiding principle of an African worldview focused on holism: achieving the integration of physical, emotional, and social events and their outcomes to create healthy, viable, daily life conditions. Moving toward maat was perceived as an ethical and spiritual journey that centered on practical strategies to maximize personal and community life. As such, maintaining optimal health comprised a critical component of living.

Striving for physical balance was considered integral to the achievement of enlightenment. In fact, "[The] ideal type was the *geru*, the self-mastered, i.e. calm, silent, controlled, modest, wise, gentle and socially active."[4] In light of this model, emphases on breath and breathing, focal points of yoga, elements of dance, and relaxation techniques support an African-derived perspective of daily life. Moreover, achieving physical balance enhances moves toward wholeness and contributes to overall wellness, particularly for Africans living in urban enclaves where diverse forms of stress undermine life chances.

Philosophical wisdom from Kemet suggests that wholeness is possible when one not only thinks—Aristotelian logic—but also feels and experiences knowledge. In fact, comprehension rests on a profound ability to integrate diverse modes of learning. This three-pronged approach to understanding life's contours reflects an African way of being in the world: balanced emphases with respect to thought, feeling and sensibility, and experience. Psychologist Wade Nobles illuminates the importance of an African-centered awareness. He states: "In discussing the 'Kemetic Origins of Psychology,' Na'im points out that the wisdom of ancient Kemet and the psychology that made it manifest was like a vast tapestry being defined by every other thread. Akbar further points out that no thread can be unraveled without destroying the entire tapestry. In effect, one must comprehend, think, feel, experience like the Ancients in order to interpret and understand ancient ideas and beliefs."[5] In light of this ancient model, healing, health, and wellness are integrated into the warp and weave of daily life.

If one interrogates the walls of the pyramids, it is interesting to note that yoga postures, meditative stances, and prayerlike hand positions are notable presences. Social scientist and African-centered scholar Marimba Ani notes: "The African and Native American worldview have similar cosmic concepts. Their intellectual traditions and thought-systems rest on the assumption of cosmic interrelationship. These conceptions form a basis of communal relations as well as sympathetic relationships with the natural environment."[6] Ani's assertions support African religious studies scholar John Mbiti's contention that an African cultural orientation is not only profoundly religious but also anthropocentric—it places human beings at the center "to look at God and nature from the point of his [her] relationship with them."[7] Mbiti does not seek to *define* religion, but to frame religion in an African context: "The point here is that for Africans, the whole of existence is a religious phenomenon; man is a deeply religious being living in a religious universe. Failure to realize and appreciate this starting point, has led missionaries, anthropologists, colonial administrators and other foreign writers on African religions to misunderstand not only the religions as such but the people of Africa."[8]

Mbiti's assertion that African ontology is "a religious ontology" frames and supports the kind of integration necessary for balanced, and, thereby healthy, living. The ontology is explained as follows: "Expressed anthropocentrically, God is the Originator and Sustainer of [humans]; the Spirits explain the destiny of [human beings]; [human beings are] the center of this ontology; the Animals, Plants and natural phenomena and objects constitute the environment in which [human beings live], provide a means of existence and, if need be, [human beings establish] a mystical relationship with them."[9]

Both Mbiti's and Ani's emphases on the interdependence between human beings and the natural environment—plants, animals, ancestors/spirits, and God—suggests that human survival, productivity, and well-being are linked to the natural world. As such, health and wholeness are achieved in the context of addressing multiple life processes simultaneously.

Mbiti notes that in African societies, "Many expressions…attribute human nature to God."[10] This conceptualization remains a telling facet of

African American religious praxis today. And it is in the context of religiosity that the sacred life of the spirit becomes intricately attached to the body as vehicle for spirit consciousness, manifestation, and actualization of good in the community. As such, health maintenance speaks to a sustained sense of integrated wellness: body, mind, and spirit.

In sum, the richness of an African-centered psychological, mental, emotional, and spiritual orientation toward life that emphasizes the interdependence of the varying modes of living serves as a foundation to establishing sound, viable health practices. That human beings in an African context are as profoundly motivated by thought, feeling, and experience attests not only to the vibrancy and adaptability of an African-centered worldview but also provides a fluid and practical or functional model to service the daily life conditions of contemporary Africans in the diaspora.

AFRICAN AMERICANS AND CRITICAL HEALTH ISSUES

Unethical social policies collide with alleged individual freedoms in the United States. In a society that fails to hold persons or institutions accountable for environmental pollution, race-based inequities, and gender hierarchies that menace and diminish the well-being of citizens and the planet, African American women are disproportionately affected. The effects of industrial waste, air pollution, and global warming exacerbate the daily life conditions of all U.S. citizens. Yet, even more profoundly, the nation's poorest, namely women, children, and most Black women experience increasingly more life-threatening health conditions than other groups.

In 2006, the U.S. population reached a staggering 300 million. Yet, despite rich economic resources, the number of U.S. citizens who cannot afford health insurance has climbed to almost one-sixth of the population. Health insurance is a measure of one's access to sound health care. African Americans represent approximately 13 percent of U.S. citizenry and experience adverse health conditions disproportionate to their numbers.

AFRICAN AMERICANS, HYPERTENSION, AND ELEVATED BLOOD PRESSURE

Among African Americans, rates of hypertension and elevated blood pressure almost double that of Whites, according to 2001–2004 statistics.[11] Among African Americans 20 years and over, an astounding 44.7 percent of Black women suffer from hypertension, in contrast to 41.6 percent of Black men; 28.8 percent of both Black men and women suffer from elevated blood pressure. African American men and women are almost twice as likely to suffer from hypertension and elevated blood pressure as are whites of both genders.

High rates of hypertension and elevated blood pressure among African American women and men illuminate the importance of honoring the body, not only to recognize the body as an ongoing witness to the sacredness of life, but also to affirm its significance as an integral site of sacred and secular convergences, both of which are needed to resist structures of domination and its resultant stress. If Black people are to maximize life chances, then we must effectively honor our bodies. Taking sensible measures to care for the physical body through thoughtful diet and exercise programs can inhibit hypertension and elevated blood pressure. Honoring the body affirms an African ontological and epistemological framework and recognizes that synergy in mind, body, and spirit sustains effective living.

AFRICAN AMERICANS' WEIGHT AND HEALTH

The general health profile for most U.S. citizens, both male and female, is consistent. The nation's citizenry is getting bigger. Over the course of the average citizen's lifetime, he or she will become overweight and unhealthy. Even the youngest group of U.S. citizens profiled, those 20 to 34 years old, have gained consistently more body fat since 1960. Health professionals estimate that diet and exercise patterns tend to persist over time. Nonetheless, habits developed during one's early years can be changed with awareness, gentle persistence, nudging, and healthy choices: activity, exercise, and diet.

In light of recent research, daily attention to health and wellness deserves priority status in black communities nationally. Between 1976 and 1980, 62.6 percent of Black women and 51.3 percent of Black men were overweight, with body mass indexes (BMIs) equal to or greater than 25. By 1994, those figures reached 68.5 percent and 58.2 percent for African American women and men respectively.[12] Statistics for 2001–2004 reveal that both females and males of African descent in the United States are increasingly more overweight than in previous years. A shocking 79.5 percent of Black women and 66.8 percent of Black men are overweight. Research has shown that controlling weight, particularly as we mature—enter midlife—may significantly reduce the likelihood of type II diabetes, hypertension, high blood pressure, heart attack, and stroke, all which affect African Americans more than Whites. Moreover, maintaining a healthy weight helps to sustain health and promote longevity, as it reflects an African-centered respect for balance among the physical, mental, and spiritual elements of our humanness.

Indeed, honoring the body as a divine gift challenges the American (U.S.) mindset with its emphases on conspicuous consumption in diverse forms: vehicular travel and food and clothing purchases. In a nation where more is either consciously or unconsciously perceived or interpreted as better, it is not surprising that people are larger than others around the world. Figures from 1976 to 1980 revealed that 31 percent of Black women were obese; a BMI greater than or equal to 30 constitutes obesity.[13] The figures have climbed significantly since then. Between 1988 and 1994 the number of obese African American women rose to 39.1 percent and by 2001–2004, that statistic grew to 51.6 percent. The 2004 statistic is 20 percent higher than the rate for White women.

Although U.S. citizens have grown larger over the last decade, the rate of growth among African Americans is cause for grave concern, particularly because structural inequities based on skin color and class status have remained constant in U.S. society. In light of this, honoring the body becomes not only a sacred act of loving oneself regardless, but also a form of resistance that helps to sustain a critical mass of African Americans.

AFRICAN AMERICANS, MORTALITY RATES, AND LIFE EXPECTANCY

On another note, the data provides a regional look at "age-adjust death rate by race, Hispanic origin, geographic division and state"[14] for three time periods: 1979–1981, 1989–1991, and 2001–2003. Annual averages are noted. Although the cause of death is not identified, the data reveals that for all persons in the United States the death rate dropped over the three categories from one million, twenty-two thousand, eight hundred to 842,700. However, when one notes the contrast between Black and White death rates, it is clear that African Americans die in numbers unequal to their representation in the society: African Americans, 1,081,600 to White Americans, 826,100.

Calculation of mortality rates with respect to region may suggest patterns as telling as the numbers reveal. New England and the mountain states reflect fewer African American deaths than do middle Atlantic, Midwest, south Atlantic, and Southern states. However, in all states except New Hampshire, the mortality rates of African Americans exceed those of European Americans fairly significantly, on an average of approximately one hundred thousand more deaths among Black than White people. The data does not identify causes.

In the United States, life expectancy at birth has increased significantly since 1900 when both sexes could expect to live about 47.3 years. In 1900, Whites lived 47.6 years in contrast to 33.0 years for Blacks. Over time that ratio has improved, with whites' projected lifespan being 78.0 years and Blacks' 72.7 years. Across all groups, women live longer than men: White females, 80.5; Black females, 76.1 years. These figures represent 2003 data. At 65 and 75 years of age, projected longevity remains fairly similar across ethnic lines.

In sum, if we consider the reality of shorter life spans of Blacks than Whites, as well as the greater prevalence of adverse health-related conditions such as obesity, hypertension, and elevated blood pressure among Black women, then it becomes clear that health consciousness is a critical concern for African Americans. Pursuing strategies that not only increase longevity but also maximize health begs attention. Moreover, if, as studies repeatedly illuminate, African American women are inordinately among the poorest U.S. citizens, and more often than any other group, fall prey to intimate partner violence,[15] then embarking on a serious mission to increase longevity needs to be a priority.

There are many connections between racism and Black women's experiences of intimate partner violence, HIV infection, drug addiction, and motherhood.[16] These social conditions, as well as the inordinate incarceration rates among African American males, place a burden on Black women.

Furthermore, coping with excessive stress is often a component of Black life in the United States. As such, it is strategically important that Black people, especially women, be cognizant of how honoring the body helps to mitigate and alleviate diverse levels of stress and dis-ease.[17] Now, let's turn to some practical strategies that can be used to eliminate day-to-day tension to maximize and sustain health.

MEDITATIONS ON THE BODY: PERSONAL ACTS OF FAITH AND HEALING

In the throes of everyday life, too often we forget to nurture and care for the sacred tabernacle of our physical being: the body. Some of us may have forgotten, or perhaps, we never really understood, that like any other achievement at work, school, home, and church, health and well-being require focus, commitment, dedication, determination, and faith. So, how do we begin?

I offer the following strategies as a form of personal meditation and exploration of your own body. This is no easy task, particularly since everywhere we turn, air-brushed, uncommonly, thin images assault us.

To get started, you must become comfortable with your own body. No two bodies are alike, nor do they respond to movement, postures, positions, and stances equally. So, please adjust suggested positions as needed. Your aim is to be comfortable before you begin any one exercise. Nevertheless, remember to focus on the breath and how it feels.

Close your eyes. Visualize a healthy, happier, peaceful you. Accept how you feel and what you look like right now. I found it helpful to look in a mirror and say, "I love myself, right here, right now. I am worthy of love." This worked for me. However, different affirmations may be better suited to your personality, sensibilities, or taste. What's important is that you affirm your sacred self orally, mentally, spiritually, and physically.

As a dancer for over two decades, I've learned that loving myself, regardless, is no easy task. I used to think that I loved myself, but every time I saw a well-toned, muscular body, one that was thinner and more defined than my own, I longed to look like the person I admired. I had not accepted my broad shoulders and large waist. I was too busy coveting the bodies of others to live fully within my own. After 20 years in the body business of dance, I had yet to accept my black body. So, I know that what I'm asking you to do takes great courage and continual but gentle nudging in the direction of your choosing: multiple levels of health and wellness.

The intent of what follows is to assist you in finding that unique space within yourself from which you can move forward with ease—slowly, consistently, step-by-step, day-by-day—toward a healthier lifestyle that includes a daily ritual of breathing and pain-free movements. Identifying ways that breath can be regulated and manipulated to increase efficient breathing and create an environment of reduced stress opens a window onto improved Black women's health.

Your personal meditation on the body must be your personal act of faith, repeated every day. In this day-by-day process, you repeatedly affirm your commitment to loving yourself, regardless. It is from this position of loving acceptance that commitment to change one's health is nourished. Remember that nothing happens overnight. Nothing happens in a vacuum. Be gentle. Be patient. Be persistent.

Life coach Iyanla Vanzant articulates critical ingredients of personal success when she asserts:

> Remember that you can trust life to give you the courage that is required to do anything or face anything...The moment that you feel that you can't take it or won't make it, reach down into the essence of your being. From that place, pull out a scream. Then pull on your power, your strength, the divinity of life within you. Tell yourself, *"This is going to make me stronger! This is going to make me wiser!"* This challenge, no matter what it is, has come to make you bigger, brighter, stronger, more loving and compassionate. *It will not break you!* Trust yourself. Trust life. You will make it through this! Our ancestors did! (emphasis mine)[18]

GETTING STARTED

Rolling out of bed right onto the floor works best for me. I've tried waiting until after work to practice breathing and exercise. However, I found that the morning ritual not only increased my energy, but also added a sense of purpose and intent that anchors each day.

I do not eat before the morning routine and have found that the hunger disappears as I focus on breathing and picturing myself in a variety of relaxing scenarios: laying on sand, falling weightlessly through the floor, being drenched by sun on a beach in the Caribbean. Visualization helps to set a mood and tone for your meditation. Use images that you know and enjoy. Remember, this is your special time, your daily rest and relaxation. Relish it. It is your gift to yourself. Let's get started.

Opening Meditations

Lying on the Floor

Lie on your back with your legs spread comfortably apart. If this feels uncomfortable, then bend your knees with the soles of both feet resting solidly against the floor.[19] Regardless of the position you choose, be sure that your lower back feels relaxed and pain free. Palms face upward as you position your arms diagonally away from the body. Just lie there. Close your eyes. Try to clear your mind. Envision white light or focus on a color. If your thoughts wander from one topic to another, gently remind yourself to return to the color you selected. *Do not judge* yourself. If your thoughts stray, just gently refocus. Remember that you are preparing for a lifelong journey into the sacred realm of your own body. Begin by maintaining the position for approximately five minutes.

Next, focus on your breath. Inhale and exhale, being conscious of taking as much air into the body as possible. Place your hands on your ribcage to make sure that it is moving when you inhale and exhale. On the inhalation *feel* the air moving into you nose, then continue by visualizing and feeling the breath moving through the various parts of your anatomy. Focus on the breath as you exhale, again feeling the air move slowly and deliberately out of the ribcage and finally through the nose. As the air is released from the body, feel your body sink into the floor, attempting to feel weightless.

Remember that this segment of your personal ritual is designed to relax the body, relax your mind, and focus your energy on the breath. On days when you feel tired, exhausted, or hurried, simply perform this exercise for 15–20 minutes. Pay attention to how your body feels. Listen to its gentle urgings. Trust that it knows what is best for you. Herein lies the sacred component of our physical being. Even five minutes of focused breathing will be tremendously beneficial before beginning your official workday.

Stretching

Breath initiates every form of exercise. In the context of breathing, you will eventually be able to feel not only the air moving within your body, but also the release and contraction of muscles. Unlike some trainers and coaches who live by the old adage, "no pain, no gain," kinesiology and physiology research over the past five decades has demonstrated that one can, indeed, stretch muscle, achieve tone, and not be racked with pain. I like to think of breath as an anchor for all forms of physical exercise. Staying conscious of breathing allows you to move past many obstacles, both physical and mental.

Now, you're ready for your next step. Bring your legs together. If you were lying with your knees bent, then straighten your legs. Keep your arms on the floor, but place them over your head, close to your ears. Note that your arms are straight, but not rigid. Feel air circulating within the body and continue to breathe normally. When you are comfortable, with your arms and legs remaining in contact with the floor, stretch up and down at the same time. It's like yawning, except you are consciously stretching away from the center of the body—the solar plexus—as you inhale. Go back toward your center on the exhalation. Rest in between. Repeat this gentle stretch three to four times. Remember there is no hurry. No rush. Focus on feeling the breath and feeling how the muscles extend and stretch to allow the bones to move. Honor what your body tells you.

Curls

Hopefully, by now you're getting the hang of being in your body. With arms placed alongside your body and legs together, take a few breaths. Make sure that your chin is not jutting forward. Feel the back of your neck resting in its natural arch, but the neck is lengthened. Gently bring both knees toward your chest. Touching your chest with your knees is not a requirement. You will get the same benefit from this posture when you work comfortably within your own physical capabilities. This is not a competition but a meditation intended to enhance your specific needs.

If and when you are comfortable bringing your knees close to or touching your chest, place your hands under your thighs and gently pull your legs closer, making a ball with your body. Be sure to inhale and exhale completely during the process. Placing your hands on the top of the legs or near your shins or kneecaps will place unnecessary pressure on these areas. Remember, your strategy is to relax into the position, to feel the breath circulating throughout your body, and to focus. Hold the curled positions for four inhalations and four exhalations; then, return to the supine position. This can be repeated several times. Again, listen to your body.

As you progress in your meditation, consider rocking from side to side as you hold the curled position. The rocking should be slow and gentle. If you feel yourself falling uncontrollably to one side or the other, that's a signal that you need to be more gentle and limit the range of motion. Repeat this four to eight times, evenly on both sides. Remember, if at any time your body signals you to stop, please listen. When you listen to your sacred physical self, you honor the body and demonstrate that you trust and respect the physical domain.

In my own daily ritual, I perform breathing exercises or asanas (postures) based on Hatha yoga techniques.[20] You may find yoga practice helpful as you move closer to your health goals. Nonetheless, this is not necessary or required. Listening to your body is the most important feature of any exercise program, especially if you seek to tap into the sacred wellspring of your personal power and vibrancy. The aforementioned rituals are intended to do just that. So, toggle along with commitment and focus, accepting slow, gradual changes.

RITUAL POSTSCRIPT

Honoring your body is intricately connected to the practice of mindfulness. Stress and its accompanying health challenges—hypertension, elevated blood pressure, eating compulsions that lead to being overweight and or obese—are not going to disappear from our lives. Hence, establishing a regularized ritual to counteract its presence is critical to health and longevity, particularly for African Americans. As noted earlier, Black people in the United States disproportionately represent those who suffer from chronic ailments exacerbated by inactivity as well as unhealthy food choices. Health is a multifaceted endeavor that requires attention to diet, exercise, and levels of stress.

As noted in a *Harvard Business Review* interview, "We all know that unmanaged stress can be destructive. But are there positive sides to stress as well?"[21] Herbert Benson's reply to this question provides a context relevant to African American health. He answers, "Yes, but let's define what stress is first. Stress is a physiological response to *any change*, whether good or bad, that alerts the adaptive fight-or-flight response in the brain and the body" (emphasis mine).[22] He goes on to highlight that "Good stress, also called 'eustress,' gives us energy and motivates us to strive and produce."[23] It is important to be mindful of this explanation as we seek to move toward optimal health.

In our efforts to manage stress, achieve longevity, and concretize rituals for daily wellness, let us remember to honor the spirit and intelligence of the body. In the ritual specificity of daily living, we have opportunities to feel the presence of spirit and to respect it in meditations on the body. I hope that each of us will learn to transfer the mindfulness applied during breathing exercises to day-to-day, moment-to-moment living. May our faith grow in the subtle but persistent life chant that emanates from the physical body.

NOTES

1. Song–dance–chant is used to contextualize the integral relationship between songs, chants, prose, poetry, ululations, music, and dance in the ontology and epistemology of African-derived cultures. The term also emphasizes the interdependence of the diverse forms of expressive communication.

2. Loving self, regardless, an integral fourth segment of Alice Walker's four-part definition of *womanist*, has yet to be explored fully within womanist scholarship. See Alice Walker, *In Search of Our Mothers' Gardens: Womanist Prose* (New York: Harcourt Brace Jovanovich Publishers, 1983), p. xii.

3. Maulana Karenga, *Selections from the Husia: Sacred Wisdom of Ancient Egypt* (Los Angeles: The University of Sankore Press, 1984), p. 91.

4. Karenga, *Selections*, p. 91.

5. Na'im Akbar, *Light from Ancient Africa* (Tallahassee, Fla.: Mind Productions & Associates, Inc., 1994), foreword, p. ii.

6. Marimba Ani, *Yurugu: An African-Centered Critique of European Cultural Thought and Behavior* (Trenton, N.J.: Africa World Press, 1994), p. 45.

7. John Mbiti, *African Religion and Philosophy*, 2nd edition (Portsmouth, N.H.: Heinemann Educational Books, 1989), p. 48.

8. Ibid., p. 15.

9. Ibid., p. 16.

10. Ibid., p. 48.

11. *Health, United States*, 2006 ed., http://www.cdc.gov/nchs/hus.htm, p. 279.

12. Ibid., p. 287.

13. Ibid., p. 288.

14. Ibid., p. 176.

15. Traci West, *Wounds of the Spirit: Black Women, Violence, and Resistance Ethics* (New York: New York University Press, 1999).

16. See Tanya Telfair Sharpe, *Behind the Eight Ball: Sex for Crack Cocaine Exchange and Poor Black Women* (New York: Haworth Press, Inc., 2005).

17. The term *dis-ease* is used to distinguish physical, mental, and emotional discomfort and stress that may result from fatigue, poor diet, insufficient exercise, racial discrimination, multiple problem solving, and multitasking.

18. Iyanla Vanzant, *Acts of Faith: Daily Meditations for People of Color* (New York: Fireside, 1993), January 31 reading.

19. Please note that any form of physical exercise, particularly if inactivity has been habitual, will challenge your body. As such, check with your medical or health professional to ascertain appropriate levels of movement. Advice from a doctor is advised for people with mild to severe health challenges.

20. The Sivananda Yoga Center, *The Sivananda Companion to Yoga: A Complete Guide to the Physical Postures, Breathing Exercises, Diet, Relaxation and Meditation Techniques of Yoga* (New York: Simon & Schuster, 1983), pp. 30–39.

21. Herbert Benson, "A Conversation with Mind/Body Researcher Herbert Benson," *Harvard Business Review* 88, no. 11 (2005): p. 2.

22. Ibid., p. 2.

23. Ibid., pp. 2–3.

PART IV

Analyzing Social Realities

CHAPTER 8

———— ⌗ ————

The Destruction of Aunt Ester's House: Faith, Health, and Healing in the African American Community

Terri Baltimore and Mindy Thompson Fullilove

Radio Golf, the final play of August Wilson's 10-play cycle depicting African American life in the twentieth century, opens with two entrepreneurs celebrating how their so-called urban renewal of Pittsburgh's Hill District will make them rich. Into this merriment comes Elder Joseph Barlow, who enters asking the question, "Are you a Christian?" He needs help to prevent destruction of his Aunt Ester's home at 1839 Wylie Avenue, once the center of activity on the Hill: he thinks a Christian might want to be of service. Harmond Wilks, though set on dreams of success, is stopped dead in his tracks by Barlow's question. Indeed, Wilks, whose intent was to be the agent of destruction, ultimately recognizes his kinship with Barlow as the center of meaning in his life.[1]

We open with Barlow's question because the salvation of community— Aunt Ester's house—is the note on which Wilson finishes his saga of black life in the twentieth century. The question hangs over the new century as yet unanswered. Furthermore, we open with that question because we approach this examination of community, healing, and faith through the same lens he used, that of the Hill District, and our story starts in 1997, the year in which the play takes place. The Hill District is located in Pittsburgh between the central downtown business district and Oakland, the city's university center. It sits on a series of plateaus and valleys, which open up to glorious views of the Allegheny and Ohio Rivers on its northern edge, and the Monongahela River on the southern edge of the neighborhood. The Hill's creative spirit has spawned Ahmad Jamal, George Benson, Lena Horne, Art Blakey, Charles "Teenie" Harris, and, of course, August Wilson. It is a place of stories about struggles faced and surmounted, of songs that transmit hope from one generation to the next, of a willingness to share our shortcomings in the hopes that the listener will not repeat the same mistakes.

We—the authors, Terri and Mindy—first met in 1997, at the Graduate School of Public Health of the University of Pittsburgh. Mindy, who had just published a paper on the psychiatric implications of displacement, was asked to speak at the university.[2] At that time, Terri worked in the Hill District as the director of a program serving with women with substance abuse issues and their families. Based on the flyer she received, she assumed that Mindy would be white and would give an academic talk about displacement that would have little relevance to her work. After attending a late afternoon meeting, Terri decided that fate would determine if she would go listen to Mindy: If a bus heading toward downtown came first, she would go home, but if a bus headed toward the university arrived first, she would go to the talk. The bus headed toward Oakland and the University of Pittsburgh came first. For a long time, Terri characterized the arrival of the Oakland-bound bus as fate or kismet. As events unfolded in the years to follow, she began to see the 54C bus as act of faith that would be connected to a chain of acts of faith.

Much to her surprise, it turned out that Mindy was neither white nor irrelevant. Terri recognized in Mindy's remarks ideas that resonated with past and present experience of the Hill. Terri caucused with Hill District elders present that day and agreed, "Mindy needs to come to the Hill to talk about displacement." Back in the neighborhood, Terri convinced others to join the effort. Human service providers, residents, and college students pooled their resources to bring Mindy to the community. Each group gave what they could—food, photocopying, mailing, space, time, and transportation. Mindy's first trip into the Hill District was born on an act of faith.

COMMUNITY, FAITH, AND HEALING

Black Nation as Community

For more than a hundred years, black people have viewed themselves as a nation-within-a-nation. The sense of black nationhood was born of exclusion and built in defiance of dehumanizing racism. That nation was once geographically contiguous, rooted in the Black Belt in the South. Migration to the cities created urban offshoots throughout the nation. Because blacks were confined to ghetto neighborhoods, the new geography of black life was one of continuity-in-discontinuity.

These neighborhoods were referred to as "the ghetto" or "the hood." More recently, the displacement that we will discuss in this chapter has forced people out of the traditional ghetto space and into new neighborhoods. The old terms have been replaced by the term "community," which we take to signify the dense social networks of black people but without the same geographic anchors.

The Community's Sentiments about Faith

We define faith as "the absolute, down-to-your-core belief that despite all the pain, disappointment and hurt, the future holds promise." Faith is a personal belief, but among African Americans it has become a shared sentiment as well. Here is what we mean by that. When people join together to do work, they initiate a collective process. Such processes depend on people coming to accord about the tasks and the ways in which they are to be accomplished. These accords are the product of many people sharing their thoughts about their experience and arriving at shared sentiments. The collective task of the African American people is liberation, rooted in being torn from home in Africa, force marched to port, consigned to a terrible ocean voyage from Africa to the United States, and trekked to a new home where the condition of slavery was imposed.

With rampant disease, little food, little water, and harsh conditions, many died along the way, some by simply letting go of the will to live. Those who held on had deep faith that they would be free one day, and they passed that faith along to their children. After generations of endurance under dire conditions, African Americans could look back and say, "We've come this far by faith," thus elucidating a guiding sentiment. This is a faith about "us"—that *we* shall overcome—it is a shared sentiment, where the term "sentiment" refers to a thought-feeling complex that resonates with individual and group strivings.[3] Fighting for liberation in the face of slavery, Jim Crow, the Great Depression, segregation, and poverty gives credibility to that assertion. More than just survival, African Americans have built great institutions and a great culture, battled for equality, and resisted centuries of racist dehumanization. These, too, add to the argument that faith works.

Sentiments that arise from collective life may be undermined when the collective itself is altered by war, epidemic disease, displacement, disaster, or other kinds of social upheaval. During such upheaval, populations are shifted and critical consensus-building networks are damaged. Without those networks it is difficult to pass along information. Without adequate sharing, groups cannot develop shared sentiments about the way to live. In the aftermath of upheaval, larger collectives are broken up into smaller groups, within which new sentiments evolve. Often these new groups come to have very different ideas about ways in which to live. These differences can be costly, in terms of the possibility of collective action for survival. The recent history of African Americans is characterized by a terrible series of unmitigated upheavals spanning more than five decades. The constant destruction has been accompanied by a constant rebuilding, notwithstanding the fact that it is easier to destroy than to build, which has resulted in a negative trajectory that has overwhelmed many people with the sense, "Why bother?"

Healing: The Code of the Rose

In 2007, a group of young artists who were painting a mural in a homeless shelter in Harlem decided to use the "code of the rose" as their theme. In this symbolism, the rose has three stages: the bud for hope, the half-opened rose for faith, and the full bloom for beauty. When the rose, which stands for the homeless people, meets the bridge, which stands for the shelter, they make first hope and faith, then beauty.[4]

The bringing together of the fractured community, with links to the past where faith was tested and found strong, appears to be a way to healing. As the young muralists concluded:

> To go from nothing to something,
> The rose and the bridge must meet.

In 2006, a friend who lived in the Hill lost her son to violence on the streets of her beloved neighborhood. She could no longer walk past the spot where he had been killed. Her confidence in the future of the neighborhood was shattered. Her faith crumbled in the face of tragedy. She was one of many caught up in the alienation engendered by community disintegration.

Aggrieved people struggling in weakened networks challenge the assumption that faith matters. Despite the weakening of faith, rebuilding of social connections and restoration of faith begins almost immediately. As our friend was struggling with grief, the community rallied around her in ways that slowly helped her reconnect with her life and her faith. Elders, sisters, friends, and children she had mothered: all had faith for her. Their prayers, calls, e-mails, letters, and tiny gestures wrapped a protective covering around her until she was able to reclaim her faith and equilibrium. The determination to hold our friend up was the same determination that allowed the people of the Hill to hold together in spite of external and internal forces that have nearly pushed the community off the face of the earth. We explore the destructive and healing processes in the following parts.

INCESSANT DISPLACEMENT

While racial oppression is always understood to be part of the black experience, it can take many forms. Urban renewal in the 1950s loomed large in the destruction of the Hill. In order to develop a better understanding of that story, Mindy began the Root Shock Project, a project that examined urban renewal in African American neighborhoods in five U.S. cities: the Central Ward in Newark; the Hill District in Pittsburgh; Northeast, Kimball, and Gainsboro in Roanoke; Mill Creek Valley in St. Louis; and the Fillmore District in San Francisco.[5] People who had lived through urban renewal situated that experience between other attacks on community life, beginning with segregation.

Segregation

All five neighborhoods were segregated, that is to say, places in which blacks had to settle because of both formal and informal policies and practices that blocked their living in other parts of the city. The stories of how these neighborhoods came into being vary to some extent. These processes of settlement were entwined with the local development of social, economic, political, and cultural organization, largely confined within the boundaries of the segregated area.[6]

African Americans had lived in the Hill District in Pittsburgh since the 1800s, a story related to us by *Pittsburgh Courier* journalist Frank Bolden. He described in some detail the long struggle by blacks to win political control of their neighborhoods, including the Hill District. This political power allowed them to fight for better services and better neighborhood life. At the same time, black residents of the Hill also devoted time and energy to the development of cultural institutions, ranging from symphony orchestras to book clubs, economic institutions such as hotels, beauty shops, pharmacies and jazz clubs, and recreation for children. Among the many comments about life in a highly developed albeit segregated neighborhood were those of Lois Cain, also a black resident of Pittsburgh's Hill District in her youth in the 1940s and 1950s. She noted:

> All the resources we needed, my mother, my grandfather, my grandmother, my father, all got it right here [in the Hill]. I am amazed at that, because now you have to kind of shop around. If you want to turn your dollar over with your people, you've got to get a list and a map. But [back then] you could stay right here, and never leave it, and get everything you needed, from party-time to church. This is my memories of the Hill, was that families stayed together.

Redlining

But residents of ghetto neighborhoods were engaged in a constant fight with forces of destruction. Among the policies that undermined neighborhood viability was redlining, introduced by the National Housing Act of 1934 and carried out by the Homeowners Loan Corporation (HOLC). The HOLC created redlining maps for more than 200 cities. These maps rated neighborhoods on the age and integrity of the built environment, as well as on the ethnicity of residents. Areas were graded A, B, C, or D. These grades were color coded. The areas were mapped according to the codes. Non-whites were considered a negative, and areas where blacks lived were given a D grade and colored red on the HOLC maps.

As pointed out by people interviewed for the study who lived in Newark's Central Ward, redlining made it difficult to get insurance or to borrow for repairs and remodeling. This meant that the built environment, including all of its elements of homes and businesses, deteriorated more rapidly than it might have, had there been adequate and continuous investment.

Urban Renewal

Discouraging investment in ghetto areas played a critical role in setting up urban renewal because a city's declaration that an area was "blighted" was the first step toward clearing land. Rutgers University urban studies professor Dennis Gale explained:

> Part of the idea behind urban renewal is that the officials in Washington realized that you would never get private capital to invest back in the city, to build new office buildings, build shops, housing, etcetera—you could never encourage them to do that as long as there were these significant numbers of minorities and low-income people in the cities...So the idea was, the only way that we can hope to get private capital back into the cities, because we can't do it alone without federal money, the only way to do it is to get rid of all the slums and deterioration. You label it as bad, you clear it all out. You have a featureless plain, and call it urban renewal. There is no longer any bad, there is nothing. And then you build from scratch.

Pittsburgh city planner Robert Pease was involved in assessing the Hill District's need for renewal. He remembered:

> There was a family there [in the Hill] who had a son the same age as my son. But I could look at the walls and see outside through the walls. And it was bitter cold...Well, the conditions in the Hill, not every family lived that way, because there was some pretty decent housing there, not expensive but decent, with indoor plumbing and all the good things. But there were a lot of slums that were overcrowded and really needed to be cleared.

Sala Udin grew up in the neighborhood Pease was describing. Born Samuel Howze, his family had multigenerational roots in the Hill. He commented:

> I think that the sense of community and the buildings are related within an old area. The buildings were old, the streets were cobblestone and old, there many small alleyways and people lived in those alleyways. The houses were very close together. There were small walkways that ran in between the alleyways that was really a playground. So, the physical condition of the buildings helped to create a sense of community. We all lived in similar conditions and had similar complaints about the wind whipping through the gaps between the frame and the window, and the hole in the walls and the leaking fixtures, the toilet fixtures that work sometimes and don't work sometimes. But that kind of common condition bound us together.

Pease and Udin: two men, looking at the same land. For one, there is nothing of value worth saving. For the other, everything had value. They represent the views of the outsider and the insider. The outsider sees old buildings, a blighted landscape, and nothing worth saving, nothing of redeeming value. The insider sees the intangible connections with people and rituals. The outsider assumes that destruction is the only way to create something of meaning. The insider knows that destruction represents the end of precious social networks. The outsider recognizes only the deficits. The insider holds on to the strengths.

Given that the outsiders have the power of government behind them, the neighborhoods were leveled—often hundreds of acres were clear-cut in a form of urban forestry designed to create the "featureless plain" that was supposed to lure investors back to the city. This so-called new land was used for many different purposes, ranging from low-income housing projects to cultural centers. The people who had lived in the neighborhoods were dispersed. The new places in which they settled tended to be heavily black and less integrated by race or class than the old neighborhoods had been. Dense high-rise housing projects, such as those erected in the Central Ward of Newark, typified the extreme isolation of very poor black people from others unlike themselves. Those with more resources settled in neighborhoods close to where they had lived prior to urban renewal.

Catastrophic Disinvestment

African Americans, dispersed by urban renewal but settled in nearby segregated neighborhoods, lived in places undermined by disinvestment of public and private resources. In the 1970s simple redlining—which labeled an area according to the potential for return on investment—was transformed into active disinvestment of public and private resources, ranging from removing supermarkets to closing fire stations. This lead to contagious housing destruction, a process of destruction that fans through dense urban areas consuming homes and other buildings inadequately protected by proper maintenance, code enforcement, and fire extinguishment.[7]

One such neighborhood was Gainsboro, a section of Roanoke, Virginia, that was marked for urban renewal but never cleared. The declaration of planned urban renewal effectively blocked investment in the area. Slowly, the area deteriorated and the housing stock fell apart. Fires destroyed buildings and forced the mostly black residents of the area out. As people left, businesses and other institutions suffered. As Evelyn Bethel, one of few remaining residents of the area, pointed out:

> The small businesses that we had where people were self-sufficient to a degree, no matter how much or how little they made, they were self-sufficient, and they had a core of ready-made customers. When the people were forced out, your business could no longer survive, so it was a devastating loss to the residents as well as the business owners.

Contagious housing destruction, as implied by its name, is a spreading process. Its progress had not been halted in the five cities examined in the Root Shock study. Indeed, whole cities, at some distance from the original urban renewal site, were endangered by destruction set off when black neighborhoods were cleared for "higher uses."[8]

Gentrification

At the same time that contagious housing destruction was eating habitat at the edges of the hollowed-out zone, other investment had started to take place in areas closest to the center. Crawford Square, on the near-downtown side of the Hill District, was such a site of new investment. Carlos Peterson, a resident of the Lower Hill prior to urban renewal, had watched as disinvestment had caused the Middle Hill, the next-over neighborhood, to sag and disappear. It was part of this site that was eventually cleared to make way for Crawford Square. He commented:

> I think the city government and urban developers waited twenty years for this area to kind of like, decline on its own, to make it easier for them to come in and redevelop the property. And I think some of the buildings could have been saved. It could have been more of what it was, but upgraded in terms of people, property, and so forth. Right now, I think that what they've developed in terms of Crawford Square, they basically razed everything. They just took everything down. And I used to call it the carcass of the Hill. You looked at the Hill and there was this carcass up there. I thought that if they could have saved the structures, because there was so much character. Now it's like looking at some sort of cul-de-sac from suburbia, you know? People don't look out their windows, they don't sit on their porches, they don't barbecue and work on their cars. You know, it's just not black folks.

Frank Bolden, who spoke about Crawford Square at some length, concluded:

> Now even today, they still haven't done anything to beautify the Hill, except they put up the Civic Arena, and they put up Crawford Village, which has homes that are too expensive for the poor people to buy or rent. Now there are a few down there but I am talking about masses of the Negroes. Now they want to continue, they want to still beautify the Hill. They are hoping to bring white people back to the city to work, because those people living in Crawford Village and so forth now, do not patronize anything in the Hill District. They patronize downtown. They are no use to us.

HOPE VI

Federal housing projects were linked into the story of serial forced displacement in many ways. Housing projects were an important social reform when first introduced in the 1930s. They offered clean, decent housing for poor and working families. Indeed, housing projects developed in that era were often models of design, especially by comparison with those erected later, which were often poorly conceived and shoddily built. Yet, however the projects started, by the 1990s many were deemed "distressed communities," a label that was applied to an array of housing types and conditions. Reminiscent of "blight," places labeled "distressed housing communities" were arbitrarily slated for destruction under the federal government's HOPE VI program.[9] At the time of our fieldwork in Pittsburgh and Newark, the HOPE VI demolition of public housing was reorganizing ghetto neighborhoods.

Ironically, people who had moved into the housing projects as a result of urban renewal were threatened with a new round of upheaval and resettlement. Muhandes Salaam Allah in Roanoke said, with some bitterness:

> I don't know whether the ultimate goal was to impoverish these black communities, but certainly anybody who has any understanding knows that if you spend thirty years in the project and you are not able to build equity, you are not going to be able to pass anything on to your children. And when you destroy a neighborhood where people own their own home, and replace it with a project, where people don't own nothing, then what is going to be the consequences in a thirty or forty year period? It's going to be that these people are going to be an impoverished group of people. And they are not participating in the American Dream. They are participating in the Housing Authority nightmare.

Bitter and Fractured

The sentiment that reverberates off the pages in the collected narratives of African Americans displaced by urban renewal and other destabilizing programs is one of bitterness: people resented the losses they had experienced. This resentment was directed at federal, state and local governments that had enacted a long series of policies that effectively undermined the integrity and functioning of urban ghetto neighborhoods. The anger was amplified by the people's sense that they had been robbed of the fruit of their efforts to achieve equal opportunity in the United States.

One example is the anger expressed by Dr. Walter Claytor of Roanoke. The Claytor family—several generations of health care professionals—had worked hard to gain education and to build facilities to house their offices. Dr. Walter Claytor described how his grandfather, a skilled builder, had come to Virginia to build the family mansion. Their large and beautiful home was a place of shelter for the family and a welcome for African Americans visiting Roanoke and unable to stay in white hotels because of segregation. The mansion burned during the era of contagious housing destruction in Gainsboro; getting restitution for this loss motivated Dr. Claytor to pursue a long and arduous lawsuit against the city of Roanoke. He eventually won a bittersweet settlement that repaid only a fraction of his loss but provided a measure of justice after many years of legalized abuse.

In addition to the feeling of bitterness was a deep reality of fractured relations. Everyone remembered large social networks, densely populated neighborhoods, and widespread agreement about aspects of community life from the discipline of children to the concern for equal rights as Americans. Little of that was left by 2001 when the Root Shock fieldwork was conducted. The Lower Hill, for example, had been cleared by urban renewal, while the middle and upper sections of the neighborhood had been destroyed by contagious housing destruction. Housing projects were slated for destruction by HOPE VI, with replacement by mixed-income projects that were geared to change the character of the Hill. Not only would fewer people be living in the area, but also they would be different people: some former residents would not be allowed to return to the new housing, and some wealthier people would be able to move in (see Figure 8.1).

Figure 8.1 Pittsburgh's Hill District

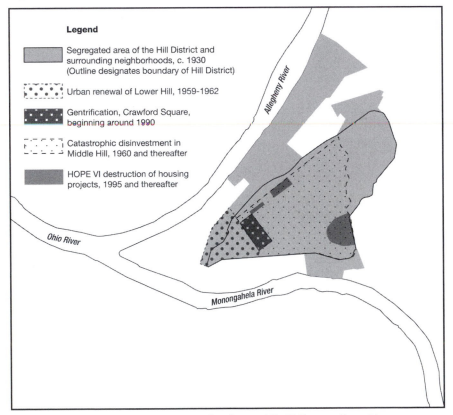

Urban renewal clear-cut the Lower Hill. The Middle Hill was affected by contagious housing destruction, which wiped out a massive amount of the built environment. HOPE VI projects led to the demolition of two housing communities: Allequippa Terrace and Bedford Dwellings. Gentrification started in the Crawford Square area and has moved northwest (by the Hill).

THE SOCIOCULTURAL DISINTEGRATION AS A RESULT OF INCESSANT DISPLACEMENT

All of the processes that we've described contributed to the destruction of neighborhoods as social and physical entities. This destruction of human habitat triggered "sociocultural disintegration," that is, the loss of social bonds and shared symbols. As social groups fell apart, hostility and stress emerged as dominant parts of daily life. What is critical for our discussion of faith is that it is undermined by massive setbacks in group life, such as those described here. De Figueiredo has proposed a "law of sociocultural demoralization" that states that: "At a given rate of sociocultural change, the prevalence of demoralization in a community is inversely associated with the sociocultural integration in that community."[10]

According to social psychiatrist Alexander H. Leighton, "Morale is the capacity of a group of people to pull together persistently and consistently in pursuit of a common purpose."[11] In his observations of men at war, he found that a group's effort depended on individuals' faith in each other's commitment to get work done. Pulling together also depended on the ability of collective processes to identify and endorse common goals. In the aftermath of upheaval, this is very difficult for groups to do.

Demoralization, then, is understood to mean the inability of a group to pull together consistently for the common good. This implies a profound loss of faith among the members of the group, which de Figueiredo calls "subjective incompetence." More recently, sociologists studying urban neighborhoods have used the term "collective efficacy" when assessing neighbors' ability to help each other.[12] They have found that violence is higher in neighborhoods in which people report a low sense of collective efficacy. We might hypothesize that violence rushes in to fill the void created by the rupture of critical social bonds, the collapse of group morale, and the failure to act because of a subjective sense of incompetence. In this scenario, aggression is the opposite of faith.

ORGANIZING IN THE FACE OF INCESSANT DISPLACEMENT

Despite being opposites, in real communities, aggression and faith and destruction and rebuilding co-exist in complex patterns. Leighton did a study of a Japanese "relocation center," one of the internment camps where Japanese-Americans were confined during World War II.[13] He observed, "Communities undergoing social disorganization also show new organization; break down and repair take place simultaneously."[14] He noted:

Many of the symptoms of social disorganization are at the same time signs of the repair process. This is a point easily missed by an administrator who does not understand the nature of men and society, with the result that he spends his energy trying to stop the repair instead of guiding it in the direction that will be least expensive and least painful to all concerned.[15]

Informed by his research, Leighton gave advice to camp administrators that enabled them to defuse hostilities, prevent riots, and promote as healthful an atmosphere as was possible under the constraints of internment.

This path is the path followed by Terri and her colleagues. The fact that the public housing communities in the Hill District—Allequippa Terrace and Bedford Dwellings—were designated HOPE VI projects had actually precipitated Terri's interest in Mindy's talk and was the reason Mindy was invited to the Hill in July 1997. As we noted earlier, Terri thought that Mindy's ideas on displacement would help the community manage the threats posed by HOPE VI.

The invitation for a one-day visit grew into a 16-month project on community displacement called "Hillscapes."[16] The project brought together the rose and the bridge at meetings, teach-ins, and a conference. Hill District folks used the time with Mindy to explore a wide range of issues and activities. First, they talked about their roots in the community and what the community felt like "back in the day." Their reminiscences were filled with tears for people, places, and rituals that were long gone and with pain about the way public policies such as urban renewal had torn sacred places asunder. And yet, through all of that pain, hurt, grief, and longing, folks had stayed in the Hill. For some, their faith anchored them there. They knew that the Hill would not be what it was during the Wylie Avenue heyday and that it would not remain the same as it was. People had remained in the neighborhood because, despite the negatives, they thought the place could be transformed.

Through exercises like mapping the community, recording stories, remembering the community's old norms, teaching college students how to respectfully enter the community, organizing tours for outsiders, and challenging the status quo, people from the H-I double L operationalized their faith.

By the time a public hearing was held on September 30, 1999, organized to discuss the plans for Bedford Dwellings, this work had had an important effect. The city officials were prepared to share their plans for the new replacement units. They had renderings and explanations. The use of eminent domain to acquire buildings in the development zone was floating in the air. Over one hundred Hill residents showed up and many registered to testify.

The tone of the meeting could have gone in many directions. It could have been a gripe session. It could have been a meeting where the community resigned itself to the role of victim. But that was not the case. People had written about their lives and understood that they could influence the process by speaking their truths. Following the metaphor of the young Harlem artists, the rose and the bridge had come together. They realized that history could repeat itself if they stayed silent. To prevent that from happening, they were determined to speak.

Residents of the Hill spoke about the pain of displacement at community meetings. They spoke about the lasting impact of displacement with college students. They spoke with children about the grief associated with displacement. Faith had kept them tethered to the community. Resolute that history should not be repeated, faith made them act. Faith made them overcome the vulnerability of bearing their hearts and souls in very public ways. Their cry was that people should not be displaced in the name of progress.

At the hearing, a very cool thing happened. Each resident speaker used similar language. No one wanted to be displaced. Folks told very personal, poignant stories about losing significant people and places when the Civic Arena (now the Mellon Arena) was built. There were ways to join the old and the new. The history, the stories, and the results were a manifestation of faith.

ENVISIONING THE FUTURE

One of the ways that the Hill is reshaping itself, as of 2007, is by reconnecting to Pittsburgh's three rivers. The idea for this project came from a very unlikely source, French urbanist Michal Cantal-Dupart. In 1998, Cantal, a colleague of Mindy's, came to the Hill. He fell in love with the community. He literally raced across the Hill, walked up and down hillsides and asked a critical question. "How did people get to the rivers from here?"

The answer came from the elders, the people who steadfastly clung to the hope that the community could be transformed. They told him that there used to be many connections to the rivers, including an incline, or funicular, that took workers down to the mills located there. It took several years and a new project called "Find The Rivers!" (FTR), for Cantal Dupart's question to be answered.

The FTR project provides an opportunity to use the Hill's natural assets—such as its plentiful green spaces and topography—to tell another story about the Hill. For newcomers, FTR is a way to talk about their community. For longtime Hill residents it's a way to use their memories and stories to tell how they used the space. The Hill was part of Pittsburgh's industrial history. Inclines, city steps (which were constructed along hillsides to connect those areas of the city that were flat), and community-made pathways were the ways residents made their way to work in the mills, train yards, produce-shipping center, and the mines. Their stories are about reawakening a part of the town's past and thinking about reconnections.

As neighborhood residents began to develop their ideas about the rivers, FTR asked landscape designers to help articulate a vision for rebuilding. From explorations and discussions the idea of a park along the north–south

Kirkpatrick Street took shape. This park would connect from river to river, adding green space to the interior of the neighborhood. These processes brought many partners to the Hill, including urban planners, landscape designers and parks enthusiasts, teachers and their classes, and many others, all eager to explore forgotten corners of the city.

Explorations, public visioning sessions, and other kinds of meetings extended the discourse on neighborhood developed during the Hillscapes work. More and more people were engaged, in one way or another, with the fate of the neighborhood. More and more people began to feel that they had a stake in what the future would be.

But, as these efforts of FTR were opening up new visions of the Hill, gentrification was moving rapidly from downtown up the slopes of the District, in the HOPE VI project areas and scattered all around. Suddenly, the Hill, because of its proximity to downtown, was valuable again, and developers were eager for the land. The poor who had endured decades of civic neglect were suddenly in the wrong place at the wrong time. This latest in the series of disorganizing pressures created many new challenges for Terri, Denys Candy, who co-directs Find the Rivers! with Terri, and others working to preserve the Hill as a historic African American neighborhood.

Two events were characteristic of the diverse challenges thrown at Terri and other Hill District leaders. The first, in March 2004, was a massive fire that destroyed Ebenezer Baptist Church, killed two firefighters, and injured 27 people. This was devastating, as the church was a historic place. The fire seemed to symbolize the vulnerability of the area, as if the last bastion of people's strength had been consumed by flames. At the same time, people's commitment to heal and rebuild helped to create new openings for revival. The two firemen, killed in the line of duty, were mourned by the firefighters and their families, as well as by the church congregation.

The church held a day of public mourning on Easter Sunday, which was celebrated just days after the fire. Church members invited the firefighters' families to join them as they held a service in a nearby church and then walked in solemn procession to the burned-out hulk of their church. People brought mementos of their great moments in the church—weddings, baptisms, and choir performances—that were displayed on the walls that were still standing. The congregation vowed to rebuild, and many in the city committed to aiding them. This created a rare and precious moment of interneighborhood and interorganizational unity. The commitments were realized and the church reopened rapidly. Its gratitude for the firefighters was manifested in a special memorial to them in the new sanctuary that opened in November 2006, creating a permanent link between the firefighters' families and the church, its new stolid walls affirming once again the right of black people to be in the Hill. It is not surprising that Reverend J.V. Alfred Winsett, pastor of the church for 33 years, told the celebrants, "The church has come this far by faith."

The second event involved a 2006 proposal to put a casino in the Hill District. This aroused popular concern. At first it seemed that the proposal was unstoppable, and that, as in previous instances, the city would roll over the Hill's concerns, forcing its will on a politically weak and vulnerable neighborhood. But many people decided to participate under the umbrella of The Hill District Gaming Task Force. The task force gathered and disseminated information so that residents could be well informed in their choices. This led to many different actions from residents of the Hill, including letter writing, sign posting, song writing, and meeting attendance. These actions were recognized by those involved with the redevelopment as signaling the need to include Hill representatives in further discussions. In 2007, then, the Hill had awakened and was claiming its territory.

But fractured neighborhoods, like the Hill, have many representatives, often at odds with each other. The reanimation of any neighborhood must go through a critical transition, fraught with danger that leadership will be snatched by greedy and selfish entrepreneurs who sell out the larger interests of the people. In addition to the many threats that accompany reorganization, the Hill suffered from random acts of violence, the ongoing destruction of historic places and trees, the displacement of longtime residents, and the unceasing building of new homes, all of which continued to undermine the sense that the Hill was winning. In fact, though many small victories could be counted, it seemed highly possible that the last vestiges of African American life in the Hill could be wiped out.

Indeed, the idea of faith is that one holds on even though the future is mired in uncertainty. Now the Hill is very much a part of conversations about harnessing the economic opportunities related to the rivers. The FTR project would not exist were it not for the residents who remained in the Hill. Their persistence and faith kept them here. And now current and future generations in the neighborhood will reimagine this community because of them. As Norman Vincent Peale once said, "Faith supplies staying power... Anyone can keep going when the going is good, but some extra ingredient is needed to keep you fighting when it seems that everything is against you."

Returning to August Wilson's final play, we are struck that the great playwright used the metaphor of Aunt Ester's house to focus our attention on the unrelenting destruction of the ghetto that characterized the twentieth century for African Americans. Battered by segregation, redlining, urban renewal, gentrification, HOPE VI, and other damaging policies, people on the Hill continue to fight for their collective survival. In the sorrow of the loss of Aunt Ester's house, we are cheered that Wilson's hero, Harmond Wilks, turns away from destruction. This is the two-sided process of destruction and reinvestment that accompanies all upheaval. Despite the real dangers in the future, it is commitment to the collective process that lights the way: this faith that, having made it this far, we shall overcome some day.

NOTES

The section on incessant displacement draws from, and follows closely, the arguments made in previous book chapters that have tackled the problem of incessant displacement, especially Wallace R. and M. Fullilove, *Collective Consciousness and Its Discontents: Institutional Distributed Cognition, Racial Policy, and Public Health in the United States* (New York: Springer Books, in press); M. T. Fullilove, "Incessant Displacement and Health Disparities," in *Toward Equity in Health: A New Global Approach to Health Inequity*, ed. B. Wallace (New York: Springer Publishing, in press). The methods and results of the Root Shock Project, as well as some of the experiences of the Hillscapes Project, are described by M. Fullilove, *Root Shock: How Tearing up City Neighborhoods Hurts America and What We Can Do about It* (New York: Ballantine/One World, 2004).

Mindy's work was supported in part by the Maurice Falk Medical fund; Robert Wood Johnson Foundation Health Policy Scholar Award; Columbia Health and Society Scholars; and the Open Society Institute. Terri's work was supported by numerous foundations and by a Hill-based nonprofit organization.

1. "Radio Golf," http://en.wikipedia.org/wiki/Radio_Golf (accessed September 28, 2007); Ben Brantley, "In the Rush to Progress, the Past is Never Too Far Behind," http://theater2.nytimes.com/2007/05/09/theater/reviews/09radio.html?pagewaanted=print (accessed September 28, 2007).

2. M. Fullilove, "Psychiatric Implications of Displacement: Contributions from the Psychology of Place," *American Journal of Psychiatry* 153 (1996): pp. 1516–23.

3. Alexander C. Leighton, who was one of the pioneers of the study of sociocultural disintegration, used the term "sentiment" in his research. His colleagues offered the following discussion of the meaning of term: "Sentiments as Leighton defines them are relatively stable and recurrent compounds of thought, feeling, and striving which relate a person to the objects in his environment. They are the emotionally-toned 'templates' through which he defines 'what is,' 'what ought to be,' and 'what is desirable'. . . Sentiments can be both individual and cultural; the latter are designated as shared sentiments" (p. 396). Jane M. Hughes, Charles C. Hughes, and Alexander H. Leighton, "Notes on the Concept of Sentiment," Appendix A, in *My Name Is Legion: Foundations for a Theory of Man in Relation to Culture*, ed. Alexander H. Leighton (New York: Basic Books, 1959).

4. Picasso Dali, "The Rose Bridge," Summer Art Works: Murals in Harlem, Creative Arts Workshops for Kids, August 16, 2007.

5. The Root Shock Project was funded by the Robert Wood Johnson Foundation. It was approved by the Institutional Review Board of the New York State Psychiatric Institute. The field work was carried out in 2001, with additional fieldwork in 2004. *Root shock* is defined as the traumatic stress reaction to the loss of all or part of one's emotional ecosystem. The results are presented in Fullilove, *Root Shock*.

6. We use the term *ghetto* to describe areas in which people were forced to live because of their group membership. Neither *ghetto* nor *segregated* is a term that specifies socioeconomic condition of an area. A segregated neighborhood might be quite well-to-do.

7. D. Wallace and R. Wallace, *A Plague on Your Houses: How New York Was Burned Down and National Public Health Crumbled* (New York: Verso Books, 1998).

8. R. Wallace et al., "Forced Displacement of African-Americans in Newark, NJ, 1970–2000: How 'Urban Renewal' Triggered an Advancing Glacier of Collapsing Public Order and Public Health, A Report of the Transect Study," Community Research Group, Columbia University and NYSPI, March 21, 2005.

9. HOPE VI was an initiative of President William Clinton's administration. Its goal was to change the face of public housing by getting rid of all barracks-style or high-rise buildings and replacing them with modern structures integrated into the neighborhood proper. HOPE VI was also designed to change communities by mixing public housing units with subsidized and market rate units.

10. J. M. de Figueiredo, "The Law of Sociocultural Demoralization," *Social Psychiatry* 18 (1983): pp. 73–78.

11. A. H. Leighton, *Human Relations in a Changing World: Observations in the Use of Social Sciences* (New York: EP Dutton, 1949).

12. R. Sampson et al., "Neighborhoods and Violent Crime: A Multilevel Study of Collective Efficacy," *Science* 277 (1997): pp. 918–24.

13. A. H. Leighton, *The Governing of Men: General Principles and Recommendations Based on Experiences at a Japanese Relocation Camp* (Princeton, N.J.: Princeton University Press, 1945).

14. Ibid., p. 332.

15. Ibid., p. 333.

16. A. Robins et al., *Hillscapes: A Scrapbook, Envisioning a Healthy Urban Habitat* (Pittsburgh: University of Pittsburgh, 1999).

CHAPTER 9

———— ✵ ————

The Unspoken, the Spoken, and the Affirmed: Meanings of Healing, Same-Gender-Loving African Americans, and Black Churches

Linda L. Barnes

These positive accounts call into question the assumption that black people and black communities are necessarily more homophobic than other groups of people in this society. They also compel us to recognize that there are diversities of black experience.

—*bell hooks*

It is in the diversities of black experience that talk of religion, sexual orientation, and healing must be rooted. Instead of speaking about a black community in tension with black same-gender-loving realities, the deeper truth lies in their profound interconnectedness. Likewise, blackness and gayness cannot be set in opposition. Because there is no individual without *both* a race *and* a sexual orientation, there can be no same-gender-loving identity without a racial identity, whatever that racial identity might be. This interconnection has particular ramifications for same-gender-loving people of color. As one man I interviewed said:

> I feel like being a gay black male, I already have two strikes against me in the society we live in, because you'll find that there are racist people out there who won't like you because you're black, and people in general out there who won't like you because you're gay. So it's like you already have two strikes against you. You have to struggle that much harder.[1]

To be asked to choose between the different parts of one's identity—to prioritize being black over being same gender loving or vice versa, or being Christian over same gender loving, as though the two are irreconcilable—presents the individual with an untenable choice. After all, as one woman said, "I am a Black lesbian. I was raised in an African American household.

I don't eat gay food, I eat soul food, I don't attend a gay church, I attend a Black church."[2]

The different ways in which these factors configure in the lives of different persons and groups means that there is no single way to talk about what healing means in relation to African Americans and homosexuality. At stake are deeply held religious worldviews and commitments, grounded in opposing readings of biblical and other religious sources. For some Christians, these readings make it impossible to do anything but condemn the same-gender-loving members of their churches; for some, it requires a conditional embrace based on not asking and not telling; for still others, it mandates an open welcome and full embrace. To date, these worldviews have often remained mutually exclusive and unreconciled.

BIBLICAL READINGS

Because many of the differences involve a foundation built on divergent English translations of the Bible, it is useful to start out with some of these examples to show how such devastating and divisive outcomes arise. Paradoxically, Hebrew, Aramaic, and Greek do not even have words for homosexual orientation, for committed same-sex relationships, or for same-gender-loving people. The Hebrew Bible cites acts of sexual violence, as when a conquered king was violated by the conquerors as an act of ritual humiliation. Two words in particular appear in relation to passages condemning specific same-sex acts. The first, *qadesh*, refers to temple prostitutes who engaged in ritual sex as surrogates for gods or goddesses in pagan temples. English translations like the King James version (KJV) of the Bible, however, simply render the terms "sodomite" or "homosexual" without any discussion of the specific context for the condemnation (see, for example, Deut. 23:17 KJV, 1 Kings 14:24, 15:12, and 22:46, and 2 Kings 23:7). The second, *to'ebah*, refers to actions condemned as foreign or pagan cult practices. To eat dairy and meat products together, for example, was *to'ebah*. Yet the KJV and the New International Version (NIV)—two translations regularly used in more conservative Christian communities—translate this term generically as "abomination," making it virtually impossible not to conclude that the Hebrew Bible condemns homosexuality across the board.

The mandate in Gen. 1:27–28 to be fruitful and multiply is often read as affirming male–female relations as the only religiously authorized and normative form of pairing to generate children. Yet presumably, if both Adam and Eve were made in God's image, either one could parent children without it necessarily requiring that the two do so together. Gen. 19 tells the story of Sodom and Gomorra, in which the people of Sodom form a mob around Lot's house, demanding that he send out the two angels for them to "know." The sin for which the city was subsequently destroyed is then assumed to have been homosexuality. Again, however, the actual attempted sin was violation of the laws of hospitality and rape of the angelic visitors (Judg. 19:14–29 is also a case involving rape).

Another verse regularly referenced is Lev. 18:22, translated in the NIV to read "Do not lie with a man as one lies with a woman; that is detestable." A more accurate translation reveals that the prohibited act is for two men to have sexual relations in a woman's bed—a restricted space limited to the woman and a specific partner—because it would make that particular bed ritually unclean. The issue is not *what* is being done, but *where*. Such verses are often quoted as evidence of God's rejection of all homosexual relationships, and it is not uncommon for some pastors to seek out the most radically exclusionary translations.

In the Christian scriptures, Paul writes to Christians in Rome and discusses the way some former Christians have returned to pagan traditions, including worship of the temple gods and involvement in ritualized sexual orgies that include same-sex encounters. What is sometimes translated as Paul's condemnation of "vile affections" more accurately refers to the orgiastic state of mind induced by some of the mystery cults (see Romans 1:26–27). For many conservative Christians, again, this is an irrefutable rejection of same-gender relationships as violations of a natural order. An alternative reading, however, focuses on the return to pagan temple practices and limits the condemned sexual behavior to heterosexual individuals engaging in same-sex relations—something indeed running counter to their own heterosexual orientation—not a commentary on same-gender-loving persons.

These and other passages, when translated as they are in the KJV and the NIV, leave one branch of Christians with virtually no alternative but to conclude that God condemns same-gender sexual behavior and, by extension, any related attraction. Consequently, individuals involved in such relationships must be viewed as having exercised their free will to choose sinful behavior. As a lifestyle choice, it then can and must be wholeheartedly rejected. A Pew Research Council poll in 2003 indicated that 58 percent of African Americans surveyed viewed homosexuality as a lifestyle choice (only white evangelicals polled higher numbers).[3] It is a view that leads clergy like Boston's Bishop Gilbert Thompson, President of Boston's Black Ministerial Alliance, to comment, "To say there is such a thing as a gay Christian is saying there's an honest thief."[4]

In contrast, alternate translations of these same passages, based on efforts to return to the original biblical languages and to rethink histories of translation, allow other groups of Christians to turn away from unilaterally rejectionist perspectives and to focus on additional biblical passages that emphasize Jesus's acceptance and embrace of all who turn to him. Within this worldview, homosexuality is intrinsic to someone's identity and being and is nothing to be rejected. This second group is more likely, as well, to accept emerging scientific explorations of the neurobiological and genetic bases of homosexuality—a view that the first group generally rejects out of hand.[5]

SOUNDS OF SILENCE…AND VOICE

For some African Americans growing up particularly during the years of legalized segregation the pressures on black communities from the outside contributed to intensified internal cohesion born of situational necessity. For example, bell hooks recalls: "The gay people we knew then did not live in separate subcultures; they lived in our small, segregated, black community where work was difficult to find, where black folks lived in densely populated neighborhoods, where many of us were poor. This poverty was important; it created a social context in which structures of dependence were important for everyday survival."[6]

Anthropologist Deirdre Crumbly remembers her grandmother saying, "You can be funny, but you can't be a fool." That is, you could be homosexual, but couldn't flout certain community norms. Everybody knew someone who was "funny," but it wasn't discussed because the person was, as she put it, "somebody's child." It was an ethos that writer Ann Allen Shockley has characterized as "Play it, but don't say it." The point was to avoid forcing a discussion in which familiar theologies would leave room for little but rejection. To characterize black communities as homophobic, therefore, overlooks the different ways in which communities sought and created ways to be inclusive.

As class differences within black communities met with emerging possibilities for the more affluent to move into new locations, some of this cohesiveness became more challenging to sustain. Even as people relocated, within faith communities what was often retained was the ethos of not asking and not telling. In this effort to accept through avoidance, what went unexamined was the impact on same-gender-loving members of the faith community. The arrangement demands, as activist Keith Boykin puts it, "a truce with the church that allows [same-gender-loving people] to serve quietly, and this conspiracy of silence enables the church to remain simultaneously the most homophobic institution in the black community and the most homo-tolerant."[7] It depended upon a necessary invisibility paralleling the racial invisibility described by Ralph Ellison, in which white Americans saw "only my surroundings, themselves, or figments of their imagination—indeed, everything and anything except me."[8]

To suffer an enforced minority status, embedded within another minority status, imposes a stigma from the very communities one expects to provide support. If the church was historically a refuge and source of upliftment, then the impact of this stigma is a particularly painful price to pay. Like all stigmas, the implication is that the person is not entirely human. If someone is less than fully human, it becomes acceptable to treat them as less and to exclude them from ordinary life activities. As one man explained, "I have to deal with the fact that I could be married with none of my family representing me there. I have to deal with that, and it hurts."[9] Such are the wounds of stigma.

This is equally true for same-gender-loving clergy. Speaking of a pastor friend, another man said, "He feels very, kinda like in limbo in a sense, because, at least for him as a minister, people look at him in the traditional black minister role. So they feel he should be a certain way and then he, as a minister, he's not even comfortable with how he goes before God and things like that." The process, as a whole, shames individuals into silence, often with emotionally damaging effects. "You have to look at yourself and say 'I'm not wrong, you know, I'm not a bad person; there's nothing bad about me in a sense but then, um, it's just like to be believe there is a higher power up there that is loving towards everyone.'" This silencing process, at its (relatively) most benign, is intended to keep everyone under one roof. Yet by ignoring this core dimension of identity, the unspoken message is that it is unspeakable.

In this book, D. Mark Wilson quotes "Herman" as describing the experience of having other congregants "sway away" from him because he is gay. The message required no speech to communicate the imposition of distance. An even more overt process surfaces when same-gender-loving people in a church find themselves confronted with having to sit through virulently homophobic sermons that both condemn them or try to preach them out of their identity. A sermon by Rev. Willie Wilson of Washington, D.C., for example, is regularly cited for its offensive descriptions of homosexual behavior and for its claim that "lesbianism is about to take over our community."[10]

Some clergy cloak homophobic preaching in the guise of "loving the sinner but hating the sin." It is, however, difficult if not impossible to separate out the actual target of the hatred, when on the receiving end. One interviewee responded by saying, "I thought I was being punished for it. God didn't like me, didn't want me to be happy. God made me sad. If God's all knowing, all powerful, so...I became so disillusioned with the whole idea of God or spirituality." Bishop Yvette A. Flunder of San Francisco characterizes the outcome of church-based homophobia as having "resulted in the destruction of self-esteem, open vicious attack against the personhood of countless individuals and their families and has produced self inflicted theological and physical violence, duplicity and inauthentic leadership (some leaders are themselves [same gender loving] SGL and or bi-sexual)."[11]

In response, as Wilson describes, some individuals leave the church altogether and seek alternate sources of support and spirituality, whether through a club or an entirely different religious tradition. Some go deeper into what has been called the "Down Low (DL)," usually referring to men who are gay but who conceal their sexual orientation and may have public involvements—including marriage—with women. As Edward Brown observes, some gay black men may present themselves as bisexual in order to gain the privileges enjoyed by heterosexual men.[12] Down Low can also refer to men who believe themselves to be heterosexual but just happen to have sex with other men. Gay men on the DL can also feel added pressure to act in hypermasculine ways. In each case, the person can present himself as straight and bypass the stigma imposed on same-gender-loving identity.

Sometimes a person chooses to come out within their family. Pressure from the white gay and lesbian movement to come out has challenged African American same-gender-loving communities in new ways. Some of this challenge has reflected racism within the white lesbian and gay communities and a related lack of understanding of the potential racialized fallout related to coming out. African American same-gender-loving individuals may be accused of betraying their race and undermining black families, for example. They may even be charged with wanting to be white since it is assumed African Americans have no tradition of homosexuality.[13] Although white gay and lesbian individuals can and do face estrangement from their families when they come out, they don't necessarily grasp the broader implications of such estrangement for their African American counterparts, for whom family networks can provide an essential buffer against the impact of a surrounding racist culture. Author Jewelle Gomez comments:

> We pay a heavy toll for being who we are and living with integrity. Being out means you are doing what your grandmother told you to do, which is not to lie. Black lesbians and gays who are out are not lying. But we pay high prices for our integrity. . . . [A]s Black gay women, we haven't been interested in removing ourselves from our families or communities because we understand the importance of that connection. . . . We straddle the fence that says we cannot be uplifters of the race and lesbians at the same time—that's what makes it so dangerous for our emotional health as Black lesbians.[14]

Some families respond with acceptance. One man characterized his grandfather as a Pentecostal minister who, nonetheless, came to terms with the homosexuality of the speaker and his cousin. No homophobic sermons were preached, no judgments rendered.

At the same time, acceptance of individuals with whom one has a direct personal relationship doesn't necessarily signify broader acceptance. For example, one black woman Baptist minister was simultaneously loving and supportive of gay friends while also voicing strongly negative views against homosexuality. Her reading of the Bible sanctioned harsh rejection of homosexuality while also calling for identification with the exploited and oppressed, for whom she is to seek justice. She saw no contradiction between these two stances.[15]

A truly deadly outcome of silence and silencing arose as the HIV/AIDS epidemic raged worldwide. Black churches faced a dilemma that seemed beyond resolution. Because the disease had become so firmly identified in the public imagination with gay men, and because homosexuality had been just as clearly bracketed in many churches as an abomination to be shunned, how could the presence of the disease in black communities be talked about? Bishop Kwabena Rainey Cheeks of Washington, D.C., recalls trying to get into churches during the 1980s, "going in the back door" by getting invited to health ministry fairs or to speak to the women's auxiliary or to the pastor.

It was the organization The Balm in Gilead[16]—an African American AIDS group that fosters HIV awareness in faith-based communities—that provided a way to reframe the issue. Balm in Gilead simply bypassed the question of how someone had contracted the disease. Instead, it defined its mission as enabling "thousands of churches to become leaders in preventing the transmission of HIV by providing comprehensive educational programs and offering compassionate support to encourage those infected to seek and maintain treatment." This approach, in turn, enabled faith communities to become centers for HIV/AIDS ministries, education, and compassion. Ironically, they could still require silence, insisting that it was unnecessary to address how the disease had entered one's body and life.

SAME-GENDER-LOVING RIGHTS AND MARRIAGE RITES

In the spring of 2004, the Massachusetts Supreme Judicial Court ruled four to three, in *Goodridge v. Department of Health,* that the "common benefits" clause in the state's constitution required that same-sex couples be granted marriage licenses. Writing for the majority, Chief Justice Margaret Marshall argued that the constitution "affirms the dignity and equality of all individuals" and "forbids the creation of second-class citizens." The court did not confer the right to marry on same-gender couples; rather, it affirmed that there were no grounds for denying that right, based on due process and equal protection under the law.

Bitter local and national debates followed, with church-based groups in particular weighing in. Despite efforts over the next few years by Governor Mitt Romney, some members of the state legislature, and the group VoteOn Marriage.org to amend the constitution to define marriage as existing only between "one man and one woman," the right to marry for same-sex couples in Massachusetts prevailed. Heading into the 2004 presidential election, conservative Christian groups mobilized not only among their own ranks, but also among heads of black churches. Rev. Al Sharpton would later charge that the Bush administration "tricked people in our community into homophobia so Bush would get re-elected. They used the gay community as a scapegoat."[17] Highly regarded groups like the Black Ministerial Alliance (BMA) in Boston and a San Francisco coalition of African American pastors issued statements opposing same-sex marriage.

Working with Kristian Mineau, president of the conservative Massachusetts Family Institute and a spokesman for VoteOnMarriage.org, the BMA supported initiatives to change the state's constitution to limit marriage to union between a man and a woman. The BMA president Bishop Thompson, also head of New Covenant Christian Church in Mattapan—one of the largest black congregations in the state—said, "We're weighing in on this because we're concerned with the epidemic rate of fatherlessness in America and in our community, and we don't think gay marriage helps that cause."[18]

Some black pastors tried to differentiate their stand against same-sex marriage from homophobia. Bishop Thompson argued, "As an American I defend the right of gay citizens to live as they choose under the law, but I do not believe that anyone has the right to change the age old institution of marriage and the family to suit a radical sexual agenda."[19] Bishop Harry Jackson Jr., founder and chair of the High Impact Leadership Coalition based in Beltsville, Maryland, defines the mission of the black church and its leaders as needing to "lead the way to protect America's moral compass and heal our nation."[20] In an interview with Tavis Smiley, host of talk shows on both public television and public radio, he said, "So what we're saying is, draw a boundary line around families, not 'We don't like gay people,' but rather, if we let this thing called family and culture in the black community keep sliding down the slippery slope it's going, what are we gonna have left? And we've got to start somewhere at changing America as far as blacks go."[21]

It is important to recognize the sincerity of these positions in their commitment to a specific vision of family and black community. That there is even recognition of the rights of same-gender-loving citizens represents a major step for these public figures. Indeed, I heard Bishop Thompson acknowledge, at a BMA meeting, that most families had gay members and friends—a new kind of public statement. In a move rarely recognized by the press, the Massachusetts coalition against same-sex marriage also voiced support for same-sex couples having access to legal protections and proposed sponsoring reciprocal beneficiary legislation to grant benefits such as hospital visitation and survivorship rights to any adult consenting couple.[22]

Nevertheless, for black same-gender-loving residents of Massachusetts, the opposition to same-sex marriage by groups like the BMA were deeply wounding. Pamela K. Johnson of Boston, for example, responded, "The idea that gay people are somehow on the list of major concerns eroding the black family is ridiculous. The real issues impacting our community impact us all, gay and straight." Christina Cobb, a financial consultant who comes from a long line of ministers, said, "When you have the Black Ministerial Alliance speaking against us, and they're the only black faces you're seeing speaking about marriage, we're up against a wall where we finally have to step up and say, 'We're not invisible.'"[23]

One of the thorniest debates sprang up over the question of whether same-sex marriage belonged under the umbrella of civil rights. Given the historic significance of the civil rights movement in rectifying racialized inequities in the United States, it was no surprise that those who argued yes found themselves confronting opposition from some black religious leaders. One of the more widely quoted responses came from Dwight McKissic, a Texas pastor and organizer of the "Not On My Watch Coalition"—a group of black pastors and leaders opposing same-sex unions. The comparison, McKissic insisted, was "insulting, offensive, demeaning, and racist." Homosexuals were "comparing their sin to my skin." The civil rights movement, he added, sprang from righteousness, while the gay rights movement sprang from "the pit of hell itself" and is a "satanic anointment," birthed from the anti-Christ who is himself homosexual.[24]

Some ministers insisted that the Rev. Martin Luther King Jr. would have been horrified at any attempt to link gay rights in general, and same-sex marriage in particular, to civil rights. Rev. Wesley A. Roberts, President Emeritus of the BMA, said, "To equate what is happening now to the civil rights struggle which blacks had to go through would be to belittle what we had gone through as a people."[25]

Author Keith Boykin, former president of the board of the National Black Justice Coalition—a Washington-based civil rights organization dedicated to fighting racism and homophobia—counterargued that Dr. King's widow, Coretta Scott King, was a strong supporter of civil rights protections for gays and lesbians. Lynn Cothren, spokesperson for Mrs. King and the King Center in Atlanta, added that, although Dr. King had not spoken publicly about his views on homosexuality, he had, in private conversations with his wife, voiced his concerns about anti-gay discrimination.[26] (It is not clear whether or not this support would have extended to marriage.)

Still, the rejection of linking gay rights to civil rights runs strong. Rev. Irene Munroe explains, "For many African Americans, the LGBTQ [Lesbian, Gay, Bisexual, Transgender, Queer] debate about the freedom to marry appears to be more than just a pimping of the civil rights movement to them. It also appears as the erasure of their history as a people who are still striving to get what they feel LGBTQ people already have—access to mainstream society."[27] Munroe adds that the feeling is intensified because so few white LGBTQ people take responsibility for their own racial privilege, and for racism among their ranks. Boykin concludes:

> True, the civil rights movement is not the same as the gay rights movement. Blacks are not the same as gays. And racism is not the same as homophobia. But that's not the point. No two groups suffer discrimination exactly the same way. Anti-Semitism, for example, differs from sexism, both of which differ from

racism. But we don't require Jews and women to prove their similarity to the black struggle in order to be protected by the law.

In the end, it matters not which group is most oppressed, which was first oppressed, or whether they are identically oppressed. What matters is that no group of people should be oppressed.[28]

The debate has divided black clergy and leadership. As we have seen, some have taken public stands opposing both the civil rights dimensions and same-sex marriage. The Rev. Jesse Jackson has limited his support to civil unions. In June 2008, Georgia's Congressman John Lewis, the National Association for the Advancement of Colored People (NAACP) Chairman Julian Bond, and the NAACP and Urban League denounced the Federal Marriage Amendment, an attempted amendment to the Constitution to define marriage in the United States as a union of one man and one woman. Sharpton and Lewis, however, have gone on to voice support for same-sex marriage. Mr. Bond has compared opposition to same-sex marriage to bans on interracial marriage, adding, "Marriage is a civil ceremony that apportions some rights and responsibilities to both parties. If for some reason you don't want me to marry in your church, that's OK, it's your church. But don't bring your religious bigotry into city hall."[29]

FROM REPARATIVE THERAPY TO WELCOMING CHURCHES

It comes as no surprise that the divergent readings of biblical sources filter throughout each of the orientations discussed so far and find expression in other equally divergent ways of thinking about healing and homosexuality in African American communities. For those who rely on KJV and NIV approaches to Biblical translation, once homosexuality is named and identified in a faith community, it is no longer invisible and there is little theological option except to try to eliminate or change it.

The very notion that homosexual identity can be removed relies on the assumption that homosexuality is a lifestyle choice that can be rejected. One approach, so-called reparative therapy, draws on psychoanalytic theory to claim that gay men are trying to heal their gender identity that was wounded by inadequate bonding to their father and excessive attachment to the mother. It assumes that heterosexuality is the only true driving force behind gender identity and sexual orientation.[30] (Note that reparative therapy has little to say about lesbian, bisexual, or transgender identity.) Also known as conversion therapy, it argues that God hates homosexual acts and has the power to change a person's orientation, having promised to answer the prayers of true believers. Consequently, prayer, conversion efforts, and related counseling are promoted as part of this therapeutic strategy by many conservative Christian therapists, ministers, and groups like Exodus International.

Actual methods also include promoting a close nonsexual bond with another same-gender adult to substitute for the seeming missing childhood bond. Ex-gay ministries have asserted high so-called cure rates primarily based on a person's not acting on his or her homosexual feelings or choosing to remain celibate. Some individuals become certain that they have transformed their sexual orientation. This conviction, however, almost always disappears over time, and can leave one depressed (sometimes to the point of attempting or committing suicide). As one man described his experience in a residence promoting reparative therapy:

> It was that experience I guess that really, really ate away at my foundation as a person. I've spent the last two years just trying to build it back up....I guess, yeah part of me still hates him [the program director] for messing up probably one of the most important points in my life....I ended up not even finishing school because I just couldn't handle it....I was too busy thinking about whether, you know, God's gonna kill me or something because of what I did.

The experience, in other cases, can actually allow the person to come to terms with, and accept, his or her homosexuality. It should be noted that professional groups like the American Psychiatric Association, the American Psychological Association, the American Counseling Association, the American Academy of Pediatrics, the American Medical Association, and the National Association of Social Workers have all banned reparative therapy.[31]

This ban holds little meaning among more conservative churches. Black pastors like Rev. Darryl Foster, founder of Witness for the World[32] in Atlanta—a ministry offering healing from homosexuality—argues that the Down Low phenomenon in the churches has resulted from the "feminization" of men in the United States and from the failure of ministers to address "sexual sin in the body of Christ." Foster says of himself, "I'm just as black as the day I was born, but I'm no longer homosexual. You can't deny that. You can look at me and immediately ascertain that I'm an African-American. However you can't look at me and make the same judgment that I'm homosexual. Because those characteristics are two different things; one is an assumed identity, one is a born identity."[33] He insists that the churches must stop ignoring the presence of same-gender-loving congregants, saying instead that, "When you ignore sin, you give it illegitimate authority to grow in the church."[34]

This approach represents a radical departure from the longstanding tradition of not asking and not telling. Instead, it pushes the question of identifying and confronting gay and lesbian church members. Pastor Michael A. Stevens Sr. of Charlotte, North Carolina, has challenged other pastors to confront "closet homosexuality" in the church.[35] In a Palm Sunday sermon in 2006, Bishop Alfred A. Owens of Greater Mount Calvary Holy Church, a black Baptist church in Washington, D.C., preached, "It takes a real man to confess Jesus as Lord and Savior. I'm not talking about no faggot or no sissy. I mean a real man who has made up their mind...I'm talking about the straight men."[36] He called all such man up to the altar, such that any man remaining seated was, by default, identifying himself publicly as gay.

Less than a year later, this kind of call took the form of one of Bishop Owens's congregants emailing him to out over one hundred church members—most of them men—as same-gender-loving. "The following people I am asking you to monitor very closely," she wrote, "and my prayer is that you will sit them down from their ministries, because they are ushering in the presence of sin, lies, a spirit of homosexuality and sexual spirits." A former church member commented, "My name was not on the list...but I think it is horrible...We give, pay tithes, dues and whatever, and this is how we are treated. This is discrimination, humiliation, and just mean."[37] Bishop Owens responded by calling a meeting of those who had been named to ask which among them sought help to be free of a homosexual lifestyle.[38] Such a choice is viewed as the most essential step toward healing *from* being a same-gender-loving person.

In a parallel move, Keith Boykin and Jasmyne Cannick wrote a series of articles profiling nine prominent black pastors known for their homophobic pronouncements, speculating over their possibly being closeted same-gender-loving individuals. Boykin explained, "When closeted public figures use their notoriety to promote vicious homophobia, I believe we have the right to expose their hypocrisy.... Your right to privacy ends when you violate my right to liberty.[39] Cannick, addressing critiques that she and Boykin had given no advance warning about their series, replied, "Well, I don't recall a memo ever coming across my desk saying that this Sunday's sermon was going to condemn me to hell.[40]

Bishop Yvette A. Flunder of San Francisco lamented the dynamics at Greater Mount Calvary and pointed to "a psychosis that permeates many churches with regard to the presence and involvement of SGL people, who have great love for God and for their church communities."[41] Bishop Flunder's church is part of a growing movement known as "Welcoming," "Reconciling," and "Whosoever Churches."[42]

Ministers like Bishops Flunder and Cheeks focus on a theology built on "the radical inclusiveness of Jesus Christ—seeing Jesus as a radical person who did not differentiate or segregate."[43] Bishop Cheeks argues that, "the 'theology of Jesus' is inclusive, but the 'theology about Jesus' is generally selective." Who, he asks, is not permitted to sit at the table of God? "Does [a church] ordain women who so diligently serve in that church? Or are they only able to serve the food, but not sit at the table? What about gays, lesbians, and bisexuals? Is it all right for them to sing in the choir or to play the piano, but not to sit at the table? Should I even mention the word transgender? Do they even get invited into the room?"[44] Rev. Dennis Wiley and

Rev. Dr. Christine Wiley, Baptist ministers in Washington, D.C., provide a supportive place for same-gender-loving parishioners. Dennis Wiley observes, "Jesus says nothing about the question of sexual orientation, but he does say a lot [about] loving one's neighbor and how we should treat one's neighbor." He argues, as well, that the church emphasizes its congregants' African roots, hoping to make them even more aware of the injuries caused by discrimination.[45]

One man described the experience of being part of a welcoming church, saying, "That's what makes my church unique, because everyone knows all the people in the church that are [gay, lesbian, bisexual, transgender] GLBT and we are not treated any differently. Um, there's never nothing in the sermon that's said to make anyone in the congregation feel uncomfortable. Pastor, she's an excellent preacher, she's great, she's fantastic. She says, 'God doesn't care who you are, what you are, and what you do, 'cause Love, God, never changes.' It's always been, it's made me feel really good, you know what I mean?"

Reconciling congregations like Union United Methodist Church in Boston have a long history of social justice and activist work. Prince Hall, founder of black Freemasonry, and David Walker, who wrote his historic antislavery *Appeal* in 1829, were both members of the congregation. The church was also a stop on the Underground Railroad network. The church, in the 1980s, called for divestiture from South African businesses. In 2000, under the leadership of Reverend Ted Lockhart, it became "the first black congregation in United Methodism to declare itself reconciling and thus welcoming to all God's children without exception to sexual orientation."[46]

Union United Methodist characterizes itself as recognizing all humans as created in the image of God, and as aspiring "to follow Jesus, who welcomed, received and stood with the oppressed, the disinherited and scorned persons of his day." Additionally, given the "particular invisibility" of "Black lesbians and gay men, and all other homosexual persons who confess Jesus Christ as Lord and Saviour" within the African American community, the church particularly affirms their full participation and seeks to advocate for their rights, needs, and concerns. "We hope," the statement of inclusion adds, "with God's grace to be instruments of reconciliation to all persons who, because of prejudice, racism, homophobia or ignorance, find themselves in exile from the family of God and the household of Christian faith and service."[47] The approach to fellowship, says Rev. Martin D. McLee, draws on meanings based in black culture. McClee has opened the church's doors for the annual Boston Pride Interfaith Service.

Because the transformation of a church can mean going against a long-standing tradition of silence, overt rejection, or both, churches like Bishop Flunder's—City of Refuge United Church of Christ—have proposed specific steps for same-gender-loving people and their allies to take, to bring about radical inclusivity.[48] Other groups and authors have addressed these issues specifically in relation to black churches.[49] It is in such lived reconciliation and welcome that healing is seen to be grounded.

CLOSING THOUGHTS

The lack of reconciliation between readings of the Bible and related expressions of theology through the different churches represents a living wound in the body of black church experience. To date, a meta-theology that would foster mutual welcome has yet to be formulated. And still, it is in the diversities of black experience that meanings of healing in relation to same-gender-loving African Americans are being articulated.

Emilie Townes has dwelled at length with the meanings of an ethic of care and the imperative of community in the course of healing. The importance of communal lament includes, I think, the need to lament the injuries unwittingly inflicted by men and women of God—not only to the same-gender-loving members of their congregations, but to the heterosexual members, and to themselves. It is to recognize the unidentified stigmata of stigma, the despair and depression of unwelcomed, unacknowledged selves. It is to look at how one can be displaced while in place. It is to look for the impact of this suffering in what Albert Raboteau refers to as both the body personal and the body social. And, it is to see that love of self, love of other, and love of God and God's people are all part of the same-gender-loving body, and therefore to be honored. It is, ultimately, to conclude that there is no one too gay for the church.

NOTES

1. Unless otherwise specified, interview quotes are from conversations with gay men of color, conducted in 2001 and 2002 by Melissa Hackman while she was a researcher with the Boston Healing Landscape Project, a program directed by the author.

2. In Tracy Baim, "Black Groups Push for Gay Marriage Rights," *Windy City Times*, May 26, 2004, http://www.windycitymediagroup.com/gay/lesbian/news/ARTICLE.php?AID=5066 (accessed February 10, 2008).

3. Christine McCarthy McMorris, "Black Pastors Bridle at Gay Marriage," *Religion in the News* 7, no. 2 (2004): http://www.trincoll.edu/depts/csrpl/RINVOL7No2/BlackPastorsGay%20Marriage.htm (accessed February 10, 2008).

4. Michael Paulson, "Black Clergy Rejection Stirs Gay Marriage Backers," *The Boston Globe*, February 10, 2004, http://www.boston.com/news/local/articles/2004/02/10/black_clergy_rejection_stirs_gay_marriage_backers?mode=PF (accessed February 10, 2008).

5. This section draws on Ontario Consultants on Religious Tolerance, "What the Bible Says about Homosexuality," http://religioustolerance.org/hom_bibl.html (accessed February 10, 2008). This source, along with related links, are particularly

useful in providing detailed analyses of how biblical passages in both the Hebrew Bible and the Christian New Testament have been translated and applied by different constituencies. See also Mary E. Wood, "How We Got This Way: The Sciences of Homosexuality and the Christian Right," *Journal of Homosexuality* 38. no. 3 (2000): pp. 19–40.

6. bell hooks, "Reflections on Homophobia & Black Communities," *Out/Look* (Summer 1988): p. 23.

7. Keith Boykin, "Whose Dream?" *The Village Voice*, May 24, 2004, http://www. villagevoice.com/news/0421,boykin,53751,1.html (accessed February 2, 2008).

8. In Mab Segrest, "Race and the Invisible Dyke," in *Dangerous Liaisons: Blacks, Gays, and the Struggle for Equality*, ed. Eric Brandt (New York: New Press, 1999), p. 49. This kind of invisibility occurs, as well, in the Nation of Islam. See Irene Monroe, "Louis Farrakhan's Ministry of Misogyny and Homophobia," in *The Farrakhan Factor: African-American Writers on Leadership, Nationhood, and Minister Louis Farrakhan*, ed. Amy Alexander (New York: Grove Press, 1998), pp. 275–97.

9. For a classic discussion of the process and effects of stigmatizing, see Erving Goffman, *Stigma: Notes on the Management of Spoiled Identity* (Englewood Cliffs, N.J.: Prentice Hall, 1963).

10. Katherine Volin, "Equality Maryland's Marylanders of Color Collective," *Washington Blade*, July 29, 2005, http://www.equalitymaryland.org/mocc/news/2005/ 2005_07_29_b.shtml (accessed February 7, 2008). In response, local gay activists cancelled a Millions More Movement meeting that had been scheduled at his church.

11. Rev. Dr. Yvette A. Flunder and Rev. Dr. Wyatt I. Greenlee, "The Fellowship's Response to Mt. Calvary (DC)," *The Fellowship*, http://radicallyinclusive.com/page_ to_print.cfm?id=2031 (accessed February 10, 2008).

12. Edward Brown II, "We Wear the Mask: African American Contemporary Gay Male Identities," *Journal of African American Studies* 9, no. 2 (2005): p. 31.

13. Michael Hendricks, "Differences in Disclosure of Sexuality among African American and White Gay/Bisexual Men: Implications for HIV/AIDS Prevention," *AIDS Education and Prevention* 12, no. 6 (2000): p. 2.

14. Jewelle L. Gomez and Barbara Smith, "Black Lesbians Look in Their Own Backyards," *Out/Look* (Spring 1990): pp. 35, 37.

15. hooks, "Reflections on Homophobia," pp. 23–24.

16. See http://www.balmingilead.org/home.asp.

17. Derrick Z. Jackson, "Bible Lessons These Clergy Forgot," *CommonDreams.org*, February 11, 2004, http://www.commondreams.org/views04/0211–02.htm (accessed February 10, 2008).

18. Paulson, "Black Clergy Rejection," 2004.

19. Ethan Jacobs, "Opening the Next Front of the Marriage Battle," *Bay Windows*, June 18, 2005, http://www.mglpc.org/printer.php?id=293 (accessed February 10, 2008).

20. See http://www.thehopeconnection.org/welcome.php.

21. Irene Monroe, "Gulf between Black, Gay Communities Narrowing," http:// www.irenemonroe.com/2007/06/21/gulf-between-black-gay-communities-narrowing/ (accessed February 10, 2008).

22. Jacobs, "Opening the Next Front."

23. Paulson, "Black Clergy Rejection."

24. Debra Dickerson, "Black Ministers Get Religion about HIV/AIDS," *Mother Jones*, October 12, 2007, http://www.motherjones.com/mojoblog/archives/2007/10/5762_black_ministers.html (accessed February 10, 2008).

25. McMorris, "Black Pastors Bridle."

26. Keith Boykin, "Miami's Black Ministers Group Distorts Gay Rights," *keithboykin.com*, August 1, 2002, http://www.keithboykin.com/arch/2002/08/01/miamis_black_mi (accessed February 10, 2008).

27. Irene Monroe, "No Marriage between Black Ministers and Queer Community," *The Witness Magazine*, June 2, 2004, http://www.thewitness.org/agw/monroe060204.html (accessed February 10, 2008).

28. Boykin, "Miami's Black Ministers."

29. Irene Monroe, "Gulf between Black, Gay Communities Narrowing," http://www.irenemonroe.com/2007/06/21/gulf-between-black-gay-communities-narrowing/ (accessed February 10, 2008).

30. Chuck Bright, "Deconstructing Reparative Therapy: An Examination of the Processes Involved When Attempting to Change Sexual Orientation," *Clinical Social Work Journal* 32, no. 4 (2004), p. 478.

31. Ibid., p. 472.

32. See http://witnessfortheworld.org.

33. Anon., "African-American Ex-Gay Pastor Explodes the Myth That Homosexuality Is No Different Than Race," *LifeSiteNews.com*, Friday May 23, 2003, http://www.lifesite.net/ldn/2003/may/03052304.html (accessed February 3, 2008).

34. Valerie Lowe, "COGIC Pastor Addresses Closet Homosexuality," *Charisma*, March 30, 2007, http://www.charismamag.com/soul-food/033007.html (accessed February 10, 2008).

35. Ibid.

36. Colbert I. King, "Gays, God and Bishop Owens," *WashingtonPost.com*, Saturday, May 13, 2006, p. A17, http://www.washingtonpost.com/wp-dyn/content/article/2006/05/12/AR2006051201657.html (accessed February 15, 2008).

37. Lou Chibbaro Jr., "Outing Campaign Roils D.C. Black Baptist Church," *Washington Blade*, January 30, 2008, http://www.washblade.com/thelatest/thelatest.cfm?blog_id=16289 (accessed February 10, 2008).

38. Flunder and Greenlee, "The Fellowship's Response."

39. Keith Boykin, "The Big Gay Outing Debate," *keithboykin.com*, October 4, 2005, http://www.keithboykin.com/arch/2005/10/04/the_big_gay_out (accessed February 10, 2008).

40. Jasmyne Cannick, "Much Ado over Outing," *Lesbian News* 31, no. 4 (2005), p. 32.

41. Flunder and Greenlee, "The Fellowship's Response."

42. Gary David Comstock, *A Whosoever Church: Welcoming Lesbians and Gay Men into African American Congregations* (Louisville: Westminster John Knox Press, 2001).

43. Anon., "Profiles in Courage: Bishop Kwabena Rainey Cheeks," *The Body: The Complete HIV/AIDS Resource*, February 23, 2006, http://www.thebody.com/african_american/profiles/kcheeks.html (accessed February 7, 2008).

44. Bishop Kwabena Rainey Cheeks, "Understanding the Radical Inclusiveness of Jesus," http://www.portofharlem.net/newsinnerlightministries.html (accessed February 7, 2008).

45. Volin, "Equality Maryland's Marylanders."

46. Anon., "A Brief History of United Methodist Church," http://www.gbgm-umc.org/unionboston/unionhistory.htm (accessed February 3, 2008).

47. Union Church Council, "Union United Methodist Church Statement as a Reconciling and Inclusive Church," http://www.gbgm-umc.org/unionboston/drftstmt.htm (accessed February 3, 2008).

48. Anon., "12 Steps to Radical Inclusivity," *The Fellowship*, http://www.radical lyinclusive.com/page_to_print.cfm?id=2008 (accessed February 10, 2008).

49. See, for example, Yvette A. Flunder, *Where the Edge Gathers: Building a Community of Radical Inclusion*, (Cleveland: Pilgrim Press, 2005), and Horace L. Griffin, *Their Own Receive Them Not: African American Lesbians & Gays in Black Churches* (Cleveland: The Pilgrim Press, 2006). For a list of self-defined welcoming churches with related links, see http://www.clgs.org/3/welcoming_churches.html.

PART V

Finding and Making Wellness

CHAPTER 10

——— ❖ ———

Seeking Help for the Body in the Well-Being of the Soul

Rosemary D. Gooden

Beginning with my own quest for healing, my chapter explores black women's beliefs about and experiences of religious, or spiritual, healing beginning with the nineteenth-century divine healing movement.[1] It ends with a discussion of forms of spiritual healing that complement, yet are distinctive from, the Christian practice of healing through the prayer of faith that includes the laying on of hands and anointing with oil for healing.

Healing has many components. It can include attending a patient and advocating on behalf of that patient to change the medical establishment. Healing can occur in unexpected and nontraditional places, namely, in prison and through informal networks of African American women outside a church setting, such as communities of women who meet to offer one another mutual support. Healing practices are also facilitated by self-help literature as well as such complementary therapies as Qigong, meditation, and aromatherapy.

There are many questions to explore. How do African Americans experience health and wholeness? What do faith and healing mean to contemporary African Americans? Who is a healer? Where does religious faith fit into the healing process?

A one-dimensional view of healing becomes multidimensional when we listen to how African American women experience mind–body–spirit healing. For instance, "Stitch 'n Bitch" groups meet to socialize and knit. The Harlem Knitting Circle was the only organized knitting group I found through an internet search. This group, unlike the Stitch 'n Bitch groups, mentors young knitters and crocheters and also knits for charity, supporting such endeavors as the Red Scarf Project for orphans.[2] The importance of these informal networks is recognized even by public health programs such as the Center for Minority Health in the Graduate School of Public Health at the University of Pittsburgh and the Arthur Ashe Institute for Urban Health.

They identified two important resources in African American communities for preventive health care and education: barber shops and beauty salons.[3]

Faith healing, conjuring, doctoring traditions, and root working remain important in the healing arts of African American women healers. Through it all, faith, whether biblical or a strong conviction rooted in various cultural experiences and belief systems, is vital to healing, health, and the hope that leads to a good life. What follows are stories of black women, past and present, seeking healing, being healed, and practicing healing.

MY STORY

My father died of colorectal cancer on Thursday, February 1, 1996, in a Catholic hospital in suburban Chicago. As he lay dying, an Episcopal priest and friend asked my mother what she wanted for my father. My mother, as one would expect, said she wanted him to be healed. This was a very different experience from what had occurred a few days earlier when a Pentecostal minister asked my father if he was saved before praying for him, leaving me angry at the way he intruded upon a somber and meaningful death vigil. When my father died, our priest said a prayer, "Ministration at the Time of Death" from the *Book of Common Prayer*. Her pastoral presence brought comfort and peace to my mother and me.

My parents had been married for 53 years and my mother was, as one would expect, absolutely devastated and overwhelmed with grief. Although individual members of my parents' church visited, prayed, and offered support, I lamented the fact that there was no organized grief support group that would help my mother deal with her bereavement. I searched for a grief support group for myself. About 18 months later, I started attending a recently organized grief support group sponsored by my diocese through its counseling center.

Bereavement was not the only health issue I faced that year. A toxic work environment led me to seek treatment for a chronic illness that manifested in acute, debilitating pain. Although I experienced some relief from prescribed medication, I began researching alternative and complementary medicine, looking for a way to cope with stress. I tried aromatherapy, Chinese herbal medicine, acupuncture, and massage therapy. I also prayed, but it seemed that God did not hear my prayers. Then I read a meditation that reflected on the words of an exorcist: "Evil is a palpable force in the universe."[4] These words were like a balm in Gilead for me. They gave me new perspective on my work-related suffering. "Deliver *me* from evil" became my healing mantra.

My personal quest for healing in my life and family led to an academic study of religion and healing. I explored the divine healing movement of the nineteenth century in a book about the life and healing ministry of evangelist Sarah Ann Freeman Mix (1832–1884). She was the first known African

American healing evangelist and the first woman known to have had a full-time healing ministry.

"GO WORK IN MY VINEYARD": SARAH MIX AND THE DIVINE HEALING MOVEMENT

Religious healing was a well-established feature of early Christianity and it is documented in church history. Along with a related belief in miracles, religious healing has been the subject of sustained debate, criticism, and controversy, beginning in the sixteenth century when the idea of a limited age of miracles emerged. By 1855 through 1890, in American Protestantism, attitudes toward miracles changed dramatically. Beginning in the mid-nineteenth century, the possibility was raised of a religious role for modern miracles as a continuing supernatural presence of God in the world. This view offered a context for a new Protestant interest in healing.

The divine healing movement in America was also known as faith healing, faith cure, or simply healing movement. It came into existence in the 1850s when an interdenominational group of lay persons and preachers, who were also active in the Holiness movement, began systematically teaching and practicing faith healing. This group included Charles Cullis, an Episcopalian homeopathic physician, William E. Boardman, a Presbyterian minister; A. J. Gordon, a Baptist missionary, Carrie Judd, an Episcopalian; and Sarah Mix. However, faith healing did not become a significant movement and religious phenomenon in America until the 1870s when the movement became institutionalized. Faith healing became institutionalized and popularized through healing homes, faith-healing conventions, and a plethora of healing magazines and newspaper articles with collections of healing testimonies.

Faith-healing advocates and practitioners believed in the ongoing relevance of the promise of Jesus in Mark 16:18: "They will lay hands on the sick, and they will recover." The promise of healing through "the prayer of faith" in James 5:14–15 is often cited: "Are any among you sick? They should call for the elders of the church and have them pray over them, anointing them with oil in the name of the Lord. The prayer of faith will save the sick, and the Lord will raise them up; and anyone who has committed sins will be forgiven" (New Revised Standard Version). Faith healing evangelists of this period did not refer to themselves as healers. Rather, they viewed themselves mainly as people of prayer who prayed with the sick and sometimes, in faithfulness to the biblical command in James, anointed with oil and performed laying on of hands.

For many faith-healing practitioners, healing of the body and the soul went together. Some used medicine in their healing practices, while others relied solely on prayer and laying on of hands. Generally, this focus on prayer remains the standard today. The belief that the laying on of hands and anointing with oil would result in healing informed the practice of the healing ministry of Sarah Mix.

Sarah Ann Freeman Mix published and edited *Victory Through Faith,* a monthly journal on faith healing. She wrote an eight-page leaflet, *In God We Trust,* and contributed articles for other faith-healing journals. Her *Faith Cures, and Answers to Prayer* was published in 1882. It includes an account of Mix's healing from tuberculosis, other healing testimonials, and a newspaper account of her ministry as a healing evangelist. Her spiritual autobiography, *The Life of Mrs. Edward Mix, Written by Herself,* was written in 1880, although the book was not published until 1884 after her death. As a faith-healing evangelist, Sarah Mix reflects a historical continuum of healing that includes not only faith healing but, equally important, a complex and multifaceted African American healing tradition that dates from Africa and continues to the present day.[5]

As historian Albert Raboteau has noted, blacks' views about healing, medicine, and religion have their roots in Africa. These beliefs and their accompanying practices were imported to the American colonies during the Atlantic slave trade and continued even as blacks adopted and assimilated Christianity and other religious traditions. Herbalism, astrology, and conjure, for example, flourished in slave quarters and were viewed not only as being compatible with Christianity, but also as complementing it.

African Americans connected faith and healing, whether or not they were actively involved in the faith-healing movement as practitioners or were ministered to by a faith-healing evangelist. In fact, the belief in God's power to heal was a long-established belief among African Americans. Sharla Fett points out this connection in the conversion narrative of a former slave woman that included an account of her healing from swollen limbs by "Doctor Jesus." She prays, asking God to relieve her misery, and testifies:

> The spirit directed me to get some peach-tree leaves and beat them up and put them about my limbs. I did this, and in a day or two that swelling left me, and I haven't been bothered since. More than this, I don't remember ever paying out but three dollars for doctor's bills in my life either for myself, my children, or my grandchildren. Doctor Jesus tells me what to do.

In her examination of black women's healing work, especially herbalism and bedside care, Fett points out that during slavery black women performed a variety of healing roles, including that of hospital nurse, midwife, and doctoress. These roles were performed within the plantation community for slaveholders and slaves alike. Whether routine everyday tasks such as nursing and treating injuries, "doctoring," or conjuration, all relied on spiritual empowerment for effectiveness, and all forms of healing were expressions of religious belief. According to Fett, "Many women healers, as well as some men, spoke in an explicitly Christian language of God working through them."[6]

Questions about the meaning of prayer, faith, and healing, however, persist. What is prayer? Is it efficacious for bodily healing? What do we mean by healing? Among the current definitions of Christian healing, Episcopal priest John Koenig provides the following definition:

> Healing events are daily signs of the divine mercy that is surging through our world and guiding it toward its final perfection. This is true whether they take place by the sharing of chicken soup, the performance of delicate surgery, or the laying on of hands in a service of worship.[7]

Margaret Guenther, an Episcopal priest, provides some insights about intercessory prayer for healing and easing the pain of suffering:

> When we pray our intercessions, we are not bargaining with God, nor are we engaged in magical thinking. It is important to remember that we cannot pray people well, even though we know situations where the most fervent prayers seemed to go unheard or were answered in a way that we cannot understand. It is cheap comfort to pretend that any amount of prayer can magically make everything all right, bring swift comfort to the grieving, and ease the pain of the suffering. It is excruciating to watch at the foot of the cross, yet if we live long enough and let ourselves experience life fully, we will find ourselves at some point in that desolate place. If nothing else, intercession holds the sufferer in the embrace of the community. The suffering is not lessened, but it is more bearable when one does not watch alone.[8]

In *Conversations with God: Two Centuries of Prayers by African Americans*, James Melvin Washington stated that prayer is conversation with God.[9] This is a basic individual view of prayer; it's how those who pray define this spiritual practice. However, Washington expands this idea by suggesting that prayer is not just a personal spiritual practice but a communal conversation that reflects the history of African Americans. Washington writes:

> It is a mistake to see these prayers only as the personal conversations that each of these African-Americans has had with God. They are certainly this. But from a cultural and social standpoint...these prayers represent major moods in the complex spiritual history of a people who have obvious reasons to be angry with God....The prayers...are attempts to converse with God about the joys, burdens and hopes of being African people in a racist society. All these prayers trusted that the Lord would make a way somehow.[10]

A case in point is the following excerpt from Fred C. Lofton's "We Need Thee, Lord Jesus, as Never Before."

> Have mercy on us, Lord. We're stealing away because the Black community seems to be under siege again—dope running rampant in our community;

hoodlums and thugs have frightened our women; our churches are being broken into; houses are being burglarized; and we seem, our Father, to be destined to destroy ourselves....Is there a Balm in Gilead? Is there a word from the Lord for those at the bottom of the ladder? Is there a word? Is there a healing word, a word of hope.[11]

"HEALING SERVICE": DR. JOHNYE BALLENGER

I know that I am not in control of everything that happens. I must do my best, of course, always...but I am not alone in the work of heal-ing...Use my hands, O Lord, I surrender to you.

—*Johnye Ballenger, MD*[12]

Dr. Johnye Ballenger, a healer and activist, provides healing service to patients in her private practice and to those she sees at the South End Health Center in Boston one afternoon a week. Ballenger's medical practice is rooted in respect for her patients. A pediatrician, Dr. Ballenger embodies respect and teaches it to her patients and to residents.[13]

The South End Health Center in Boston serves black, Asian, white, and Latino families Dr. Ballenger greets each patient by introducing herself, ask-ing their name, and asking "How may I help today?" Respect and care of patients also are extended to their families when they bring their children to the clinic. Ballenger becomes an activist whose healing service includes advocacy for the patient.

The Martinez family is a case in point. Rosa Martinez, a 10-year-old pa-tient from Revere, Massachusetts, needed follow-up care after her appoint-ment. Dr. Ballenger spent an inordinate amount of time on the phone trying to arrange follow-up care at a hospital that was much nearer the Martinez home so Mrs. Martinez and her three young children would not have to travel through the snow back to Boston the next day. Although she encountered resistance from other doctors, Dr. Ballenger succeeded in getting further care for Rosa Martinez. When asked about other doctors who may look down on her efforts, Dr. Ballenger responded: "I don't *allow* there to be hierarchy! I'll be a slave to no one. You can't *disrespect* me!"[14] This, I suggest, is an example of self-healing, an ongoing practice, even as one seeks to heal others. And this is not unique to Dr. Ballenger or other physicians. It's part of what it means to be African American in the United States.

Dr. Ballenger chose to work at Boston City Hospital for her pediatric resi-dency. It was the place she wanted to be. She described her professional goals in this way: "I was very happy at BCH. I wanted to give respectful care to patients who didn't always get it. I also knew that I could model that kind of care to other health professionals, including doctors. Actually, what I really wanted to do...was give the care that I would want if I were the patient."[15]

When she talks about her experiences with adolescents who behave in a manner that is disrespectful of themselves and others, Dr. Ballenger says she treats these patients with respect and compassion. Her Catholicism is part of her response to them: "There is Christ, the deity in all of us, and I try to address the divinity in everyone. I always have in the back of my mind, the depth of my soul, the search for that part of the person that transcends the outer body." [16]

Dr. Ballenger's description of one seminar shows that she is consistently compassionate and respectful. Indirectly, she teaches respect. Respect extends to her students to whom she tries to teach respect for self, for one another, and for the patient. In the seminar, Dr. Ballenger demonstrated a key aspect of practicing medicine: relationships. She explained: "Good practice also requires that doctors enter into 'relationships' with their patients, that they actually 'see' them. Good practice requires that doctors be respectful, tender, and gracious."[17]

Dr. Johnye Ballenger embodied all of these characteristics. Moreover, Dr. Ballenger practiced faith healing. Can the doctor heal the sick with faith? Yes. Her story will help African American women preparing for a professional career in medicine and healing in a racist and sexist profession and society.

HEALING THE DISFIGURED: REV. CAROLYN YARD

That's one thing about working here…You develop a lot of strength. But I don't think it's my own strength. I think it's because God has placed me here. This is where I'm supposed to be.

—*Rev. Carolyn Yard*[18]

I learned about Rev. Carolyn Yard, the first official chaplain at the Burn Center of New York Hospital–Cornell Medical Center, in the late 1990s, the period of my quest for personal healing and the beginning of my academic study of religion and healing. What struck me immediately was her decision to work in the Burn Center. Like her colleagues, initially, she did not want to work there but changed her mind when she saw there was a need. After praying about it, she decided that she would meet that need as the chaplain.

Her journey to chaplaincy in a burn unit was one of self-healing. Following two surgeries, on both wrists, for carpal tunnel syndrome, Yard was unable to continue her insurance job that included rigorous travel and writing lengthy reports. Her specialty was helping disabled persons resume productive lives. She soon would continue doing this in another capacity.

Yard, who had always wanted to be a nurse, enrolled in United Christian College and earned masters and doctorate degrees. Her studies enabled her to develop the pastoral skills she would need to be a hospital chaplain. "It's like it was my destiny," says Yard. "The pieces just came together." Rev. Yard brings gifts of healing through listening and empathizing with her patients. Her ministry goes far beyond helping burn victims cope with disfigurement, pain, and mortality. Like Dr. Ballenger, Yard has a caring relationship with her patients and their families. Her first encounter with a burn victim was with a four-year-old boy who had been doused with lye by his mother who was aiming at her boyfriend. The lye ate much of his left eye and the skin around his eye. Yard assured the mother that God had forgiven her. The two women forged a relationship that included regular contact nearly a year and a half after the accident.

Rev. Carolyn Yard is influenced by two rich traditions in her chaplaincy ministry. One is that of the Seventh-Day Adventists, which has a rich heritage of health reform dating from the nineteenth century; the other is a contemporary emphasis on available resources for health and wellness. Now a "born-again Pentecostal," Yard brings the charismatic tradition to her ministry. How does a chaplain deal with the pain that burn victims endure? Douglas Martin, the journalist who interviewed Yard wrote: "The impact of burns sears to the core of people's conception of identity, going to the very meaning of being human. If you believed you were formed in the image of God, what are you now? What kind of God would allow this to happen?" Yard sees her mission as to help those whose suffering is often tormenting and to offer them emotional and spiritual support.

Yard discusses a 48-year-old man who scalded his feet and didn't seek treatment immediately. When he finally came to the burn center, he couldn't breathe without a ventilator, and the pain was unbearable. Yard prayed "that God [would take] him out of here. [She] came in Monday and he had died. It was a relief." Yard views this as "a form of healing."[19]

Yard continues her chaplaincy at the Burn Center of New York Hospital–Cornell Medical Center. In 2003 she was appointed to the Board of the New York Regional Organ Donor Network. Her primary responsibilities include reviewing policies and programs and educating minority communities about the importance of organ donation A recent program was a symposium, "African-Americans and End of Life Care Decisions," held at an African Methodist Episcopal (AME) church in Jamaica, New York. Yard also participated in another symposium, "Saving the Body and Soul: Religious, Cultural and Ethical Perspectives on Organ and Tissue Donation." Organ Donation is one of the health care issues about which African American communities need more awareness.[20]

LAYING ON OF HANDS: REV. DIANE LACY WINLEY

Women find it easier to use prayer and mediation to find energy, strength, and healing.

—*Rev. Diane Lacy Winley*[21]

In June 1999, the *New York Times* included a supplement on Women's Health, which included an article by Winifred Gallagher, entitled "Seeking Help for the

Body in the Well-Being of the Soul." As an African American woman, I was deeply moved by and gratified to read about Rev. Diane Lacy Winley, also African American, who, at the time, was the coordinator of the Wellness Center at Riverside Church in New York City. She was also identified as a board member of New York City's Health and Hospitals Corporation. She is still a board member and is now co-pastor of Good-Shepherd-Faith Presbyterian Church, a multicultural congregation that worships in English and Korean.[22]

The photograph that accompanied the article got my attention right away. Winley is shown looking attentively at an African American woman who is kneeling during a Sunday morning "laying on of hands" service in a chapel at Riverside Church. Most of those who attend this Sunday morning service are women. Meditation, accompanied by aromatherapy and music, opens the service followed by communion with laying on of hands. At the conclusion of the service, congregants gather in the Wellness Center to discuss a variety of health issues, including nutrition and cancer. The following is its mission statement, stated on the web site: "Based on God's call to wholeness, the Wellness Center is committed to helping the staff, congregation and community attain and maintain high level wellness and explore the many dimensions of healing for the body, mind, and spirit." The web site also states: "The Wellness Program has been developed in the tradition of Christian healing and wholeness, and offers a wide variety of groups and services in an ecumenical and interfaith spirit through spiritual practice, education, small groups, and health maintenance and prevention services."[23] They offer a range of programs: a writers' workshop, acupuncture, holistic health and healing, Qigong, and healing touch and prayer.

The mission of the Wellness Center illustrates reframing healing as wellness, self-healing, and complementary medicine. Healing Touch and Prayer, a Writers' Workshop, and Qigong, for example, show how in the Christian tradition the concept of healing and faith for healing is expanded. This healing ritual is an example of expanding the concept of healing and enhancing the traditional laying on of hands with aromatherapy, music, and meditation at a Sunday morning church service. Prayer includes meditation. As Ann and Barry Ulanov write in their book, *Primary Speech: A Psychology of Prayer*:

> Everybody prays. People pray whether or not they call it prayer. We pray every time we ask for help, understanding, or strength, in or out of religion. God hears all the voices that speak out of us—our vocal prayer, the prayer said in our minds, the unvoiced longing rising from our hearts, the many voices of which we are not conscious but which cry out eloquently. The God to whom we pray came to us in the flesh and speaks to us now in the flesh of our human self and our world. And even if we do not pray to the God of Scripture or traditional religion, still, every time we call for help or understanding from forces beyond us, we pray to some thing that one way or another seems to respond to us in terms of our humanity.[24]

SISTERLY MEDICINE

> We have to remember that healing takes place in the present.
>
> *Dr. Julia Boyd*[25]

Several well-known black women are community healers: psychotherapist Dr. Julia Boyd, editor Susan L. Taylor, and well-known author Iyanla Vanzant. I would add that they are also cultural workers whose healing work reflects a theme found in the work of Lee Butler, a pastoral theologian. Butler defines the wide impact of healing: "Healing restores the body and the spirit to a harmonious relationship...Healing is the process of being restored to a life of relationships...Healing transforms relationships and restores a person to life. When our wounds are healed, our relationships are open, trusting, and loving."[26]

These relationships are attested to in some of the self-help literature of these authors, especially Iyanla Vanzant, whose writing addresses her need for personal healing from low self-esteem, domestic abuse, and other illnesses African American women suffer. Her works are food for the soul and lead readers on a journey to wellness. As the popularity of these books shows, healing narratives have an effect that is just as powerful as laying on of hands.[27]

In another book, *In The Company of My Sisters: Black Women and Self-Esteem*, Julia Boyd discusses affirmations as a healing ritual that she practices daily. She encourages them as a daily practice, a practice that also reframes the concept and practice of prayer. According to Boyd:

> Affirmations are like silent prayers that we can use for self-healing and self-empowerment. They can be used at any time and in any situation where there is a need for personal strength. But the most important feature of affirmations is that using them allows us to stay in the present. We have to remember that healing takes place in the present.[28]

Boyd lists the following affirmations that, she says, have helped in her healing process:

> I am in the present light of the Goddess. She will protect me and comfort me.
> I am a worthwhile person.
> I am a Black woman of dignity.[29]

Along with Julia Boyd, whom I had the pleasure to meet in Chicago, I was inspired by the writings of Susan L. Taylor during what seemed to be one of the lowest points of my career. I looked forward to reading Taylor's monthly column "In the Spirit," in *Essence* magazine where Taylor was then editor-in-chief. Occasionally I would tear columns out of the magazine and carry them with me. When Taylor's book, *In The Spirit*, was published, I was overjoyed.[30] Taylor's book enabled me to hope. Every night my husband read a chapter aloud to me. Sometimes he chose the chapter, sometimes I did. These chapters brought comfort. For example, in "New Beginnings," Taylor writes:

God's kingdom isn't in the heavens or in the hereafter.

God is wherever you are. The kingdom is right here, right now, Closer than your next breath. Any healing that you need can take place within you, in the stillness of your being. No special prayers or chants or mantras are needed here. All you must do is get quiet and ask the Holy Spirit to give you understanding and peace.[31]

I found a connection that I hadn't experienced through traditional prayer. I normally would not have gravitated toward the writings of Boyd and Vanzant. Nor would I have considered these writings, along with Taylor's, as having anything to do with healing, especially personal healing. But Susan L. Taylor, Julia Boyd, and Iyanla Vanzant, spoke to me on a very deep level and were an essential part of my healing journey. In their book on gender and race issues among African Americans, Johnetta Betsch Cole and Beverly Guy-Sheftall write:

In their writings and public appearances, both Taylor and Vanzant shy away from what might be labeled as "feminism," but they center their teachings on issues that haunt many African American women. The "medicine" they prescribe for problems that range from sexual abuse to low self-esteem are grounded in Afrocentric notions of healing and personal empowerment through spiritual growth.[32]

There are many other books and Web sites written by black women that provide inspiration and healing. For instance, Susan Newman and Renita Weems address African American women's healing from an explicitly Christian context. Both are ordained ministers; Newman in the United Church of Christ, and Weems in the AME church. Susan Newman wrote *Oh God: A Black Woman's Guide to Sex and Spirituality*.[33] The publishers describe the latter book this way:

With OH GOD! Dr. Newman shows that women of faith do not have to live divided lives. She offers frank discussions about sex both in and out of marriage; about being honest about your spiritual and erotic needs; about making personal choices; and about acknowledging the holiness of your body. OH GOD! *opens new paths to healing and reconciliation for women of faith looking to live in wholeness of spirit and body.* (emphasis mine)[34]

Along with her books, Newman is the director of the Washington office of Balm in Gilead, an organization "whose mission is to improve the health status of people of the African Diaspora by building the capacity of faith communities to address life-threatening diseases, especially HIV/AIDS." Newman is a healer on many fronts.[35]

Similarly, Dr. Renita Weems writes a column for Beliefnet, a Web site about all things spiritual. Some of the titles for her column include: "New

Love, Old Habits" (May 31, 2007); "Apologies Aren't Enough" (April 13, 2007); and "The One That Got Away" (March 19, 2007).

Newman and Weems are reframing healing and wellness along with what it means to be women of faith. They have taken the gospel to cyberspace and formed a gathering place for women who are seeking to deal with "matters of church, race, sex, values...and, Oh Yeah, God."

CONCLUSION

Use my hands, O Lord.

—Dr. Johnye Ballenger

Today the healing ritual of laying on of hands is as vital as it has always been. Faith and healing are augmented by challenging the medical establishment, whether it be another doctor, a resident, or a national movement to encourage blacks to be organ donors. The healing arts among African American healers are practiced for the benefit of self, community, and the world. Healing also focuses on wellness and hope.

We have to address and change the dismal predictions about our lives because we've got songs to sing, pictures to paint, poems to recite, children to teach, books to write, pies to bake, hair to braid, flowers to grow, business to run, and people to love. There's a whole lot of living left in us yet.

Please take this medicine and pass it on.

NOTES

The title of my chapter is from Winifred Gallagher, "Seeking Help for the Body in the Well-Being of the Soul," *New York Times*, Sunday, June 13, 1999, sec. WH, p. 23.

1. The divine healing movement in America, also known as faith healing, faith cure, or simply healing movement, which emerged during the Holiness revival of the 1860s, did not become a major movement in American Protestantism until the 1870s.

2. Afi-Odelia Scruggs' book, *Beyond Stitch & Bitch: Reflections on Knitting and Life*, as well as blogs and *Black Purl*, a knitting magazine published by an African American female, expand knitting from an individual act to a communal one.

3. See the Web site http://www.cmh.pitt.edu for Center for Minority Health in the Graduate School of Public Health at the University of Pittsburgh; Laura A. Linnan and Yvonne Owens Ferguson, "Beauty Salons: A Promising Health Promotion Setting for Reaching and Promoting Health among African American Women" in *Health Education & Behavior* 34, no. 3 (2007): pp. 515–30; http://www.Newsday.com, "D.C. Barbers and Stylists Clip Away at Illness," *The Washington Post*, December 11, 2007; Richard Perez-Pena, "Hair Styling, Plus Cancer Education, *New York Times*, November 6, 2003.

4. Author Unknown. "April 20, 1999," *Forward Day by Day* February–April, (Cincinnati, Ohio: Forward Movement Publications), p. 80.

5. From Rosemary D. Gooden, ed., *Faith Cures & Answers to Prayer by Mrs. Edward Mix* (Syracuse, NY: Syracuse University Press, 2002).

6. Cited in Gooden, *Faith Cures*.

7. John Koenig, "Healing," in *Practicing Our Faith: A Way of Life for a Searching People*, ed. Dorothy C. Bass (San Francisco: Jossey-Bass Publishers, 1997), pp. 149–62.

8. Margaret Guenther, *The Practice of Prayer. The New Church's Teaching Series, Vol. Four* (Cambridge, Mass.: Cowley Publications, 1998), pp. 55–56

9. *Conversations with God: Two Centuries of Prayers by African Americans*, ed. James Melvin Washington (New York: HarperCollins Publishers, Inc., 1994), p. xxxi.

10. Ibid., p. xlvii.

11. Fred C. Lofton, "We Need Thee, Lord Jesus, as Never Before," in Washington, *Conversations with God*, p. 269.

12. Sara Lawrence-Lightfoot, *Respect: An Exploration* (Cambridge, Mass.: Perseus Books, 2000), p. 82.

13. Ibid., pp. 67–89.

14. Ibid., p. 67.

15. Ibid., p. 79.

16. Ibid., p. 76.

17. Ibid., p. 89.

18. Douglas Martin, "Healing the Burned with Hope: A Hospital Chaplain Helps the Disfigured Beneath the Skin," *New York Times*, December 3, 1996, B1–B2.

19. Ibid.

20. Ibid.

21. Gallagher, "Seeking Help for the Body, p. 23.

22. Ibid.

23. www.riversidechurchny.org/renewa/?wellness.

24. Ann Ulanov and Barry Ulanov, *Primary Speech: A Psychology of Prayer* (Atlanta: John Knox Press, 1982), pp. 1–2.

25. Julia A. Boyd, *In the Company of My Sisters: Black Women and Self-Esteem* (New York: Dutton, 1993).

26. Lee H. Butler Jr., *A Loving Home: Caring for African American Marriage and Families* (Cleveland: The Pilgrim Press, 2000), p. 31.

27. Iyanla Vanzant, *Acts of Faith: Daily Meditations for People of Color* (New York: Fireside, 1993).

28. Boyd, *In the Company of My Sisters*, p. 144.

29. Ibid.

30. Especially *In the Spirit: The Inspirational Writings of Susan L. Taylor* (New York: Amistad Press, 1993).

31. Ibid., 25.

32. Johnetta Betsch Cole and Beverly Guy-Sheftall, *Gender Talk: The Struggle for Women's Equality in African American Communities* (New York: One World Ballentine Books, 2003), p. 126.

33. www.sincerelysusan.com/pressinfo.html.

34. www.balmingilead.org.

35. www.beliefnet.com/author/autho_149.html.

CHAPTER 11

Too Gay for the Church, but Always at Home in the Club: Health, Spirituality, and Social Support among Adult Black Gay Men at Oakland's Cable's Reef

D. Mark Wilson

When it comes to identifying how faith, spirituality, and wholeness is understood and shaped among African Americans, many social and theological researchers would not dare to walk down this road of study without stepping into the doors of the black church. From classical sociological studies such as W.E.B. Du Bois's *The Philadelphia Negro* and E. Franklin Frazier's *The Negro Church in America* to more contemporary theological writings on African Americans by Peter Paris and Archie Smith Jr., African American churches are described as having two primary roles in strengthening spirituality and health among African Americans.[1] According to this history of social and theological research, African American churches are viewed, first, as spiritual centers that preserve and pass on spiritual traditions, rituals, and practices of healing, as well as an African-derived worldview of God's interrelatedness in every aspect of human life. Second, African American congregations are also seen as centers of social, economic, and communal life wherein African Americans are not only protected from the "hostilities" of racial segregation and white racism, but where African Americans also create political networks, extended family relations, and systems of social support systems.[2] These latter networks, relationships, and systems of support are crucial to the survival and wellness of African American people as a whole. In terms of spirituality and health, systems of social support help the church in the African American community function as a therapeutic center, wherein African Americans are reminded by other "sisters" and "brothers" in the community of the following maxim heard in African American churches: "God will make a way out of no way."

As a child of the African American church—the black Baptist branch in particular—it is impossible for me to enter into this discussion on health and spirituality without affirming how important the church has been to me and to the history of my ancestors. From my great-grandparents' experiences as slaves in the United States, to my nieces, nephews, and my African American undergraduate students in the current hip-hop generation, black churches continue to be places of healing, spiritual nurture, and care. In my conversations with these younger African Americans, I still find their approach to health quite similar to the approach of Mother Omelia Jackson, my "Grandma," who would first use a home remedy and take matters of health to God in prayer before consulting with the preacher or seeking healthcare from hospitals and doctors.

I also cannot enter this discussion without highlighting the important role of church in mobilizing social change within African American communities in the early and modern civil rights movement and in spawning economic development projects, jointly planned by African American churches and city and state governments.[3] Were it not for this kind of social activism and economic development in congregations such as Hartford Memorial Baptist Church of Detroit, where I served as youth minister between the years of 1985–1992, I would not have had the resources or people support to help youth in and around the congregation find answers to struggles with faith and health concerns, such as teen pregnancy, sexually transmitted diseases, HIV/AIDS, violence and abuse, and teen suicide.

Yet, similar to the feminist critique of womanist theologians (black women theologians, whose scholarship critiques and "unmasks" dominant structures of racism, sexism, and heterosexism in theology and congregational life to empower, liberate, and unearth the voices, suffering, faith, and hope of African American women),[4] which highlights how black women in black churches and in the feminist movement are oppressed by joint hegemonic systems of patriarchy and racism, the question I raise in this chapter concerns how the spirituality, healing, and social support tradition of African American churches is challenged when sexual orientation is added into the equation. Along with my identity as a child of the African American church and my work as a sociologist, I share with many others in African American churches the identity of being black, Christian, and gay, an identity that Smith identifies as a "spiritual refugee" among African Americans.[5] In other writings, I describe myself as "unashamedly black, unapologetically Christian, and proudly gay," which echoes the expression "unashamedly black and unapologetically Christian," coined by my friend and mentor Rev. Dr. Jeremiah Wright of Trinity United Church of Christ, Chicago, Illinois.[6] Much like black women and like my lesbian, gay, bisexual, transgender, intersex, and queer (LGBTIQ) brothers and sisters, I too live daily with the hurt, the pain, and the wounds of rejection from black churches. Those wounds of rejection for being a gay man among African Americans are not less painful than the wounds of racism I receive for being a black man in the United States. Along with racial discrimination, I too have experienced a spiritual distance within my own black community, a spiritual distance best described for me and other LGBTIQ people in the lyric of the black gay poet Essex Hemphill, who died from HIV/AIDS-related complications in 1995: "I cannot go home ['to the black church, the black family, the black literati'] as who I am, and that bothers me!"[7]

When it comes to black churches serving as the central institution for the health, spiritual wholeness, and social well-being of African Americans, do all "us black folk" enjoy this spirituality and wholeness equally, particularly if we are gay and aging? Were we to roll back the clock from church on Sunday morning, to conversations at a black gay nightclub on Saturday night, the answer to this question might sound like this discussion shared in a focus group interview I conducted, in the summer of 2007, with black gay men who are clientele at the Cable's Reef—a gay nightclub in Oakland, California, and an essential social space for black gay men:

James (Jim): My name is James, and I live in San Pablo California, I'm not much of a person who goes to church. I don't think the church has been very supportive of gay rights. I think there's more oppression in the African American church. And so, as a result of that, I look to other places for my sense of spirituality and support. I have a wide array of support from my other African American gay brothers, and ironically enough I connect with them at the local club, which was Cable's Reef. I don't think the bar is just a place for picking up someone for a one-night stand or just for getting your sexual freak on, so to speak. I think it's really a place where you can meet people, where you can network and really have dialogue and conversation. It's not always about being a party all the time.

Eddie: Uh, my name is Eddie, and I was born in Illinois. I'm very much into family, family ties, and traditional family, and family means a lot to me. I am now in the gay life and I love it. I didn't start "testing the waters" until after I divorced. So I was married and had a beautiful son, and was raised that you get a good education, you get a good job, you find a good lady to marry, you have a family, and I went through all this here. I thought this was it, all hot dogs, apple pie and the American way. And as time went on, something said you know you have this urge to be somewhere else. So, I never really looked for family or for church for my gay needs. In the church, I look for a spiritual support. I don't look for a gay support from the church. Because I didn't grow up looking for it or thinking that it was there, or knew that I could go there and find it. So, my relationship with the church was my relationship with God, with me and my God. And I still have a firm belief in that. And I try to raise my son and give him that background, and you know once you get grown you do what you have to do.

In March 2007, Cable's Reef not only celebrated its twenty-fifth anniversary but also ended its long history of being the last significant social space for African American gay men to close and shut its doors in the San Francisco Bay Area. This ethnographic study examines what spirituality, health, and wholeness has meant to adult black gay men like James, age 55, and Eddie, age 59, whose conversations about faith, spirituality, and sexuality were more likely to happen at Cable's than in an African American congregation.

Contemporary cultural scholars and theologians of the ecological perspective have emphasized the intersectionality and interrelatedness of social structures, institutions, and ideas through which social identities, such as race, gender and sexuality, are framed.[8] These theoretical perspectives broaden the more narrow structural view of social institutions and formal organizations, which might lead one to assume that one institution has ultimate say over matters regarding spirituality and faith. Cultural dimensions and alternative spaces that interact with social structures are not to be dismissed. In this regard, the African American church in this chapter is interpreted as having only partial control over individual experiences and decisions about spirituality and health, particularly when it comes to matters of sexuality. The cultural and ecological theoretical frameworks influence how I understand what emerges as complex experiences, multilayered performances, and varied identities used by this group of gay black men as they "navigate" and live between institutions of the African American community.[9]

James and Eddie's experiences with health and healing are shaped by a social web that includes many people, ideas, and institutions, larger than the church pulpit, more expansive than the Sunday School room, and broader than the choir stand or the church pew. The spirituality, faith, and understandings of wholeness of these gay men include exchange and interaction with friends and systems of support, which they find in their friendly neighborhood gay bar.

THE STUDY

The comments that James and Eddie shared above were expressed in a focus group interview on health and spirituality that I conducted with adult black gay males over 50 years of age and who were regulars at Cable's Reef. So many of the social spaces and events, clubs and parties, body images and representations of LGBTIQ people in media target the younger LGBTIQ "club kids," those roughly between ages 18 and 30. In this study, therefore, I wanted to unearth the experiences with finding supportive communities for an older group of African American gay men, whose social experience is not only influenced by homophobia within churches, but also by ageism in the LGBTIQ local and global community, since they are no longer the desired group of the "young and restless" pretty boys admired, sexually objectified, and used as tools of marketing a sexualized, "wild, crazy, and drug-driven" representation of identity in LGBTIQ social life, politics and national/global cultures.

Ethnographic research methods and qualitative analysis were used to reveal ideas, beliefs, and major themes about spirituality and health within this population of African American gay men, and to highlight the kind of social practices in which their beliefs about spirituality and health cause them to engage. Men in the focus group were recruited through internet contacts by one of the regulars from Cable's Reef. Eight persons were contacted, including both women and men; however, only four men showed up.[10] Therefore, with such a small number of participants, I am careful, in this chapter, not to create some grand, universal theory. The purpose of this ethnographic study is to unearth in a preliminary way the rich narratives, stories, and conversations about spirituality, health, and wholeness of these few gay men and to qualitatively investigate the following question: Where does one find a healthy place of support and spiritual nurture when one is black, gay, and over 50? (I wonder if this research question has anything to do with my context of turning 50 in three short years from now?)

As James states, his approach is to avoid the African American church altogether and to find "support and a sense of spirituality" at the club, through networks he can create at Cable's Reef. In Eddie's experience, neither the church nor the family is a setting where he finds support for his needs as a gay man. Yet, the church continues to be a central place for his "spiritual support" and important for shaping his "belief and relationship with God," which he passes on to his son. At Cable's Reef, when it comes to conversations about faith, spirituality, and wholeness, James and Eddie characterize that spirituality and wholeness are not formed in a vacuum, by one single, monolithic community (namely the African American church). Rather, the relationship between faith, spirituality, and wholeness is a dynamic process, involving communities, institutions, and social organizations through which black gay men navigate their lives.

Many important themes emerged from this focus group conversation. For the purpose of this chapter, I shall limit my discussion and explore two themes that emerged as central and key to understanding the relationship between healing and spirituality. As they journey between the church on Sunday and the nightclub when the mood hits and the beat from the jukebox calls, black gay men, first, find a cultural space at Cable's to heal, to release pain, hurt, and rejection and to process and critique homophobic experiences through which they have suffered in churches. Second, at Cable's, black gay men work to preserve their spiritual beliefs and ideas, which inform how they create wholeness and practice forms of healing. The following discussion highlights how club life helps to keep the faith of black gay men resilient and alive and how their deep commitment to spirituality enables them to create networks of social support at Cable's, for other African American gay men and their families.

IS THERE A "BALM" FOR THE UNUSUAL CHILD?: CABLE'S REEF IS MORE THAN A BUILDING

As if it were enough to live with what W.E.B. Du Bois calls the "unreconciled strivings" in the "double consciousness" and "warring ideals" of being both African and American, Smith adds to this complexity the dilemma of African Americans "navigating" between "deep pain" from a long history of economic exploitation in the United States and creative "hope" African Americans find and create in black churches, black families, and black culture.[11] When it comes to deep pain for African American LGBTIQ people who navigate between, at least, the social realities of racism, class, gender inequality, and homophobia, the picture becomes more harmful and complex. Perhaps no other writer expresses the complex outcome of this pain and internalized oppression better than the black gay poet and leader of the 1980s Black Gay Literary Movement, the late Marlon Riggs: "anger unvented / becomes pain unspoken / becomes rage released / becomes violence / cha, cha, cha."[12] The pain of internalize oppression for LGBTIQ people often becomes violence expressed toward self rather than confronting the harm LGBTIQ people receive from and within their own spiritual family, the black community and the national and global heteronormative culture.

During our discussion, Herman (a 63-year-old black gay man and regular at Cable's) begins to speak to this pain and self-destructive violence due to internalized oppression. First, he shares his pride for being gay identified from the day of his birth:

> *Herman:* My name is Herman. I was born in Asheville, North Carolina, fourth day of September 1943. And on my birth certificate, it got written "unusual child" on my birth certificate. Uh, huh, it say, "unusual child" on my birth certificate. And when I was in my single digits [in his childhood years] my mother took me back to the doctor and tried to ask the doctor why do it say that. And the doctor say, "Just let it be, that's just him." I was born gay [proudly]. I never been married, I don't have kids, I don't even want a woman. So I'm straight gay!

Citing the doctor's entry of "unusual child" on his birth certificate, sexuality and same sex attraction were clear to Herman very early on in his life. Herman does not describe for the group what being identified medically as an "unusual child" means, even after being prompted to say more about this.[13] But however proud he is about being legally "unusual" and being "straight gay," he shares in the same exclusion and pain experienced by "the children" (an underground and alternative term that African American LGBTIQ folk sometime use to distinguish themselves as separate from the dominant language of "gay and lesbian" in the LGBTIQ movement)[14] of the black church and community, particularly the "unusual children." Exclusion and internalized oppression from the church became suicide for some, which has motivated Herman, even more, to find a place of healing and hope at Cable's Reef:

Herman: Then I got that gift of music thing too. I started playin' [piano in church] when I was four years old. I saw the notes on the staff and all that. [In] my experiences with the churches, they can tell that I'm gay, but they sway away [from me], like I can feel when somebody [does that]. I can feel it real strong. I can feel the way they approach me. They sway away real quick from me. They do that right now. I can tell, when you say something, they just move away from you, because, you know, I'm gay. The preachers preach against gays when I was comin' up. And they still do that. Talkin' about they a abomination of God. I never did think about that. I just felt good about myself. Some people couldn't deal with it, they commit suicide. I never did think that way. [That's why] I like going to Cable's. You can meet people, see people comin' there...you could be supported. If everybody was together.

The Negro spiritual claims, "There is a Balm in Gilead," but where is the balm for the "unusual children" of the African American community, from whom church members "sway away," and at whom clergy continue to hurl derogatory slurs as "abominations to God?" Such actions further distance us from the community that we need and from the divinity within that would facilitate good health and wholeness among us. While Herman feels good about himself, his reference to others who have turned the church's hatred and exclusion against themselves and committed suicide challenges research on African American faith communities to question whether black congregations are solely places of healing, wholeness, and hope or rather "death-dealing" social institutions.[15]

There may be "a balm in Gilead." But for these gay men that balm is more likely to be found in the spirituality of clubs like Cable's. Is there a place for the spirituality of the so-called unusual child? Perhaps not so often at church, but there is a spiritual balm, a place of healing and welcome at Cable's, clearly indicated in the comments that Eddie shares:

Eddie: You know, Cable's was a place that I could go and have a kindred mind and a kindred spirit. People who had similar things or same things in common, and that I could relate to, and I could talk to openly and people understood what I was talking about. I refer to the spiritual that to me means, that it's not about the building, I learned that a long time ago, that it's not about the building, it's about what's in here [points to his heart]. When I go down to Cable's, and I talk to Herman, and I talk to Marlow and we talk about anthems, and we

> talk about hymns, and we talk about something like this here, some-
> times you never know what's happening in my life that really makes
> me feel good, it really does do something for me, and I'm getting that
> at Cable's not at the church. Not at the building.

In terms of responding to pain, rejection, and suicide, Cable's Reef serves
as a site for these gay men to reestablish, reconnect, replace and re-create
the bonds and ties of community, broken between them and between other
African Americans in institutions like churches and families. Similar to their
ancestors, African slaves, whose African spirituality continued traditions of
extended family and created alternative, sacred spaces in "de bushes" to se-
cretly "steal away" and be free from the racially exclusive, "death-dealing"
structures of white congregations,[16] these men are too called at times to "steal
away" to a place outside of the heterosexism of African American churches,
where they can find "a kindred mind," "a common spirit" and other LGBTIQ
people who share a common identity and social struggle.

In Eddie's words, Cable's is more than a material organization. Beyond its
physical building, Cable's is a spiritual center that unites hearts and minds,
similar to what he describes as his longtime teaching and understanding of
spirituality and faith not tied down and limited by the structure of the building and organization. What really matters at Cable's is what happens in the
hearts of its clientele and in the conversations that either celebrate and share
testimonies of their spirituality and faith in God or gives them the honesty
to stand up, "read" (i.e.—a gift we black gay men have inherited from black
women, our mothers and big sisters; to "read" is to talk back, "play the doz-
ens," "cap," or battle a heterosexist opponent using our verbal skills, much
like Deejay battles in hip-hop culture), and critique homophobic messages
from their churches.

> *Eddie:* Sometimes we talk about going to church, we always talk about going to
> the church as being a filling station, somewhere where you get fueled to
> carry you on through the week or something, to carry you over and then
> you go back and get this fill up again. I go down to Cable's and I get
> the spiritual connect when I start talking with my sisters and brothers in
> Christ at the bar. And we start talking about how God's been to us, and
> how he's blessed us and how things have been happening to us [Marlow
> lifts and waves his hands in praise] then you understand all of a sudden,
> you might be at the bar or what ever, but you realize you have something
> in common, and [what's] common is that spiritual part. That's a part of
> all of us, and that we all recognize. That's what I get at Cable's in the
> gay community. There's a support that we can get from and give to one
> another, without having to be at the church house, be up under the cross,
> and be up in the building and say we goin' to church and we goin' to wor-
> ship. When I go to Cable's sometimes, and we sit there, we start singing
> songs, and we start talking about the "amen choir."

While Eddie talks about testimonies of "God's goodness" and hymn singing heard around Cable's bar, Marlow finds at Cable's the space to perfect his "discipline" to "read" and to speak honest and "brazen truth," a verbal discipline he, in turn, uses in his spiritual critique of homophobic messages in the structure of African American churches:

> *Marlow:* In respect to Cable's Reef, that was a meeting ground. It was like "the library" of meeting peoples and enjoying life. A place where you could go in, mingle with people, enjoy like and see [the books]—not read! Well, "read" too! [Group breaks up into laughter]. "Reading" determines your discipline as a homosexual. I have come through many ups and downs. But I believe in God. I strongly believe in God and whatever he has for me to do, I do. I got escorted out of the church because the pastor spoke and said, "That's why God put AIDS in the community." And I stood up and called him A LIAR. I called him a liar with the FULLNESS of my VOICE [looking sternly, as he remembers "reading" the pastor]. And I said, "You are a liar," cause God did not give us this disease, it's how we live our lives that has brought these things on. I'll be honest with you. I don't bite my tongue. I speak my mind because I believe in the word of God. But when you start making erroneous statements and you're going to tell me that God put this disease out there, it's like when whites were exploiting blacks with the [Tuskegee] syphilis epidemic that had to go all the way to the Supreme Court.

Marlow's spirituality, expressed in his "strong belief" in God and in "what God has for him to do," demonstrates the encouragement he receives at Cable's to move from a place and an identity of the victimized unusual child to the identity and place of a powerful, God-inspired, gay man, with the subversive style and prophetic language and voice to read heteronormative and AIDS-phobic culture in African American churches. The kind of education and of social support practiced at Cable's, as gay men in the focus group stated, continues the formation of their religious belief and spiritual identity.

"HIV/AIDS IS IN THE CHEESE": GOOD SAMARITANS HEALING DISTRUST AND REACHING OUT TO OTHERS AT CABLE'S REEF

HIV/AIDS education and prevention has found a primary challenge in African Americans' distrust of the healthcare industry.[17] In response, adult gay men at Cable's have used the religious teachings of their youth to provide accurate information and create systems of care and social support, which one would hope to find in black churches. Instead, race conspiracy theories and street narratives about HIV/AIDS are alive and well within African American churches and within the larger African American community. This thinking is demonstrated in the following excerpt, as the group defines what they see as the greatest need for healing and wholeness among African American adult gay men:

> *Jim:* As I get older, what I see is that there's a disconnect in the African American gay community, and the disconnect is because there's a whole generation of black men that are gone because of HIV and AIDS, you know. So, you've got the younger group over here, and you've got the older group over here, but in between that, there's nothing. I think you can see it in the bar. In Cable's there's that transition that needs to happen, from that generation up to the next. In between, there's that piece that's missing, you know, and there's no mentoring going on with the younger gays. The older ones are up there cocktailing at the bar and the younger ones in the back there dancing. So there's not that interchange that should be happening. I think a big part of that is a result of the epidemic, the ravages of that disease on the African American gay men, you know, just wiped out a whole generation of black men.

> *Herman:* But I know somethin' about that. I know a lady and she works in politics. Now she told me that they put that [HIV/AIDS] out there. And she said they were doin' it through that cheese and butter, that came from that there government. I didn't believe that, but it seemed like it, because if they put the syphilis out there, what you think they gonna do. Where they put the syphilis? Was that Mississippi? In the water? The government, [yeah] the government did that.

> *Eddie:* They did that with a group of blacks in the army. And it wasn't [just] Tuskegee, but it was back during that time where they actually infected the men [black soldiers] with syphilis.

> *Herman:* That's what made me think that that's what they doin'... She woke me up to that. She said [that HIV/AIDS was in the cheese and butter].

> *Eddie:* And I understand your point [he and Jim laugh]. I will not dispute [begins to laugh and joke], but there's so much of HIV/AIDS in Africa, and they didn't have the government's cheese and butter [group breaks into laughter].

> *Marlow:* That's the ignorance of education within the African American community. She was giving [or "given"?] false information. The people were accepting that false information that was being fed [to them].

> *Jim:* Well, but it was true to her. And you can't really knock a lot of black people, because of what they've been through. It wasn't only Tuskegee. It's been a lot of stuff that has been done. So that's why there's distrust [among us].

Upon hearing this dialogue and exchange, my own reaction was to laugh like Eddie and Marlow, to disregard Herman's statement about HIV/AIDS strategically distributed to black Americans through the Federal Government's cheese and butter program, as "ignorance in education." However, I was led in a different direction through my conversations about HIV/AIDS conspiracy theories with Leroy Blea, Chief of Prevention Services Section, in the Public Health Division of Health and Human Services, in Berkeley, California.[18]

Blea maintains that Herman's view about syphilis and HIV/AIDS parallels metaphors used to describe "the environment" and "substandard health care and education" he often hears among communities of color and the poor.[19] Here metaphors depicting disease in the water and in the butter and cheese may symbolize that health disparities among black, brown, and poor people are faults not of the black, brown, and poor people themselves, but rather effects of environmental racism in the government's unequal distribution of nutritious food and sustaining a healthy environment. James's comment seems to express the same sentiment, as he affirms the distrust among African Americans toward the government's health care system. Such distrust is to be expected given the history of substandard health care, cutbacks in prevention programs and education, and what James calls "lot of other stuff" that African Americans have and continue to face, on the account of racial, economic, and environmental inequality within the United States. How can healing what James calls "the disconnect" between younger and older African American gay men be facilitated without addressing the disparities in HIV/AIDS healthcare that has "wiped out" a whole generation of black gay men to serve as role models for the younger generation? How can healing the disconnect between African American LGBTIQ folk and heterosexuals in the black community be facilitated without addressing the common myths and similar distrust of health care shared among African Americans regardless of class, gender, sexual orientation, or age? And with the role that black churches, and faith communities in general, play in shaping myths and stigmas about HIV/AIDS and toward LGBTIQ people, what alternative role might nightclubs, like Cable's, play in creating communities that healthy and whole?

Some answers to these questions emerge in what the gay men in this study do for one another at Cable's Reef in their efforts to preserve the spiritual understanding and interpretation of faith that they either learned during their years growing up in churches or learned in rejection of their church's' teachings about sexuality. Ironically, however, pain, hurt, and rejection from the church has taken away neither the spiritual resilience nor the understandings about God of these gay men. When asked why they continue to attend churches in the African American community, the following responses characterize their deep commitment to African spirituality and to the history and social life of African American people:

Interviewer: Why are there still so many African American gays and lesbians at church on Sunday morning?

> *Marlow:* Why? Because we believe! We believe in our roots from slavery. Where we were brought up, those of us who are African American, we were brought up to believe in a one true God. So we have carried on, but yet within this development and growth we have been able to venture into another dialogue.
>
> *Jim:* You know, it's like, for me, it doesn't have anything to do with one's sexuality. I think that everybody needs the embrace of the church. That's been our spiritual bastion, you know. That's been the only thing we've had, basically, you know, from slavery. So uh, I think it's sort of culturally engraved. We need it, whether you gay, straight, bi-sexual.
>
> *Eddie:* Trans...
>
> *Jim:* Or what!

The attempt to destroy culture, community, and family during slavery facilitated a spiritual understanding, ritual, and social practice among African Americans about the need for everyone to be embraced. This spiritual understanding and ritual practice continued at Cable's, as black gay men worked to make others healthy and whole. For Eddie this meant practicing the example of the good Samaritan, a spiritual and social practice he learned growing up in his family and church:

> *Eddie:* My spirituality is in how I deal with people and in how I help people. I was raised to be the good Samaritan, to give a hand when you see a needed hand. My spirituality is my religious upbringing to reach out and to help others, to do for others, and not to always be on the receiving end. And if I can reach out and do that, then I feel like I'm contributing. The spiritual support and connect to another, do I give that to people, at the club? Do I give that to people at my job or wherever? As far as the club is concerned? As far as the gay life? Do I do that? Yeah! When we talk about let my light shine, when somebody walk up to me and say, "Well you're a Christian, huh?" now I'm sitting at a bar, having my cocktail and enjoyin' myself, and I thinkin' that this person is coming over here to talk with me is...I say, um hm [interested in me]. Then they say, "You know, there's something different about you, you're not like the others in here, and I just wanted to let you know that I appreciate that. And the way you carry yourself and thank you for being you." And I've never opened my mouth and the conversation I wanted to have with them, that was not the conversation. But anyway, there are things that you can do and be a help to others, and be support spiritually, but it comes from what you have gotten from within that goes out to others.

The metaphor and example of being a good Samaritan, with the spiritual teachings about helping others in need, is the place where social outreach, HIV/AIDS education, mentoring, and social support of other LGBTIQ persons and their families began for these gay men at Cable's. For Eddie, good Samaritan spirituality is played out in the interrelated human interaction that has occurred for him within the institutional structures of Cable's, the family, and the church. For James, this kind of spirituality is not limited to structures of the church, family, or the club but is linked, through his individual work, to larger formal, economic, and political social networks and structures in the city of Oakland.

> *James:* Yeah, I think so, because I think it has to be [to Eddie] and I appreciate your input on individual efforts of spirituality, because, hey, it's starts there. You know, it starts with individuals, but I think it needs to be a collective approach to where you know, people coming together in terms of their spirituality. And forming some sort of, creating, and forming some sort of network, you know, that can be, instrumental in helping people in different ways. Um, you know, maybe it's not always the church that has to be the gateway for this. It can be other, uh, established organizations. And spirituality just doesn't reside in the church. [Proudly] I don't go to church, but I think I'm spiritual. It's more of a feeling? An emotion you know? And sometimes I find it hard to put it into words, but I know that it's something that moves me, and I feel, but I'm not sure how to, uh…To, to uh, want to make a difference in somebody's life. Want to be, uh, instrumental in creating some good, doing some good, bringing about a positive result.

For James, spirituality is doing something good and creating some "positive results" for black LGBT people and African Americans as a whole, particularly in prevention and educational work around HIV/AIDS. His expression this kind of spirituality is carried out through formal structures and organizations, such as county hospitals and city public health agencies, to which he is linked and to which he has built networks with Cable's:

> *James:* For me that [spirituality] translates into wiping out HIV and AIDS. You know, putting an end to the epidemic. One of the things that's important for me about Cable's is the work I do. I am the director for HIV testing prevention and education at Alameda County Medical Center Highland Hospital, so we have a grant, which is to reach out into the gay community, to reach out and provide prevention tools and materials. So I made this connection with Cable's to bring condoms, lubricants, literature, and referrals for testing for HIV into the African American gay community. So in result of that I've been really able to start to grow once again that relationship with a lot of people in the bar. Surprisingly enough I would say that 75 percent or 80 percent of the people who come to that club are HIV positive. And it's important for me to make sure that my brothers are being safe, and not spreading the virus. And one of the things I want to bring to them is to say that it's okay to be sexually active and get your freak on, but let's do it safely. And as result of that, from that has grown

more appreciation of Cable's as a venue for African American men to come together to socialize and have dialogue about a number of things that's important.

While James's expression of spirituality has involved creating formal organizational networks between city public health agencies and Cable's to "wipe out HIV/AIDS," spirituality for others in the group is expressed through more informal kinds of networks, relationships, and practices of social outreach and support. These networks are not necessarily linked to the kind of economic or political structures to which James is connected but instead emerge and gradually are woven together as the spiritual and social needs of those who have entered Cable's arise. Informal networks, relationships, and kinds of outreach and support are based on the spiritual teachings under which these gay men were raised in black churches and black families, particularly in the teaching about helping one's neighbor and friend. In this regard, men in the focus group share how material goods with the poor and homeless are exchanged, and how spiritual support around death and grief has been shared and has become a regular spiritual practice at Cable's Reef:

Herman: I come out of a big family. There's 10 of us. We were all raised to share. I just helped somebody yesterday, gave them some brand new shoes, a suit, I'm always sharing what I have. I get blessed by doing that. [Those blessings] come right back to me. I got a car given to me, furniture, piano, all that was given to me. I like helping people. That's the way I was raised.

Eddie: We are supporting each other. I know a couple of people who will come [into Cable's]. And I don't know what their ulterior motive is, but I have seen them helped. People get a home, get a roof over their head. I've seen them get clothing, I've seen them get avenues [through Cable's] where they can go down and get welfare or [supplementary security income] SSI and others at Cable's who show them the rope of how to get in and how to get into the system and get things done. There are people who I do help, get them clean clothes, food, give them somewhere to go. Do you need to come by the house? I have people who come by the house and they do my gardening. They do things around the house and I'm helping them because they say, they can get some money, that I just need a place to say, and I can get a place to stay for the night. Because of my upbringing, because of what my faith says, I can use that spiritual part to then be a help to someone else.

Marlow: I'm a witness! I have been down and out. I'll give you an example. I was homeless and Cable's Reef was the hub.

Eddie: Marlow is serious. I use to drive by the freeway, where he was sleepin' up under and I would wave to him and sometime share with him. He's an example at Cable's who can show you, take you down that path, and show you where you been, where you might want to go, and where you might not want to be. There's a fine example of someone who said you know what, let me get this together.

The poor and homeless who find help, wholeness, and support at Cable's are sometimes strangers who walk into to the club. Sometimes those poor and homeless are black gay men themselves—like Marlow, who at one time was homeless—and other longtime friends who are in need yet share their material resources to lift up one another.

But their informal networks and spiritual practices do not end with the exchange of material goods. Spirituality at Cable's continues to translate into practices of social and spiritual support that black gay men have provided for LGBTIQ and heterosexual friends with ailing parents, for their own family members, and for grieving African American mothers, who entered the club for support when their gay sons died.[20] In this latter instance, Cable's has functioned like a church community in the lives of these black gay men, their parents, and their friends. Several comments highlight this, as members of the focus group reflect profoundly upon the social outreach and spiritual care they once observed, while sitting around the bar at Cable's:

> *Jim:* And sometimes spirituality happens down at Cable's when people die, and that may be the only place where they get recognition, that they had a life, that they were appreciated, that somebody liked them, or loved them, it happen right there in the Cable's.
>
> *Marlow:* When family gets together...
>
> *Jim:* Yeah, we they get together and honor somebody's life, when they pass on. Right now there's one individual who's very, very sick, I'm not gonna name, names, and he's getting ready to have chemotherapy because he's got cancer in his nodes. Everybody who knows about him is coming together, and getting him all the support and love and making sure, "You gonna pull through this, you're going to be okay." You know. So he comes in looking for that. And there are people there ready to hug him and embrace him, go to the doctor with him, I call him everyday and say, "I'm goin' call you even if you don't want to talk to me."
>
> *Eddie:* And that same young man, I don't think he'd mind if you mentioned his name, because I call him my nephew. But that same young man, when he called and told me, he lost his mother a couple of years ago, this young man is having still having problems [with losing her]. He's just as much Christian as I am, or whatever. He don't know how to let go. I say baby your mother is safe in Jesus arms and you still trying to hold on to her here. Let your mother go and be at peace, and you go on and live your life, and do what you have to do. And he's still holding on. But that's the same support that we're givin' to him.

Marlow: And I'll give you a good example of that. Recently, one of our members [refers to him like a church member], Robbie Lee, who lost both of his parents, but none of us were able to give back, to give him any support. So I sat down at my computer, and type up [some words]. I asked the Lord for the right and proper words, and Eddie's a witness to this because I forwarded him a copy of it, and gave it to him. I emailed these words to him and I got a letter from him, a thank you card, from him the other day, saying, "Thank you for the support," that I had given him and his family. And then that day I called him on his phone and talked with him. He said, "It snowing and we don't know if we can put the body in ground right now." And I said, "Wait a minute, let me tell you what we did when my father died, back in that area, 'cause we're from the same area. He's from Delaware and I'm from Pennsylvania. And what it was like tryin' to dig in that grave through all that snow. So it was that support there. But I had paid no attention to it. I didn't feel obligated, but I felt that was something within me that said, "Reach out and touch."

Eddie: One of the things Jim mentioned, and I wanted to touch on it if I may, is the support we do when a mother walks into that club. [The mother of a gay friend walked into Cable's], and I tell you, they stop everything in that club because the Bartender talk with that mother, and said, "This mother has an announcement to make that she lost her son and her son is no longer with us." And she says, "But you're the only family my son talked about. And I want to thank you for all your love and support you gave him. And if anything that you like to do to help us with the service as far as being part of that service will you please [help], because it will make him so happy. And you have already lifted up my spirit just knowing [that you were there]." So when somebody walks in and says something like that, you know that you have touch somebody. We were supporting [her] and not aware that we were doing it. We never look at ourselves as being supporting. We just come down there and....

Jim: We just do that naturally.

Eddie: Yeah...

"RUMORS OF OUR DEATH HAVE BEEN EXAGGERATED" A CONCLUDING THOUGHT:

In an essay entitled, "Can the Queen Speak? Racial Essentialism, Sexuality and the Problem of Authority" my friend, colleague, and fellow African American gay cultural scholar Dwight McBride examines the exclusion of African American LGBTIQ voices and social experiences in scholarship focused on African American communities Reflecting upon his own personal context and social location in this regard, McBride writes:

Having come to age in a small rural black community where any open expression of gay or lesbian sexuality was met with derision at best and violence at worst; having been socialized in a black Baptist church that preached the damnation of "homosexuals"; having been trained in a African American studies curriculum that provided no serious or sustained discussion of the specificity of African American lesbian and gay folk; and still feeling—even at this moment of writing—the overwhelming weight and frustration of having to speak in a race discourse that seems to have grown all too comfortable with the routine practice of speaking about a "black community" as a discursive unit wholly separate from black lesbians and gay men—all of this has led me to the conclusion that as a community of scholars who are serious about enacting political change, healing black people, and speaking truth to black people, we must begin the important process of undertaking a more inclusion vision of "black community" and of race discourse.

While spirituality and practices of social support among black gay men at Cable's may not be any different from what other African Americans historically have done to restore wholeness and good health within the African American community, this study, as does McBride's essay, challenges black theological discourse and social research on African Americans to undertake a more inclusive vision of the black church and the spirituality and faith of black LGBTIQ folk. It comes as no surprise that black gay men like James, Eddie, Marlow, and Herman face the pain of hatred and exclusion in African American congregations. Black churches are part of the network, web, and social institutional fabric of a larger heterosexist society. Like other traditional social institutions and organizational structures, black churches too play a major role in transmitting dominant ideas about sexuality invented by a heteronormative culture.

Are LGBTIQ folk excluded in black churches? That's not so difficult to answer: Yes! What LGBTIQ person isn't treated unfairly in the United States and the global world? Yet, to focus solely on this question, as so many of us do in scholarship that addresses homophobia in congregations, among African Americans in particular, narrowly leads us not to value and appreciate the many social places, identities, relationships, culturalscapes, and institutional structures through which black LGBTIQ people live, navigate, and respond. Research on African Americans and black LGBTIQ people is challenged in this study to view the experience of religion and sexuality not in monolithic and binary, either-or categories (either the church or the club), but to a more complex theoretical analysis (both the church and the club). Black gay men such as James, Eddie, Marlow, and Herman face the pain of homo-hatred within African American churches, but "rumors of their death are exaggerated."[21] So often the tendency of both heterosexual and LGBTIQ theologians and social researchers is to authoritatively speak for black LGBTIQ people and about our oppression in one location—the black church—rather than to listen, hear, and take seriously what we have to say about the many places in which we express our faith, spirituality, and activism (Can "the queen speak" for herself? Yes she can!).

This analysis on Cable's Reef demonstrates that gay men in the African American community have utilized alternative structures and cultural dimensions to continue to nurture their ideas, their relationships, and their spiritual and social practices. Even with the exclusion and pain they receive in African American churches, there is a "river" and a deep spiritual commitment that continues to flow through them whether they are at church or at the bar.[22] And sometimes the pain and exclusion they experience at church is critiqued and healed in conservations, songs, and in formal and informal networks and social support at Cable's Reef, which they share with each other: (1) to support their younger and older friends, (2) to support black mothers who wander into the club with little or no help from the church when their gay sons die, and (3) to support the poor and homeless of the African American community from whom society has shunned, avoided and "swayed away." And with the closing of Cable's Reef, and the closing of black nightclubs and black cultural spaces in general, given ecological shifts and changes, from where will other places of healing and support for black LGBTIQ folk emerge? The word has come out recently that Cable's new owners will make it an upscale nightclub, called The Vibe, not just for the black gay community, but the LGBTIQ community in general. As the new club emerges from a new generation, will it welcome the kind of deep spiritual commitment and social outreach that Jim, Eddie, Marlow, and Herman have experienced and helped to shape? Will it be the church outside of the black church that it once served for these and other black LGBTIQ folk? With few churches to welcome us, from where will other places of healing and support emerge?

> *Jim:* So you had this little geographical area where you know there was all this interchange was going on, where you could walk out the back door of Cable's and you go around and walk down to Bellas, and not too far was Whispers.
>
> *Eddie:* And up the street there was Ollies, a women's club...
>
> *Marlow:* Then there was the Eagle Creek, that was the only black-owned-and-operated bar in the City of San Francisco. But now all the libraries are closed!
>
> *Eddie:* That was our support, and we did not know that that was our support. Until all of a sudden it's not there anymore, and it's like, "Oh, so what happened?"
>
> *Jim:* I don't think much, I don't think we realize how important Cable's was until it closed. That's when we realized that it was a spiritual hub, that it was a social hub, it was a networking hub, it was a place

that you could be embraced for when stuff like this happened, you know… it was our church!

Marlow: Cable's Reef Baptist Church! [Group laughs]

Jim: [reflectively] It was our church,… it was our church…

NOTES

1. W.E.B. Du Bois, *The Philadelphia Negro* (New York: Schocken Books, 1967); E. Franklin Frazier, *The Negro Church in America* (New York: Schocken Books, 1963); Peter Paris, *The Spirituality of African Peoples* (Minneapolis: Fortress Press, 1995); Archie Smith, *Navigating the Deep River* (Cleveland: United Church Press, 1997).

2. Frazier, *The Negro Church;* C. Eric Lincoln and Lawrence Mamiya, *The Black Church in the African American Experience* (Durham, N.C.: Duke University, 1990); Andrew Billingsley, *Mighty Like a River: The Black Church and Social Reform* (New York: Oxford Press, 1999).

3. Aldon Morris, *The Origins of the Civil Rights Movement* (New York: Free Press, 1984); Billingsley, *Mighty Like a River.*

4. Emile Townes, *In a Blaze of Glory: Womanist Spirituality as Social Witness* (Nashville: Abingdon Press, 1995); Katie G. Cannon, *Katie's Cannon* (New York: Continuum Publishing Company, 1995); Delores Williams, *Sisters in the Wilderness: The Challenges of Womanist God-Talk* (New York: Orbis, 1993); Jacquelyn Grant, *White Women's Christ and Black Women's Jesus: Feminist Christology and Womanist Response* (Atlanta: Scholars Press, 1989).

5. Smith, *Navigating the River,* pp. 35–53.

6. D. Mark Wilson, "Celebrate the Voices of Your Identity and Pride," in *Fifty Ways to Support Lesbian and Gay Equality,* ed. Meredith Maran (Maui: Inner Ocean Publishing, 2005). For reference to Rev. Dr. Jeremiah's Wright coined expression, see the Trinity United Church of Church Web site: http://www.tucc.org/about.htm.

7. Essex Hemphill, "Introduction," in *Brother to Brother: New Writings by Black Gay Men,* ed. Essex Hemphill and Joseph Beam (Boston: Alyson Publications, 1991).

8. Clifford Geertz, *The Interpretation of Cultures* (New York: Basic Books, 1973); Ann Swidler, *Talk of Love: How Culture Matters* (Chicago: University of Chicago, 2001); Smith, *Nagivating the Deep River.*

9. For discussion on navigating between institutional structures, see Smith, *Navigating the Deep River.*

10. The purpose of this study to unearth the rich narratives, stories, and conversations about spiritual, health, and wholeness of these few gay men, and to qualitatively analyze themes that emerge from these narratives. Efforts to include black lesbian women in this discussion were made, as I had preliminary discussions with one of the leaders a black lesbian group of women over 50 in Sacramento, California, whose faith and spirituality is expressed through their outreach to younger black lesbians in the clubs. Much more conversation and trust was needed to be established with the women of this group before I could be invited in, which time constraints did not allow. Therefore, given these times constraints, given that Cable's is almost exclusively black male (with transgender persons on the margins), and given that the

construction of separate social spaces for gay men and lesbian women in African American communities still seem to carry some importance, this study lacks the crucial and well-needed dialogue across gender lines needed within the African American community, and among black LGBT persons in particular.

11. W.E.B. Du Bois, *The Souls of Black Folk* (New York: Penguin Books, 1989), p. 5; Smith, *Navigating the River*, pp. 54–81.

12. Marlon Riggs, "Tongues Untied" in *Brother to Brother: New Writings By Black Gay Men*, ed. Essex Hemphill and Joseph Beam (Boston: Alyson Publications, 1991).

13. Is he transgender or intersexed?

14. Being "one of the children" is a term used between African American LGBTIQ people, to our efforts to distinguish our cultural language from the language of the dominant white LGBTIQ culture and movement. Other terms such as "the kids," "being in the life," "family members," "PLU (people like us), and "yo-mosexuals" for the hip-hop gay "kids" are used as well, yet these terms vary, given generation and region of black LGBTIQ people. As a black gay man coming out in the late 1970s to mid-1980s, I learned to identify as "one of the children," which describes both women's and men's community, and "being in the life," which refers to all oppressed street communities, rather than mainstream white theoretical pejorative terms such as "queer." See Joseph Beam, "Introduction," in *In The Life: A Black Gay Anthology* (Boston: Alyson Publications, 1988).

15. At the time of this writing, I've received word that a black lesbian woman and member of a black Methodist church in Houston, Texas, just committed suicide. For another discussion on suicide among LGBTIQ persons in African American churches, see D. Mark Wilson, "I Don't Mean to Offend, but I Won't Pretend: The Making of Family for Gay Men in an African American Church," in *Tending the Flock*, ed. Bernie Lyons and Archie Smith (Louisville, KY: Westminster John Knox, 1998). In this publication, I share the story of one of my interviewees, a black gay professional in the church, who committed suicide. Do African American congregations and other communities of faith have a responsibility for helping their LGBTIQ members find healthier choices in replace of suicide? What part to black churches play here?

16. For discussion on the use of African spirituality to preserve African extended family tradition and alternative places of worship, see Du Bois, *The Philadelphia Negro*; Dwight Hopkins, *Shoes That Fit Our Feet* (Maryknoll, NY: Orbis Books, 1993), pp. 13–48; Cheryl Sanders, *Empowerment Ethics for a Liberated People* (Minneapolis: Fortress Press, 1995).

17. Stephen Thomas and Sandra C. Quinn, "The Tuskegee Syphilis Study, 1932 to 1972: Implications for HIV Education and AIDS Risk Education Programs in the Black Community," in *Readings in the Sociology of AIDS*, ed. Anthony Lemelle et al. (Upper Saddle River, NJ: Prentice Hall, 2000).

18. Conversation with Leroy Blea on July 9, 2007.

19. See Susan Sontag, *Illness as Metaphor and AIDS and Its Metaphors* (New York: Picador, 2001), for discussion use of cultural metaphors to stigmatize cancer and HIV/AIDS.

20. Were these mothers more welcomed at the club than at church? Where was their support from African American pastors and congregations?

21. Upon hearing that Marlow was part of the focus group, one black gay scholar, who's connected to this circle of friends at Cable's, said to me: "I didn't know Marlow was still alive!" This stresses even more the need to conduct community-based research that connects itself to the social realities and daily experiences of people thought to be dead.

22. Smith, *Navigating the Deep River*.

———— ✴ ————

CHAPTER 12

Healing Hearts and Broken Bodies: An African American Women's Spirituality of Healing

Stephanie Y. Mitchem

Harriet Tubman herself had been enslaved but escaped to the North. She returned to the South in the mid-1800s to aid the escape of over 300 other black people. A story about the legendary Tubman's work as a conductor on the Underground Railroad is often told. While assisting one difficult passage of a group of enslaved people from the South to the North, a few escapees decided they wanted to return. Tubman pulled her shotgun on them, forcing them to choose to continue to freedom—or die. Either way, the safety of the entire group was assured. Healing comes in all forms.

Healing—of self or of others—is an act of power. Like all powers, healing can be used in more positive or more negative ways. For African American women, healing is a power informed by a distinct spirituality. Two sets of images, one in photographs and the other in words, highlight some of the facets of this discussion of healing and black women. The first images are two photos, and the contrast between them tells important stories about who black women are. The first photo is of a group of black women in the Virgin Islands, taken around 1900. In that photo, a woman is seated outside a rough cabin, her hair in loose, nappy glory, while another woman stands behind her taming the hair into braids. In the background, a third woman holds a child and looks on. Both the woman standing and the woman holding the child have finished their own dress, their hair tamed and tightly bound under scarves. The careful blankness on the face of the seated woman implies a certain resentment of this photographic invasion of her private moment of grooming. All three women wear aprons, clearly of the serving class.

The second photo is of a single black woman, a professional and artistic shot of the U.S. Secretary of State, Condoleezza Rice. In this photo, Rice wears a shoulder-baring black formal and sits at a grand piano, looking out the windows of her high-rise apartment. Her face is turned away from the camera, her straightened hair showing. The shot is taken so that there is a sense of looking down into the private space of the woman.

The two photos stand in stark contrast for me, especially considering what the women in the first photo and their descendants sacrificed to produce the seemingly successful results of the second. Most black women today do not know either of these extremes, although many may resonate with the seeming situation of the first group and aspire to the success of the second woman. How many black women today still feel invaded in their private moments by the observations of others? How many are actually afforded the seeming courtesy given to only one of those women? Has the success of the seated woman created any significant meaning for other black women? Or is one's success a denial of the past? For black women, healing has to happen in the spaces in between the two photos. But what is healing? Separating from, forgetting, or denying past pains?

The second group of images is from a book by a Canadian scholar, Katherine McKittrick. She weaves a complicated analysis of black women's geographies across the African Diaspora where space, location, and place are both physical and imaginative. As black women and their families have been continually displaced, and as patterns of domination attempted to define all black people as less than human, McKittrick uses the word "demonic" to define these experiences. She does not use demonic as related to devils. "In mathematics, physics, and computer science, the demonic is a non-deterministic schema; it is a process that is hinged on uncertainty and non-linearity because the organizing principle cannot predict the future."[1] This unknown factor demonstrates for McKittrick how, in spite of patterns of domination and colonization, black women have found ways to alter their assigned "place" by struggling with meanings: "ownership of the body, individual and community voices, bus seats, women, 'Africa,' feminism, history, homes, record labels, money, [and] cars."[2] McKittrick's ideas of geographies and the demonic define some of the ways black women reimagine and reshape their lives. The very process of reimagining their own or their families' lives are acts of both defiance and healing. These images set up a discussion of black women's healing and spirituality because, somewhere between these two photos, most black women live and struggle with the demonic, chaotic, and soul-eating factors that affect them and their families. To explore these images, we will consider some of the dimensions of black women's healing and then look more closely at their work of healing.

SPIRITUAL AND EMBODIED DIMENSIONS OF BLACK WOMEN'S HEALING

Healing involves acts of power. The power of healing is used by black women to re-create worlds and meanings, thereby resisting other usually negative definitions. Such re-creation can happen in great social events like the Civil Rights Movement, where many people came together to reorder meaning. But unseen and often unrecognized, black women have built black communities' structures of resistance and self-esteem that allowed the grand movements to happen. There are small and ordinary ways in black women's everyday lives that this reshaping happens.

I have been in many black women's homes where the better furniture is fitted with plastic covers. I have been in other black women's homes where anyone entering must take off their shoes at the front door to protect the white carpeting. Both plastic coverings and stocking feet underline the point: that which is seen as good in black women's value systems is safeguarded from harm. In homes, space is carved out to demonstrate comfort or beauty, thereby repositioning the humanity of the inhabitants, at least in that one space. Some would argue that such struggles are not exclusive to black women; however, American social structures establish conditions that are unique and unhealthful to African Americans. Therefore, finding a way to hold onto values in the face of a world that attempts to destroy the spirit of black people means safeguarding the good, and this is indicated in one small way by creating safe homes. This safeguarding is part of black women's healing work, contradicting the smaller idea of healing as only that of curing a single physical symptom. Social conditions are formed from living black in America. These conditions establish black women's material realities and create the need to heal the parts of life that are broken. These conditions did not end in the photo of the serving women combing hair in the 1900s but continue to this time, and are reflected in the material realities of black women today.

For instance, the importance of obtaining an education as a way out of poverty has long been known among African Americans. Data from the Institute for Women's Policy Research underscores this long-held belief when considering the dramatic impact of a college education on poverty rates:

> Women of color received the largest college premiums. While a white woman with a four-year degree experiences an earnings increase of 77 percent over her high school graduate counterpart...the earnings of African American women jump to 92 percent when compared to high school graduates of their own racial/ethnic group....Just some exposure to higher education decreases the poverty rate for African American women tremendously—from 41 percent among those without a high school degree down to 17 percent for those with some post-secondary education...Completing college reduces poverty rates even further as only 5.3 percent of African American women...with at least a bachelors degree live in poverty.[3]

From these numbers, the way out of poverty then would seem to be clear. Yet, most black women do not have options of separating from the past or making upper-middle-class incomes; obtaining postsecondary education often becomes impossible. Conditions of elementary and secondary schools in black communities, existing poverty in black enclaves, and black women's daily lives, including care of children, siblings, or parents, militate against getting the education to get out of poverty. The impact of these very real conditions on the health and well-being of black women is disastrous.

For 20 years and more, the Black Women's Health Project, now called the Black Women's Health Imperative, has advocated for changing these conditions in one way or another.[4] A study by the Black Women's Health Imperative point to the health conditions of black women but also to underlying reasons that are less understood.

> Compared to other racial/ethnic groups, African American women are disproportionately affected by cardiovascular disease, some forms of cancer, hypertension and diabetes. Lifestyle risk factors such as obesity, lack of physical activity, tobacco use and diets high in sodium are well known contributors to these chronic diseases. However, sociocultural factors (e.g. discrimination, domestic violence, stress and depression) also hypothesized to contribute to the aforementioned diseases and behaviors are less often examined in large-scale studies with African American women.[5]

This study by the Black Women's Health Imperative emphasizes the limits of the research that has been done to comprehend the realities of African American women's health. Researchers sometimes aid in misunderstanding black women's lives because they insert their own interpretations, sometimes based on racist prejudgments. So, a few researchers express bafflement by the disparities in black women's health and economic conditions, charging that enslavement ended in the 1880s, civil rights were guaranteed in the 1960s, and affirmative action policies existed for two decades. Therefore, any problems that black women and their families have must be their own fault. A few other researchers may want to deny or ignore the disparities and may forecast that, in the future, these gaps will no longer exist: it is just a matter of time and gaps will end as black women and their families get the educations and jobs and then take full advantage of all that American society has to offer. But full participation is not a just matter of choice. These kinds of statements are simplistic ways to avoid the deeper discussions of social needs. In spite of the theories, black women have had to deal with these situations whether researchers understand them or not. Like Harriet Tubman, making black families and communities move to different locations has required determination, great strength, and ability to create spaces and actions that bring about healing.

Black women begin their healing work from a holistic, embodied spirituality that deals honestly with these realities. Healing, in a black women's context, is not just about curing physical ills but necessarily includes healing the past, the present, work, income, family, community, spirit, mind, and emotions. This wider, more integrated view of healing aims for wholeness and originates from a configuration of black culture that defines relationships holistically. Such views are practical, creative, enriching, and life giving. The values inherent in these ideas inform black women's spirituality.

A black women's spirituality is reflective of African American ways of understanding the world and life. From a black cultural view of life, human existence is not carved into separate compartments of body and soul, sacred and profane. Instead, all the assorted pieces overlap into a cosmos that is understood as integrated and whole: each portion of life is interwoven, inter-related, and interdependent. For instance, an older black woman who had played a significant role in the Civil Rights Movement challenged some black college students: "If you think you pulled your own self up by your bootstraps, forget it. Remember those on whose shoulders you stand." To be aware of those who paid the high price for the seeming success of black Americans today is recognition of the connections between the people of the present and those of past generations. This idea is counter to the self-made American myth, in which an individual can accomplish anything on her or his own merit and effort. But, for black Americans, ancestors of the past are not just distant memories.

Throughout this country's history, with or without the support and recognition of differences, African Americans have continued to focus attention and handle events in culturally specific ways. At the core of these constructions is a view that each human life is interconnected with the other—living and deceased and unborn—as well as with nature and the divine. These relationships have a compelling reality that demands honor and action. To fail to do so constitutes a form of sin that damages the physical and emotional, thereby creating illness. These relationships form the core of healing in these black perspectives.

The idea of relationships that stretch and compel over time can be seen in Lalita Tademy's fictionalized account of her ancestors in *Cane River*.[6] She begins the tale with her own pull from her ancestors to leave a lucrative job and write the stories of enslaved women in her family. Maya Angelou expresses a sense of connectedness to the past in the oft-cited poem "And Still I Rise," expressing obligation to the present moment based on the lives of those in the past. Julie Dash's film *Daughters of the Dust* artistically portrays the web of connections in one African American community in South Carolina's Sea Islands.

Womanist theologian Jacquelyn Grant identified the impact of spirituality in the story of the escaped slave Harriet Tubman, who would return to help many other slaves escape. Tubman reflected on the moment of decision:

> I looked at my hands, to see if I was the same person now I was free. There was such a glory over everything, the sun came like gold through the trees, and over the field, and I felt like I was in heaven...To this solemn resolution I came;

> I was free and they should be free also; I would bring them all here. Oh, how
> I prayed then, lying all alone on the cold, damp ground.[7]

Human interconnections, relationality with the divine, and the compelling obligation to act are all seen in this one brief excerpt.

While Tubman's experience was centuries away from that of African American women today, embodied spirituality is retained over time through the condition of black women's lives. Nothing seems as dramatic as Tubman's story, but these chronic, persistent experiences of invisibility, isolation, and rejection create contemporary crises wherein African American women draw on embodied spirituality.

In the same ways, holistic views of life inform African Americans' ideas about healing. Healing is not just curing one physical condition or a set of symptoms. Rather, healing involves correctly balancing the energies of the self in community; the energies among community members, including the deceased or unborn; and the energies between humans and the divine, by whatever name this divine being is known. These views indicate the central importance of relationships in healing processes and in healing acts. The body itself is not viewed as an isolated set of parts and functions. The body has meaning because of connections with the past, the future, the family, and the divine. These black culture–based understandings of the body and healing contrast sharply with concepts of institutional medicine.

Black women's spirituality can be considered embodied because it deals with material realities. A black women's spirituality of healing is framed in families, in communities, and across generations. This view of healing is formed from black women's learned values of strength and possibilities. Black women, in line with the women pictured in the 1900s photo, learn the terror of caring in the midst of their own vulnerabilities. Relationships are the spiritual geographies of black women's healing work.

Today, too many Americans experience health care as a set of impersonal business relationships. These relationships are formed by the culture of biomedicine, in which the all-powerful healer enacts a cure on a passive sick person. Curing a single body or mind's condition rather than working for healing that includes personal integration, social balance, and spiritual correction is a cultural gap between Western biomedicine and black Americans' ideas of wellness. From a black cultural view, balancing all the dimensions of life is nothing more than a sacred act in itself—and this wellness balancing act often comes back to black women.

A black women's spirituality is integral to understanding such healing. A black women's healing spirituality demonstrates agency, not passivity. Byllye Avery, the founder of the National Black Women's Health Project, highlights the importance of agency: "Each of us has agency. Agency is the power within us to change ourselves and the world around us. Connecting with our sense of agency takes us on a lifelong journey of empowerment—for ourselves and others. Agency is one of our most precious gifts...and one of our most awesome responsibilities."[8]

BLACK WOMEN'S HEALING WORK

Understanding healing in a black women's framework begins in homes. African American women are most often the ones who are responsible for care of homes. Their care can create nurturing, subversive space for those present to grow. Black women's nurturing activities are often misunderstood, interpreted as evidence of a male-castrating matriarchy. The matriarchal role has even been proposed as the primary reason for social problems among African Americans, as was argued in the 1960s by a white senator from New York.

> [Daniel] Moynihan reported that the "matriarchial structure" of the Negro family seriously retards the progress of the group as a whole, and imposes a crushing burden on the Negro male and, in consequence, on a great many Negro women as well." Because too many black families are headed by single moms they are "pathological" and spell doom for the progress of the race.[9]

This view is part of the bad press black women receive. Like any bad press, there is a kernel of truth to be uncovered in this view, which is found in the importance of mothering by black women.

The healing aspects of black women's mothering are found through the gifts given from mother to child: glad rags, food for thought, and understanding the strength of pliancy. Black women may find ways to help those under their care to stir revolutions for personal or communal growth. This may involve dreaming new, preferred futures. The purpose of opening to new dreams is healing: becoming whole in spite of the way that the world may perceive black women and children. Black mothers may use story, song, and proverb to communicate these ideas. Parenting is serious business. Part of what is communicated is an attitude toward life: speak up; walk tall; you can if you try. These are communicated in families and across the wider black community.

As one example, social worker Joyce West Stevens noted the importance of sassiness for black girls.

> Black girls' sassy conduct is a central feature of identity exploration. The common inference of sassiness is defiant conduct. Notwithstanding considering a strengths perspective of sassy conduct, a counterpoint inference is candidness, courage, determination, and assertiveness—clearly strengths needed to challenge racial/gender stereotypes and biases and to master bicultural competence. Hypothetically, sassiness can be a promising phase in the development of black girls.[10]

The learned behavior—sassiness—of black girls becomes an important way of learning about the world, of erecting barriers against pain, and of defining self. Sassiness is as protective of black girls' vulnerabilities as the development of young black women's *attitude*. Attitude is sassiness grown up and is characterized by quick comebacks, argumentativeness, or biting humor. Attitude is also learned and helps younger women establish personal style, negotiate new areas of school or work, and is again protective. A white male colleague defined his experiences of encountering attitude when he stated, "If a black woman is mad at you, you might as well be dead." Such attitude is a protective stance, a kind of preventive medicine against the world's cruelty. Both sassiness and attitude are modes of black women's operations in the world as independent agents. Such self-protection may seem a flimsy barrier with which to negotiate the world, but it can serve to maintain mental health, resiliency, and identity.

These ways of self-protection also become important as black women move into the working world. Work is important, not only for possible income but also for self-expression and fulfillment. But many black women have experienced limits as to the types of work available, often service-related roles. Yet it is also expected that black women "naturally" are good at service. One white woman from the South told me of the response to her childhood question about why the black housekeeper was not taking care of her own family: "Black women like to take care of us." And it is expected that black women will work. The essentialized concept of the welfare mother in the American imagination is often that of a black teen mother having indiscriminate sexual relations resulting in multiple babies and therefore getting government handouts. This mythical welfare mother would rather bear multiple children than go to work. The irony of this image is that the stay-at-home mother seems to be an ideal, even the reason, that welfare was created in the twentieth century—until it referred to black women.

The idea that black women are supposed to work has long been developed in the United States, over against the view of white women who were held up as those who should be protected. The normalizing of black women's labor can be seen in the historical instance of the Black Mammy Memorial School in Athens, Georgia, in the early 1900s. The original charter glorifies the figure of mammy.

> The women who fill the places that the "OLD BLACK MAMMY" filled will bring credit not only to herself but to those who had the care of her training, and also her race.... The Black Mammy was trained in a school that passed with the institutions of her day. Where shall those who received her mantle be fitted for the places that were dignified by the industry, purity and fidelity of those distinctively Southern characters whom the South loved and will ever hold in tender memory? Shall not her MEMORIAL...perpetuate not only her memory but her SPIRIT of SERVICE?[11]

This memorial was one part of the overall construction of black American women's identities in the white imagination and integral to the related idea that black women were *meant* to work. These socially constructed identities continue to haunt black women. Today, black women must make a living in a rapidly changing, globalized economic climate where they continue to be undervalued. In obtaining higher education or seeking employment, they often must try to achieve without the mentorship and other forms of social capital that support professional development. Whatever the academic or popular thinking, black women continue to deal with their day-to-day realities, standing like Harriet Tubman, between two photos of a painful past and an impossible future. Surviving these realities requires healing work.

While black women learn to negotiate the world, the culturally derived spirituality that defines all life as interconnected is still present and operative. Relationships are integral to healing in families, as the mother-to-daughter advice shows. Healing and nurturing happens in families as black women create those spaces for rejuvenation and resistance. Encouragement may be given or subversive wisdom may be imparted. A primary black cultural view is that family is a wider institution than the nuclear structure of mother–father–children. In black views, the concept of family is more fluid, and so-called fictive kin can become more important than birth families. But family is itself important, and the ties are honored by the importance of family reunions in black traditions. Such patterns reflect the sense of interconnectedness that comes from a holistic view of the interrelated cosmos.

Additionally, there is also healing that occurs on a larger scale, for and in communities, exemplified by Harriet Tubman leading people to freedom. There is a healing hope to correct the results of poor education, underemployment, and racism. While much credit is given to Oprah Winfrey for opening a girls' school in South Africa, millions of black women can tell stories of their unrecognized giving for the life of others. Black women's giving and nurture are healing values hidden behind the terrible stereotype of mammy, a stereotype that not only normalized black women's labor but also devalued the healing gifts that black women bring. This devaluation happens not only as white people view black women—black women's gifts are often overlooked by black communities. As an example, the stories of the Civil Rights Movement are often told from the perspective of the leadership of black men. It has only been in the last 20 years that the stories of black women's leadership, giving, and healing during this time are being celebrated.

Black women use prayer in their healing work. When I graduated from college, a black woman gave me a plaque that said "Prayer changes things." She told me that was all I needed to know. At the same time, black women do not view prayer as a weak withdrawal. Prayer, as an expression of a strong spirituality, is an active engagement with the conditions of life. I met two women, Evangelist Cleopatra and Evangelist Earma, who call themselves healers and prayer warriors. One explained that "The prayer warrior get things from God that the others don't get....A prayer warrior is alert. I can't change, I'm in the word of God." Their spiritual actions are only possible through God's gift, and, as Evangelist Cleopatra stated, "You don't get this [gift of God] by looking pretty [but by] living a consecrated life to God."

Black women have developed the personal strength to continue and grow while still nurturing others. But there has been a terrible price to their well-being. Loneliness, as well as increased incidence of illness, despair, and anger, are a few results that come from always being and doing for everybody else. In fact, learning to care for self becomes a particular spiritual struggle for black women. The following poem circulated on the internet:

> On August 15, 1999, at 11:55 p.m., while struggling with
> the reality of being a human instead of a myth, the strong
> black woman passed away.
> Medical sources say she died of natural causes, but those
> who knew her know she died from being silent when she
> should have been screaming, milling when she should have
> been raging, from being sick and not wanting anyone to know
> because her pain might inconvenience them.
> She died from an overdose of other people clinging to her
> when she didn't even have energy for herself.
> She died from raising
> children alone and for not being able to do a complete job....
> Sometimes she was stomped to death by racism & sexism,
> executed by hi-tech ignorance while she carried the family
> in her belly, the community on her head, and the race on
> her back![12]

Healing self from constant service, caring for everybody else, and doing more than is good for self is a challenge that black women often face. If we can find ways to heal, we have even greater potential, as black feminist bell hooks states:

> Black women have the potential to be a community of faith that acts collectively to transform our world. When we heal the woundedness inside us, when we attend to the inner love-seeking, love-starved child, we make ourselves ready to enter more fully into community. We can experience the totality of life because we have become fully life-affirming. Like our ancestors using our powers to the fullest, we share the secrets of healing and come to know sustained joy.[13]

The potential for becoming aware of and using black women's gifts of healing are, as hooks states, tremendous. The bodies broken by experiences of racism, classism, and sexism, by the effects of undereducation and unemployment, and by being too strong and too misunderstood have healed others. Now, healing ourselves may provide a greater gift to the world.

NOTES

1. Katherine McKittrick, *Demonic Grounds: Black Women and the Cartographies of Struggle* (Minneapolis: University of Minnesota Press, 2006), p. xxiv.

2. Ibid., p. 3.

3. Avis A. Jones-DeWeever, and Barbara Gault, *Resilient and Reaching for More: Challenges and Benefits of Higher Education for Welfare Participants and Their Children* (Washington, D.C.: Institute for Women's Policy Research, 2006), p. 5.

4. As did the project, the organization assisted black women more informally through support groups and conferences that invited reflection on identifying personal needs for healing. As the imperative, the organization focuses its efforts now on research that supports changing existing health conditions.

5. "Our Research," http://blackwomenshealth.org (accessed December 2006).

6. Lalita Tademy, *Cane River* (New York: Warner Books, 2002).

7. Cited in Jacquelyn Grant, "Womanist Jesus and the Mutual Struggle for Liberation," in *The Recovery of Black Presence, an Interdisciplinary Exploration*, ed. Randall C. Bailey and Jacquelyn Grant (Nashville: Abingdon Press, 1995), p. 129.

8. Byllye Avery, *An Altar of Words: Wisdom, Comfort, and Inspiration for African American Women* (New York: Broadway Books, 1998), p. 8.

9. Traci C. West, *Wounds of the Spirit: Black Women, Violence, and Resistance Ethics* (New York: New York University Press, 1999), p. 135.

10. Joyce West Stevens, *Smart and Sassy: The Strengths of Inner-City Black Girls* (New York: Oxford University Press, 2002), p. 84.

11. June Patton, "Moonlight and Magnolias in Southern Education: The Black Mammy Memorial Institute," *The Journal of Negro History* 65, no. 2 (Spring 1980): p. 154.

12. Anon, "The Strong Black Woman Is Dead." Available at http://www.youtube.com/watch?v=stdswNCDvv0.

13. bell hooks, *Sisters of the Yam* (Boston: South End Press, 1993), p. 190.

Bibliography

Akbar, Na'im. *Light from Ancient Africa*. Tallahassee, Fla.: Mind Productions & Associates, Inc., 1994.

Ani, Marimba. *Yurugu: An African-Centered Critique of European Cultural Thought and Behavior*. Trenton, N.J.: Africa World Press, Inc., 1994.

Avery, Byllye. *An Altar of Words: Wisdom, Comfort, and Inspiration for African American Women*. New York: Broadway Books, 1998.

Baim, Tracy. "Black Groups Push for Gay Marriage Rights." *Windy City Times*, May 26, 2004, http://www.windycitymediagroup.com/gay/lesbian/news/ARTICLE. php?AID=5066.

Barfield, Thomas, ed. *The Dictionary of Anthropology*. Oxford: Blackwell Publishers, Ltd., 2001.

Barnes, Linda, and Ines Talamantez, eds. *Teaching Religion and Healing*. Oxford: Oxford University Press, 2006.

Beam, Joseph, ed. *In the Life: A Black Gay Anthology*. Boston: Alyson Publications, 1986.

Benson, Herbert. "A Conversation with Mind/Body Researcher Herbert Benson." *Harvard Business Review* 88, no. 11 (November 2005): pp. 53–58.

Berlin, Ira. *Many Thousand Gone*. Cambridge, Mass.: The Belnap Press of Harvard University Press, 1998.

Biddick, Kathleen. *The Typological Imaginary, Circumcision, Technology, History*. Philadelphia: University of Pennsylvania Press, 2003.

Billingsley, Andrew. *Mighty Like a River: The Black Church and Social Reform*. Oxford University Press: New York, 1999.

Boykin, Keith. "The Big Gay Outing Debate." *keithboykin.com*, October 4, 2005. http://www.keithboykin.com/arch/2005/10/04/the_big_gay_out.

———. "Miami's Black Ministers Group Distorts Gay Rights." *keithboykin.com*, August 1, 2002, http://www.keithboykin.com/arch/2002/08/01/miamis_black_mi.

———. "Whose Dream?" *The Village Voice*, May 24, 2004, http://www.villagevoice. com/news/0421,boykin,53751,1.html.

Brantley, Ben. "In the Rush to Progress, the Past Is Never Too Far Behind." http://theater2. nytimes.com/2007/05/09/theater/reviews/09radio.html?pagewaanted=print.

Bright, Chuck. "Deconstructing Reparative Therapy: An Examination of the Processes Involved When Attempting to Change Sexual Orientation." *Clinical Social Work Journal* 32, no. 4 (2004): p. 478.

Brown, Edward II. "We Wear the Mask: African American Contemporary Gay Male Identities." *Journal of African American Studies* 9, no. 2 (2005): p. 31.

Brueggemann, Walter. "The Costly Loss of Lament." *Journal for the Study of the Old Testament* no. 36 (1986), pp. 57–71.

———. "The Formfulness of Grief." *Interpretation: A Journal of Bible and Theology* XXXI, no. 3 (July 1977), pp. 263–75.

Bullard, Robert D., ed. *Confronting Environmental Racism: Voices from the Grassroots.* Boston: South End Press, 1993.

Camino, Linda. *"Ethnomedical Illnesses and Non-Orthodox Healing Practices in the American South: How They Work and What They Mean."* Ph.D. diss., University of Michigan, 1986.

Cannick, Jasmyne. "Much Ado over Outing." *Lesbian News* 31, no. 4 (2005): p. 32.

Cannon, Katie. *Katie's Canon.* New York: Continuum Publishing Company, 1995.

Casey, Nell, ed. *Unholy Ghost: Writers on Depression.* New York: HarperPerennial, 2002.

Catechism of the Catholic Church. 2nd ed. Washington, D.C.: United States Catholic Conference, Inc., 1997.

Chakrabarty, Dipesh. *Provincializing Europe, Postcolonial Thought and Historical Difference.* Princeton, N.J.: Princeton University Press, 2000.

Cheeks, Kwabena Rainey. "Understanding the Radical Inclusiveness of Jesus." http:// www.portofharlem.net/newsinnerlightministries.html.

Cheng, Anne Anglin. *The Melancholy of Race: Psychoanalysis, Assimilation, and Hidden Grief.* New York: Oxford University Press, 2001.

Chibbaro, Lou Jr. "Outing Campaign Roils D.C. Black Baptist Church." *Washington Blade,* January 30, 2008, http://www.washblade.com/thelatest/thelatest. cfm?blog_id=16289.

Chireau, Yvonne P. *Black Magic, Religion and the African American Conjuring Tradition.* Berkeley: University of California Press, 2003.

Cole, Luke W., and Sheila R. Foster. *From the Ground Up: Environmental Racism and the Rise of the Environmental Justice Movement.* New York: New York University Press, 2001.

Comstock, Gary David. *A Whosoever Church: Welcoming Lesbians and Gay Men into African American Congregations.* Louisville, Ky.: Westminster John Knox Press, 2001.

Cone, James H. *Risks of Faith: The Emergence of a Black Theology of Liberation, 1968–1998.* Boston: Beacon Press, 1999.

Danquah, Meri Nana-Ama. *Willow Weep for Me: A Black Woman's Journey through Depression.* New York: Ballentine/One World, 1999.

———. "Writing the Wrongs of Identity." In *Unholy Ghost: Writers on Depression,* ed. Nell Casey. New York: HarperPerennial, 2002.

Davis, David Brion. *The Problem of Slavery in the Age of Revolution, 1770–1823.* Ithaca, N.Y.: Cornell University Press, 1975.

"Depressed Mood." http://www.allaboutdepression.com/dia_12.html.

Dickerson, Debra. "Black Ministers Get Religion about HIV/AIDS." *Mother Jones*, October 12, 2007, http://www.motherjones.com/mojoblog/archives/2007/10/5762_black_ministers.html.

Du Bois, W.E.B. *The Philadelphia Negro*. New York: Schocken Books, 1967.

———. *The Souls of Black Folk*. New York: New American Library, 1982.

Einhorn, Robin L. *American Taxation, American Slavery*. Chicago: University of Chicago Press, 2006.

Ellis, Normandi, trans. *Awakening Osiris: The Egyptian Book of the Dead*. Grand Rapids, Mich.: Phanes Press, 1988.

Ephirim-Donkor, Anthony. *On Becoming Ancestors*. Trenton, N.J.: African World Press, 1997.

Erasmus, Charles. "Changing Folk Beliefs and the Relativity of Empirical Knowledge." *Southwestern Journal of Anthropology* 8 (1952): pp. 411–28.

Fabrega, Horacio. "On the Specificity of Folk Illnesses." In *Culture, Disease and Healing: Studies in Medical Anthropology*, ed. David Landy. New York: Macmillan Publishing Co., 1977, pp. 273–78.

———. "Some Features of Zinacatecan Medical Knowledge." *Ethnology* 10 (1971): pp. 1–24.

"Fighting 'the Blues' in African Americans." http://www.healthyplace.com/Communities/depression/minorities_9.asp.

de Figueiredo, J. M. "The Law of Sociocultural Demoralization." *Social Psychiatry* 18 (1983): pp. 73–78.

Flunder, Yvette A. *Where the Edge Gathers: Building a Community of Radical Inclusion*. Cleveland: Pilgrim Press, 2005.

Flunder, Yvette A., and Rev. Dr. Wyatt I. Greenlee. "The Fellowship's Response to Mt. Calvary (DC)." *The Fellowship*. http://radicallyinclusive.com/page_to_print.cfm?id=2031.

Fogel, Robert William, and Stanley L. Engerman. *Time on the Cross*. 2 vols. Boston: Little, Brown, and Company, 1974.

Foster, George. "Disease Etiologies in Northwestern Medical Systems." *American Anthropologist* 78 (1976): pp. 771–82.

Frazier, E. Franklin. *The Negro Church in America*. New York: Schocken Books, 1963.

Freud, Sigmund. "Mourning and Melancholia." In *Sigmund Freud 11: On Metapsychology*, ed. Angela Richards, trans. James Strachey. New York: Penguin Books, 1984, pp. 245–68.

Fullilove, M. "Psychiatric Implications of Displacement: Contributions from the Psychology of Place." *American Journal of Psychiatry* 153 (1996): pp. 1516–23.

Fullilove, M. *Root Shock: How Tearing up City Neighborhoods Hurts America and What We Can Do about It*. New York: Ballantine/One World, 2004.

Geertz, Clifford. *The Interpretation of Cultures*. New York: Basic Books, 1973.

George, Nelson. *Post Soul Nation: The Explosive, Contradictory, Triumph and Tragic 1980s as Experienced by African Americans (Previously Known as Blacks and before that Negroes)*. New York: Viking Press, 2004.

Gilroy, Paul. *The Black Atlantic: Modernity and Double Consciousness*. Cambridge, Mass.: Harvard University Press, 1993.

———. *Postcolonial Melancholia*. New York: Columbia University Press, 2005.

Glave, Dianne, and Mark Stoll, eds. *"To Love the Wind and the Rain": African Americans and Environmental History*. Pittsburgh: University of Pittsburgh Press, 2006.

Goffman, Erving. *Stigma: Notes on the Management of Spoiled Identity*. Englewood Cliffs, N.J.: Prentice Hall, 1963.

Gomez, Jewelle L., and Barbara Smith. "Black Lesbians Look in Their Own Backyards." *Out/Look* (Spring 1990): pp. 35, 37.

Grant, Jacquelyn. *White Women's Christ and Black Women's Jesus: Feminist Christology and Womanist Response*. Atlanta: Scholars Press, 1989.

————. "Womanist Jesus and the Mutual Struggle for Liberation." In *The Recovery of Black Presence: An Interdisciplinary Exploration*, ed. Randall C. Bailey and Jacquelyn Grant. Nashville: Abingdon Press, 1995, pp. 129–42.

Griffin, Horace L. *Their Own Receive Them Not: African American Lesbians & Gays in Black Churches*. Cleveland: The Pilgrim Press, 2006.

Gutman, Herbert G. *The Black Family in Slavery and Freedom, 1750–1925*. New York: Pantheon Books, 1976.

Hall, Arthur, and Peter Bourne. "Indigenous Therapists in a Southern Black Urban Community." *Archives of General Psychiatry* 28 (1973): pp. 137–42.

Hallman, David G., ed. *Ecotheology: Voices from South and North*. Maryknoll, N.Y.: Orbis Books, 1994.

Health, United States. "2006 Edition." http://www.cdc.gov/nchs/hus.htm.

Hemphill, Essex. "Introduction." In *Brother to Brother: New Writings by Black Gay Men*, ed. Essex Hemphill and Joseph Beam. Boston: Alyson Publications, 1991.

Hendricks, Michael. "Differences in Disclosure of Sexuality among African American and White Gay/Bisexual Men: Implications for HIV/AIDS Prevention." *AIDS Education and Prevention* 12, no. 6 (2000): p. 2.

Hofrichter, Richard, ed. *Toxic Struggles: The Theory and Practice of Environmental Justice*. Philadelphia: New Society Publishers, 1993.

Holloway, Karla F. C. *Moorings and Metaphors: Figures of Culture and Gender in Black Women's Literature*. New York: Rutgers University Press, 1992.

Homans, Peter. *The Ability to Mourn: Disillusionment and the Social Origins of Psychoanalysis*. Chicago: University of Chicago Press, 1989.

hooks, bell. "Reflections on Homophobia & Black Communities." *Out/Look* (Summer 1988): p. 23.

————. *Sisters of the Yam*. Boston: South End Press, 1993.

Hopkins, Dwight. *Shoes That Fit Our Feet*. Maryknoll, N.Y.: Orbis Books, 1993.

Hurston, Zora Neale. *Mules and Men*. New York: HarperPerennial, 1990.

Jackson, Bruce. "The Other Kind of Doctor: Conjure and Magic in Black American Folk Medicine." In *American Folk Medicine*, ed. Wayland D. Hand. Berkeley: University of California Press, 1976, pp. 259–72.

Jackson, Derrick Z. "Bible Lessons These Clergy Forgot." *CommonDreams.org*, February 11, 2004, http://www.commondreams.org/views04/0211–02.htm.

Jacobs, Ethan. "Opening the Next Front of the Marriage Battle." *Bay Windows*, June 18, 2005, http://www.mglpc.org/printer.php?id=293.

Jones-DeWeever, Avis A., and Barbara Gault. *Resilient and Reaching for More: Challenges and Benefits of Higher Education for Welfare Participants and Their Children*. Washington, D.C.: Institute for Women's Policy Research, 2006.

Karenga, Maulana. *Selections from the Husia: Sacred Wisdom of Ancient Egypt*. Los Angeles: The University of Sankore Press, 1984.

King, Colbert I. "Gays, God and Bishop Owens." *WashingtonPost.com*, Saturday, May 13, 2006, A17, http://www.washingtonpost.com/wp-dyn/content/article /2006/ 05/12/AR2006051201657.html.

Kleinman, Arthur. *Patients and Healers in the Context of Culture*. Berkeley: University of California Press, 1980.

Landy, David, ed. *Culture, Disease and Healing: Studies in Medical Anthropology*. New York: Macmillan Publishing Co., Inc., 1977.

Leighton, A. H. *The Governing of Men: General Principles and Recommendations Based on Experiences at a Japanese Relocation Camp*. Princeton, N.J.: Princeton University Press,1945.

———. *Human Relations in a Changing World: Observations in the Use of Social Sciences*. New York: EP Dutton, 1949.

———. *My Name Is Legion: Foundations for a Theory of Man in Relation to Culture*. New York: Basic Books, 1959.

Lidell, Lucy, with Narayani and Giris Rabinovitch. *The Sivananda Companion to Yoga*. New York: Simon & Schuster, 1983.

Lincoln, C. Eric, and Lawrence Mamiya. *The Black Church in the African American Experience*. Durham, N.C.: Duke University Press, 1990.

Long, Charles H. "Passage and Prayer: The Origins of Religion in the Atlantic World." In *The Courage to Hope, from Black Suffering to Human Redemption*, ed. Quinton Hosford Dixie and Cornel West. Boston: Beacon Press, 1999, pp. 11–21.

———. *Significations, Signs, Symbols, and Images in the Study of Religion*. 2nd ed. Aurora, Colo.: The Davies Group Publishers, 1999.

Long, Margaret Geneva. "Doctoring Freedom: The Politics of African American Medical Care, 1840–1910." Ph.D. diss., The University of Chicago, August 2004.

Lowe, Valerie. "COGIC Pastor Addresses Closet Homosexuality." *Charisma*, March 30, 2007, http://www.charismamag.com/soul-food/033007.html.

Mbiti, John S. *African Religion and Philosophy*. 2nd ed. Portsmouth, N.H.: Heinemann Educational Books, 1989.

McDowell, Deborah E. "The 'Self and the Other'": Reading Toni Morrison's *Sula* and the Black Female Text." In *Critical Essays on Toni Morrison*, ed. Nellie Y. McKay. Boston: Hall, 1998, pp. 77–90.

McKittrick, Katherine. *Demonic Grounds: Black Women and the Cartographies of Struggle*. Minneapolis: University of Minnesota Press, 2006.

McMorris, Christine McCarthy. "Black Pastors Bridle at Gay Marriage." *Religion in the News* 7, no. 2 (2004): http://www.trincoll.edu/depts/csrpl/RINVOL7No2/ BlackPastorsGay%20Marriage.htm.

Mechanic, David. "The Concept of Illness Behavior." *Journal of Chronic Diseases* 15 (1962): pp. 189–94.

Mitchell, Faith. *Hoodoo Medicine: Sea Islands Herbal Remedies*. Berkeley: Reed, Cannon and Johnson, 1978.

Mitchem, Stephanie. *African American Folk Healing*. New York: New York University Press, 2007.

————. *African American Women Tapping Power and Spiritual Wellness*. Cleveland: The Pilgrim Press, 2004.

Monroe, Irene. "Gulf between Black, Gay Communities Narrowing." http://www.irene monroe.com/2007/06/21/gulf-between-black-gay-communities-narrowing/.

————. "Louis Farrakhan's Ministry of Misogyny and Homophobia." In *The Farrakhan Factor: African-American Writers on Leadership, Nationhood, and Minister Louis Farrakhan*, ed. Amy Alexander. New York: Grove Press, 1998, pp. 275–97.

————. "No Marriage between Black Ministers and Queer Community." *The Witness Magazine*, June 2, 2004, http://www.thewitness.org/agw/monroe060204.html.

Morris, Aldon. *Origins of the Civil Rights Movement*. New York: The Free Press, 1984.

Morrison, Toni. *Beloved*. New York: Penguin Putnam, Inc., 1987.

————. *Playing in the Dark: Whiteness and the Literary Imagination*. Cambridge, Mass.: Harvard University Press, 1992.

"Mystical Stigmata." http://www.newadvent.org/cathen/14294b.html.

Ontario Consultants on Religious Tolerance. "What the Bible Says about Homosexuality." http://religioustolerance.org/hom_bibl.html.

Painter, Nell Irvin. *Creating Black Americans, African-American History and Its Meanings, 1519 to the Present*. New York: Oxford University Press, 2006.

————. "On Soul Murder and Slavery." http://www.pbs.org/wgbh/aia/part4/4i3084. html.

Paris, Peter. *The Spirituality of African Peoples: The Search for a Common Moral Discourse*. Minneapolis: Fortress Press, 1995.

Patton, June. "Moonlight and Magnolias in Southern Education: The Black Mammy Memorial Institute." *The Journal of Negro History* 65, no. 2 (Spring 1980): pp. 150–54.

Paulson, Michael. "Black Clergy Rejection Stirs Gay Marriage Backers." *The Boston Globe*, February 10, 2004, http://www.boston.com/news/local/articles/2004/02/10/black_clergy_rejection_stirs_gay_marriage_backers?mode=PF.

Payne-Jackson, Arvilla, and John Lee. *Folk Wisdom and Mother Wit: John Lee—An African American Herbal Healer*. Westport, Conn.: Greenwood Press, 1993.

Perry, Phyllis Alesia. *Stigmata*. New York: Hyperion, 1998.

"Profiles in Courage: Bishop Kwabena Rainey Cheeks." *The Body: The Complete HIV/AIDS Resource*. February 23, 2006, http://www.thebody.com/african_american/profiles/kcheeks.html.

Raboteau, Albert J. "The Afro-American Traditions." In *Caring and Curing: Health and Medicine in the Western Religious Traditions*, ed. Ronald L. Numbers and Darrel W. Amundsen. New York: Macmillan Publishing Co., 1986, pp. 539–62.

"Radio Golf." http://en.wikipedia.org/wiki/Radio_Golf.

Ranger, T. O. *Dance and Society in East Africa*. Berkeley: University of California Press, 1975.

Ranger, T. O., and Isara Kimambo, eds. *The Historical Study of African Religion*. Berkeley: University of California Press.

"Religious Faith Has Big Impact on Reducing Depression among African Americans, University of Chicago Research Shows." http://www.news.uchicago.edu/re leases/05/050413.data.shtml.

Riggs, Marlon. "Tongues Untied." In *Brother to Brother: New Writings by Black Gay Men*, ed. Essex Hemphill and Joseph Beam. Boston: Alyson Publications, 1991.

Roberts, John W. *Odunde Presents. From Hucklebuck to Hip-Hop: Social Dance in the African American Community of Philadelphia*. Philadelphia: Odunde, Inc., 1995.

Sanders, Cheryl. *Empowerment Ethics for a Liberated People*. Minneapolis: Fortress Press, 1995.

Schoenbrun, David L. "Conjuring the Modern in Africa: Durability and Rupture in Histories of Public Healing between the Great Lakes of East Africa." *American Historical Review* III, no. 5 (December 2006): pp. 1403–439.

Segrest, Mab. "Race and the Invisible Dyke." In *Dangerous Liaisons: Blacks, Gays, and the Struggle for Equality*, ed. Eric Brandt. New York: New Press, 1999.

Sherman, Charlotte Watson, ed. *Sisterfire: Black Womanist Fiction and Poetry*. New York: Harper Perennial, 1994.

Smith, Archie. *Navigating the Deep River*. Cleveland: United Church Press, 1997.

Snow, Loudell. "Folk Medical Beliefs and Their Implications for Care and Patients." *Annals of Internal Medicine* 81 no. 1 (1974): pp. 82–96.

———. *Walkin' over Medicine*. Boulder, Colo.: Westview Press, 1993.

Stevens, Joyce West. *Smart and Sassy: The Strengths of Inner-City Black Girls*. New York: Oxford University Press, 2002.

Stewart, Carole Lynn. "Challenging Liberal Justice: The Talented Tenth Revisited." In *Re-cognizing W.E.B. Du Bois in the Twenty-First Century: Essays on W.E.B. Du Bois*, ed. Mary Keller and Chester Fontenot Jr. Macon, GA: Mercer University Press, 2007, pp. 112–41.

"Stigmata." http://www.answers.com/topic/stigmata.

"Stigmata." http:www.newadvent.org.

"Stigmata, Stigmatist." http://www.catholicforum.com/Saints/define10.htm.

Stuckey, Sterling. *Slave Culture: Nationalist Theory & The Foundations of Black America*. New York: Oxford University Press, 1987.

Swidler, Ann. *Talk of Love: How Culture Matters*. Chicago: University of Chicago Press, 2001.

Tademy, Lalita. *Cane River*. New York: Warner Books, 2002.

Thomas, Stephen, and Sandra C. Quinn. "The Tuskegee Syphilis Study, 1932 to 1972: Implications for HIV Education and AIDS Risk Education Programs in the Black Community." In *Readings in the Sociology of AIDS*, ed. Anthony Lemelle et al. Upper Saddle River, N.J.: Prentice Hall, 2000.

Townes, Emilie M. *Breaking the Fine Rain of Death: African American Health Issues and a Womanist Ethic of Care*. Eugene, OR: Wipf and Stock, 2006. First published 1998 by Continuum.

———. *In a Blaze of Glory: Womanist Spirituality as Social Witness*. Nashville: Abingdon Press, 1995.

Townes, Mary M. "Looking to Your Tomorrows Today." In *Embracing the Spirit Womanist Perspectives on Hope, Salvation, and Transformation*, ed. Emilie M. Townes. Maryknoll, N.Y.: Orbis Press, 1997, pp. 3–8.

Trinity United Church of Christ. http://www.tucc.org/home.htm.

Vanzant, Iyanla. *Acts of Faith: Daily Meditations for People of Color*. New York: Fireside, 1993.

———. *Until Today! Daily Devotions for Spiritual Growth and Peace of Mind*. New York: Simon & Schuster, 2000.

Volin, Katherine. "Equality Maryland's Marylanders of Color Collective." *Washington Blade*, July 29, 2005, http://www.equalitymaryland.org/mocc/news/2005/2005_07_29_b.shtml.

Walker, Alice. *In Search of Our Mothers' Gardens*. New York: Harcourt, Brace and Company, 1984.

———. "Everyday Use." *In Love and Trouble: Stories of Black Women*. New York: Harcourt Brace and Company, 1967, pp. 47–59.

Wallace, D., and R. Wallace. *A Plague on Your Houses: How New York Was Burned Down and National Public Health Crumbled*. New York: Verso Books, 1998.

Warren, Barbara Jones. "Examining Depression among African American Women Using Womanist and Psychiatric Mental Health Nursing Perspectives." Womanist Theory and Research Website, University of Georgia, http://www.uga.edu/~womanist/warren1.2.htm.

Watson, Wilbur. *Black Folk Medicine: The Therapeutic Significance of Faith and Trust*. New Brunswick, NJ: Transaction Books, 1984.

West, C. S'thembile. "African Aesthetics: A Pervasive Presence in U.S. Culture." In *Babu's Magic: Dance, Rhythm, Culture: An African Perspective*. Minneapolis: Minnesota Dance Alliance, 1994.

West, Traci C. *Wounds of the Spirit: Black Women, Violence and Resistance Ethics*. New York: New York University Press, 1999.

Westermann, Claus. *The Psalms: Structure, Content and Message*. Translated by Ralph D. Gehrke. Minneapolis: Augsburg Publishing House, 1980.

Williams, Delores. *Sisters in the Wilderness: The Challenge of Womanist God-Talk*. New York: Orbis Books, 1993.

Wilson, D. Mark. "Celebrate the Voices of Your Identity and Pride." In *Fifty Ways to Support Lesbian and Gay Equality*. Maui: Inner Ocean Publishing, 2005.

———. "I Don't Mean to Offend, but I Won't Pretend: The Making of Family for Gay Men in an African American Church." In *Tending the Flock*, ed. Bernie Lyons and Archie Smith. Louisville, Ky.: Westminster John Knox Press, 1998.

Wood, Mary E. "How We Got This Way: The Sciences of Homosexuality and the Christian Right." *Journal of Homosexuality* 38, no. 3 (2000): pp. 19–40.

Index

About the Editors and Contributors

EDITORS

STEPHANIE Y. MITCHEM is Associate Professor at the University of South Carolina. She is the author of *African American Women Tapping Power and Spiritual Wellness* and *Introducing Womanist Theology,* as well as numerous articles and book chapters.

EMILIE M. TOWNES is the Andrew W. Mellon Professor of African American Religion and Theology at Yale Divinity School. She is an ordained American Baptist Minister and hails from Durham, North Carolina. Townes was the first African American woman to be elected to the presidency of the American Academy of Religion in 2005. She is the former Carolyn Williams Beaird Professor of Christian Ethics at Union Theological Seminary in New York. Her previous books include *Breaking the Fine Rain of Death: African American Health and a Womanist Ethic of Care* and *Womanist Ethics and the Cultural Production of Evil.*

CONTRIBUTORS

TERRI BALTIMORE is the Vice President of Neighborhood Development for the Hill House Association, a 40-year-old social service organization based in Pittsburgh's historic Hill District neighborhood. Responsible for developing partnerships, creating arts programming, and organizing specialized programs, she is also the cofounder of Find The Rivers! (FTR), a project that reconnects the Hill District neighborhood to the rivers and the rest of Pittsburgh.

LINDA L. BARNES, Ph.D., is a medical anthropologist, historian, and religion scholar whose work bridges these disciplines. An Associate Professor of Family

Medicine and Pediatrics at Boston University School of Medicine (BUSM) in Boston, Massachusetts, she teaches about issues in crosscultural patient care. She also directs the Boston Healing Landscape Project, an institute for the study of religions, medicines, and healing based at BUSM that focuses on culturally and religiously grounded complementary and alternative medicines among minority and immigrant patient communities served at Boston Medical Center. In addition to articles in medical and medical anthropology journals, her books include *Religion and Healing in America* (2004, coedited with Susan S. Sered), *Needles, Herbs, Gods, and Ghosts: China, Healing, and the West to 1848* (2005), and *Teaching Religion and Healing* (2006, coedited with Ines Talamantez).

YVONNE CHIREAU is Professor in the Department of Religion at Swarthmore College, where she teaches courses on African American religions, American religious history, and folk and popular religions. She is the author of *Black Magic: Religion and the African American Conjuring Tradition* (2003) and the coeditor of *Black Zion: African American Religions and Judaism* (1999). Her work has focused on diversity in African American religions, women and gender in American religion, the intersection of religion and magic in black religious experience, and folk and popular religious expressions. Her most recent work is a collaborative project that engages African American religions and conceptualizations of the body across traditions, practices, and contexts. Her current research also involves explorations of visual culture and religion in contemporary graphic media.

MINDY THOMPSON FULLILOVE is a research psychiatrist at New York State Psychiatric Institute and a professor of clinical psychiatry and sociomedical sciences at Columbia University. She has published five books and numerous articles, largely concerned with race and health in the United States. Her current work focuses on the connections between the organization of cities and mental health.

ROSEMARY D. GOODEN is Lecturer in Modern Church and Mission at Seabury-Western Theological Seminary and serves on the board of the *Anglican Theological Review*. She holds a doctorate from the University of Michigan. Dr. Gooden edited and wrote the introduction for *Faith Cures, and Answers to Prayer* (2002), a reprint of the healing testimonies of Mrs. Edward (Sarah) Mix and her previously unpublished spiritual autobiography.

DWIGHT N. HOPKINS is Professor of Theology at the University of Chicago Divinity School. He is the author of *Being Human: Race, Culture, and Religion; Shoes That Fit Our Fit: Sources for a Constructive Black Theology; Down, Up & Over: Slave Religion and Black Theology;* and *Black Theology USA and South Africa: Politics, Culture, and Liberation.* He is coeditor of *Walk Together Children: Black and Womanist Theologies, Church and Theological Education;* and *Another World Is Possible: Spiritualities and Religions of Global Darker Peoples.*

CAROLYN M. JONES is an associate professor of Religion and in the Institute for African American Studies at the University of Georgia. She is the coeditor, with Theodore Trost, of *Teaching African American Religions* and the author of numerous essays on the works of Toni Morrison, Harper Lee, Albert Murray, and others. Her research interests are in Arts, Literature, and Religion, particularly in Southern racial-ethnic minority women's religions, and in postmodern and postcolonial theory.

CHARLES H. LONG was trained as a Historian of Religions at the University of Chicago. During the two decades he taught there and in other academic positions, he participated in the training of two generations of scholars in the History of Religions and in the development of Studies in Religion in the international academic community. Among his published works are *Alpha, The Myths of Creation* and *Significations, Signs, Symbols, and Images in the Interpretation of Religion.* He has been a visiting professor at the University of Queensland in Australia, the University of Cape Town in South Africa, Tsukuba University in Japan, as well as at major universities in the United States. He became Professor Emeritus at the University of California, Santa Barbara, in 1996.

ARVILLA PAYNE-JACKSON, Ph.D., is a Professor in the Department of Sociology and Anthropology at Howard University. Her areas of interest are sociolinguistics, medical anthropology, oral histories, and ethnographic evaluation. She has published several books on Jamaican and African American ethnomedicine, as well as articles in her other fields of interest. She has conducted research in the Caribbean, Latin America, Africa, and the Southeast Lowlands of the United States. She is also the Executive Producer of the first comprehensive documentary on African American Folk Medicine, *African American Folk Medicine: A Story of Folk Medicine in America,* which was part of a commissioned exhibit for the Ellis Island–Statue of Liberty Museum Exhibit on "Immigrants' Health Contributions" (New York, New York, 1994).

C. S'THEMBILE WEST was born and raised in Harlem, New York. She earned a Ph.D. in African American Studies from Temple University, Philadelphia, in 1994. A former Fulbright-Hayes scholar to the southern Africa region, S'thembile writes and performs poetry with jazz musicians and teaches at Western Illinois University in Women's Studies, African American Studies, and English.

REV. D. MARK WILSON, Ph.D., is an ordained American Baptist Minister and former Pastor of McGee Avenue Baptist Church in Berkeley, California. He is a graduate of Howard University, Harvard Divinity School, and the University of Michigan, where he received his Ph.D. in Sociology. Rev. Wilson is currently the Assistant Professor in Ministry and Congregational Leadership at the Pacific School of Religion (Berkeley, California) and a Lecturer in the Department of Sociology, at the University of California, Berkeley.